W9-BXG-113

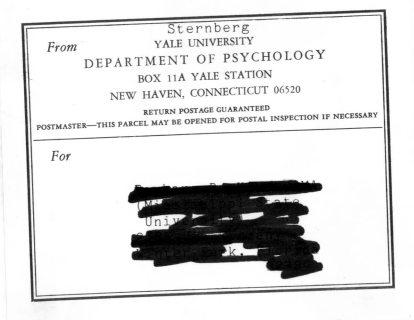

From   Sternberg
YALE UNIVERSITY
DEPARTMENT OF PSYCHOLOGY
BOX 11A YALE STATION
NEW HAVEN, CONNECTICUT 06520

RETURN POSTAGE GUARANTEED

POSTMASTER—THIS PARCEL MAY BE OPENED FOR POSTAL INSPECTION IF NECESSARY

For

The Triangle of Love

THE

TRIANGLE OF

LOVE

Intimacy, Passion, Commitment

ROBERT J. STERNBERG

Basic Books, Inc., Publishers

NEW YORK

Library of Congress Cataloging-in-Publication Data

Sternberg, Robert J.
  The triangle of love.

  Includes index.
  1. Love—Psychological aspects. 2. Intimacy
(Psychology) 3. Commitment (Psychology) I. Title.
BF575.L8S78 1988   306.7   88-19281
ISBN 0-465-08746-9

This book is dedicated

to the people in my life

who have taught me what love is.

CONTENTS

PREFACE

THIS BOOK is the result of a gamble I made in the early 1980s: that I could turn my energies as a theoretician and researcher to the study of love and come up with something that would be neither trivial nor a rehash of what was already known. When I started to study love, I endured, I hope good-naturedly, the expected remarks about midlife crisis and the decline of mental powers that hits some psychologists after the age of thirty. In time, however, as my research progressed, the jests were replaced by serious questions about it. In this book I summarize my findings.

Writings on love can be so jargon-laden and esoteric as totally to miss the point, or so vacuous as to amount to little more than inspirational homilies. I have tried to avoid these two perils both by presenting in fairly nontechnical terms much of the theory and research on love that form the foundation for the psychology of love, and also by showing the practical implications for our daily lives. I have concentrated on the meaning of the scholarly work; the technical data can be found in the journal articles and other publications cited in the notes. In focusing on my own "triangular" conception of love as the interaction of three components—intimacy, passion, and commitment—I draw on my own work as well as that of the most respected investigators in the field.

I deal in this book primarily with the heterosexual love

of a partner—spouse, lover, or close friend—and discuss liking as well as loving. I also deal, though much less fully, with the love of children and parents. Although much of what I say doubtless applies as well to homosexual love, the large majority of participants in my own and others' studies have been heterosexual, and I have been reluctant to generalize further.

The research I cite in this book, done by myself and my collaborators, involved primarily New Haven–area adults of widely varying age, background, and experience. Although these samples were geographically limited, throughout the book I draw on the research of many other investigators besides myself, using thousands of subjects from elsewhere in the United States or from Canada. In addition, my exemplary vignettes present a wide range of individuals, some of whom are not from the United States. In sum, I believe that the large and diverse total population upon which I base this study is representative of the experience of people across the United States and Canada.

I begin, in chapter 1, with the issues that face us all when we seek to understand love, and describe my initial empirical investigations. These investigations led to my triangular theory of love, described in chapter 2. In chapter 3, I elaborate on the evidence for the theory, and in chapter 4 present other viewpoints about love and its relationship to liking. Because both liking and loving often start with some kind of attraction, I discuss, in chapter 5, what lies behind attraction itself. But, since what initially attracts a person does not always continue to do so, I discuss in chapter 6 how what matters in love changes over time, and in chapter 7 widen my focus to include a variety of accounts of how relationships themselves change over time. In chapter 8, I put the theory

Preface

and data into practice, with some guidelines for creating and sustaining love.

I am grateful to my collaborators in love research—Michael Barnes, Susan Grajek, and Sandra Wright. I also want to thank those established scholars in the field who, on learning that a researcher on human intelligence wanted to study love, supported my endeavors. Among them, I thank especially Ellen Berscheid, Keith Davis, Elaine Hatfield, and Harold Kelley. Judith Greissman, my acquisitions editor at Basic, has been both a great supporter and a critic in all phases of my preparation of the book; and Phoebe Hoss, my copy editor, has done an outstanding job of making it more lucid than in its earlier versions. Sandra Wright, my administrative assistant, was generous and patient in typing up and commenting on successive versions of the manuscript; and Elizabeth Neuse, my research assistant, helped in some of the data analyses.

Some of what I have learned about love I have learned in the usual ways of scholars—through books, journal articles, and my own research. But most of what I have learned has been from people I have known, many of whose stories—with their identities disguised—I encapsulate in brief vignettes. Hence, it is to all of these men and women that I have dedicated this book.

RJS
January 1988

The Triangle of Love

In the examples I cite throughout this book, all names and identifying characteristics have been changed.

In Quest of Love

LOVE is one of the most intense and desirable of human emotions. People may lie, cheat, steal, and even kill in its name—and wish to die when they lose it. Love can overwhelm anyone, at any age—as it did this forty-year-old psychologist:

I still remember when she told me we were through. I couldn't believe it. She was serious. I should have seen it coming, but I didn't. I remember everything: what she looked like, what the room looked like, how I felt. It's burned into my memory. I wanted to die. I really wanted to die.

A few weeks later, she entered a restaurant where I was eating with some friends. I lost my breath and thought I was going to collapse. I somehow got away and stumbled out to the parking lot. She looked so lovely, and she wasn't mine any more. I would have done almost anything to get her back, but she just wouldn't have me.

I still don't really understand what happened, but I'm over her now. We're even friends. It took a few years, maybe five or six.

What did this man have? What did he lose?

My own scholarly interest in love actually grew out of my research on intelligence. Freud once said that the two major domains of life are work and love. I had spent a number of years studying a critical aspect of success in work, and felt ready in my early thirties to start studying the "other half" of life—love.

I started, perhaps inevitably, by applying concepts in the study of intelligence to the study of love. Obviously, the content of love has little, if anything, to do with intelligence. The connection was not one of content at all, but of structure. I wondered whether alternative *structural* models of intelligence might be applied to love and, perhaps, to other constructs as well. Let me elaborate.

Three Structural Models of Love

In applying theories of intelligence to the study of love, I aimed to discover whether love is a single thing or many things, even though to the person in love the many things may feel, subjectively, like a single thing. And if love is many things, what are they and how are they related? It seemed to me that three early theories of intelligence—those of Charles Spearman, Godfrey Thomson, and Louis Thurstone, in the 1920s and 1930s—might be applied to the study of love (see figure 1.1).[1]

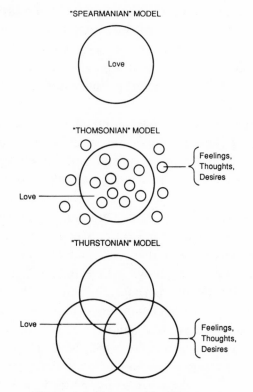

Figure 1.1 *Three models of love.*

LOVE AS A UNITARY, UNDIFFERENTIATED EXPERIENCE

In the early 1900s, Charles Spearman, a British psychologist, proposed that "all branches of intellectual activity have in common one fundamental function (or group of functions), whereas the remaining or specific elements of the activity seem in every case to be wholly different from that in all the others."[2] His idea, then, is that there is both a general factor which pervades all intelligent performance, and a set of specific factors as well, which, being relevant only to single tasks, are unimportant. The core of Spearman's theory is g, or the general factor that allegedly pervades all of intelligence. Spearman suggested that g might be an expression of some sort of mental energy, but he was never able to be more precise.

In terms of this structural model, love can be conceptualized as the single g—that is, as an undifferentiated "glob" of highly positive and emotion-charged experience which cannot be dissected. To experience love would be to experience this glob. I sometimes refer to this view of love as the "Senator Proxmire view," in honor of the Wisconsin senator who conferred on a famous love researcher his Golden Fleece Award, chastising the researcher for even studying love in the first place. Like many other people, perhaps, Proxmire believed that love should be left to poets and novelists, that it neither can nor should be studied scientifically. The senator was wrong, however. In some cases, the findings of scientific research provide a new kind of demonstration of what the novelists have already told us; while in others, we can learn through scientific discovery facts about love we are unlikely to learn in any other way.

It is possible, of course, that although we experience love as a unitary rush of emotions, the facts are otherwise. Love may really be many things rather than a single thing, the many being lost in subjective experience—a possibility the Thomsonian model allows for.

LOVE AS A SAMPLING OF OVERLAPPING BONDS

Godfrey Thomson, another British psychologist, soon pointed out that Spearman's theory was not the only theory consistent with Spearman's data: in other words, although analysis of scores from a number of ability tests produced a general underlying factor in those tests, intelligence could still be many things. Thomson, arguing that the general factor obtained by Spearman could indicate a mathematical rather than a psychological unity, saw the mind as possessing an enormous number of bonds, including reflexes, habits, and learned associations. Performance on any one task would activate a large number of these bonds and on related tasks, such as those used on mental tests, would activate overlapping subsets of these bonds. In other words, the same bonds would be used again and again, carried over from performance on one test to performance on another. Thus, while statistical analysis of a set of tests may point to a general factor, in fact what is common to the tests may be a multitude of bonds.

In this model, love may be thought of as a set of feelings, thoughts, and desires that, when experienced together, yield the composite experience we label love. According to this view, though, love is not unitary; rather, it can be decomposed into a large number of underlying bonds that tend to occur together in certain close relationships, and that in combination result in the global feeling of love.

Suppose, for example, that all loves have in common feelings such as strong attachment to, high regard for, and desire to be with, a loved one. Each time you love somebody, these three feelings—attachment, high regard, and desire to be with that person—should occur together. While you may experience them as a unit and be unable to distinguish among them, they are, according to the Thomsonian model, separable at a deep psychological level and can be teased apart by careful psychological analysis.

LOVE AS A SET OF PRIMARY FACTORS

Louis Thurstone, an American psychologist at the University of Chicago, proposed in the 1930s a theory of intelligence comprising seven primary and equally important factors, including verbal comprehension, word fluency, spatial visualization, number, memory, reasoning, and perceptual speed. The underlying idea was that intelligence is composed of a relatively small set of interrelated primary mental abilities.

In terms of this notion, love is a small, stable set of feelings, thoughts, and desires that are of approximately equal importance in the overall feeling we describe as love. Love is not one main thing, whether decomposable (Thomson's model) or not (Spearman's model), but rather a set of primary emotions that are best understood separately rather than as an integrated whole. All contribute simultaneously to the experience of love. According to this notion, a global thought or feeling (such as intelligence or love) can be separated into multiple overlapping factors, but the factors always contribute to that global thought or feeling.

One way of looking at this view would be to imagine giving people a score on each of several attributes, such as the amount one cares for the other, the amount one wishes to be with the other, and the amount one supports the other. These scores, added up, would indicate how much one loves the other.

Why should it matter which of these models best characterizes love? Suppose your goal is to assess how your relationship is going. If the Spearmanian notion is correct, then all that would matter to your assessment is your global feeling of how things are going—the overall feeling of love you have for your partner. No further analysis would be necessary. If the Thomsonian model is correct, then this global analysis is insufficient. You need to know what the "bonds" are, and evaluate your relationship in terms of each of them. You may find that, although your global feeling is not quite what you would like, you have quite a few of the elements of a successful loving relationship. Or, you may find the opposite—that your global feelings are based on relatively few elements. If the Thurstonian model is correct, then it is not enough to make a checklist of the various elements in your relationship. You would want as well to evaluate how much of each you have, and to realize that whatever your global feelings are, they are deceptive because there is no true "general factor" underlying love.

In our research, we sought to test these alternative models of love.

Testing the Models of Love

My first study was done in the early 1980s in collaboration with Susan Grajek, at the time a predoctoral student in the department of psychology at Yale.[3] We advertised in a local newspaper for people to participate, at five dollars per hour, in a study on love in close relationships. Potential recruits were eligible to participate only if they were eighteen years of age or older, had had at least one love relationship (by their own account), and described themselves as primarily heterosexual. We limited our study to heterosexual participants because we believed data from homosexual and heterosexual participants would have to be analyzed separately; and in order for such separate analyses to be viable, we would need fairly large numbers of each. But past experience of other researchers led us to believe that we would not get enough homosexual participants to make separate analysis of their data viable. The final participants were thirty-five men and fifty women from cities and towns in southern Connecticut. The greater number of women than men probably reflects the fact that men are more likely to be working during the hours we were testing.

Our participants ranged in age from eighteen to seventy, with an average age of thirty-two. The majority (seventy-eight) were white Caucasian. The participants varied widely in religion. They came from a variety of living situations: fifty-seven were single, sixteen were married, six were divorced and again single, two were divorced and remarried, three were widowed, and one was separated. It is likely, I think, that our many single participants were looking for guidance in their own search for love, and hoped to find it through self-analysis and our feedback to their participation in our experiment.

Of the sixty-seven participants not living with a spouse, twenty-one were living with their parents, eighteen were living alone, ten were living with a roommate, nine were living with a lover, and nine were living with their children. The number of significant heterosexual love relationships in which the participants had been involved ranged from 1 to 15, with an average of 2.8.

Of several questionnaires administered to our participants, the first concerned family background. Participants were asked about such factors as age, gender, marital status, current living arrangements, and the number of "significant" heterosexual love relationships they had had.

In Quest of Love

In one of several questionnaires, we asked participants to provide certain information regarding their three most significant heterosexual love relationships—for example, how long they had been in each relationship, how happy in it, how satisfied with it, and so on. Our greatest concern, however, was with the most recent relationship: When did it begin and end? Why did it end and who had ended it? How often did they see each other, and what did they do when they saw each other? We asked our participants to rate the quality of their relationship on a seven-point scale (1 = low; 7 = high) for the following dimensions: intensity, significance, similarity of partners, complementarity of partners, extent of the lover's satisfaction of the participant's needs, extent of the participant's feeling "through with" the relationship (for those that had ended), the participant's self-esteem during the relationship, and overall satisfaction with the relationship.

We also administered several scales of liking and loving, of which the two most important were the Liking and Loving Scales constructed by Zick Rubin and a scale of interpersonal involvement developed by George Levinger and his colleagues.[4] Items on the Rubin scales are worded as questions and pertain to characteristics of the loved one (for example, "How easily can _____ gain the admiration of others?") and feelings the rater has for the loved one ("How concerned are you about _____'s welfare?"). Participants in the study were asked to use a seven-point scale for each item, with 1 the low rating (for example, "Not at all concerned") and 7 the high ("Extremely concerned").

Although in the past the Rubin scales have been used to study only relationships between spouses or lovers, we asked our participants not only to use the scale to characterize their relationship with a spouse or lover, but also to characterize their relationship with mother, father, sibling closest in age, and best friend of the same sex. We did the same with the Levinger scale, which consists of phrases describing potential aspects of loving relationships (such as, "Sharing deeply personal ideas and feelings" or "Offering emotional support to other"). Again, subjects provided ratings on the seven-point scale for the same relationships that were rated for the Rubin scales. For the Levinger scale, however, we also asked participants to rate each phrase for what they considered to be the ideal romantic love relationship. Finally, we administered a set of personality tests in order to seek out any correlations between aspects of loving and personality characteristics.

Our study relied heavily on questionnaires, partly because they provide fairly large numbers of responses from participants in a relatively short time. Also, the data thereby obtained are numerical, and therefore amenable to statistical analysis and to psychological interpretation. Questionnaire data can be useful in psychological research, as long as their limitations are clear: that there is no guarantee that what a person says is exactly what he or she feels, or even that one knows what one feels well enough to express it.

As for other sources of data, we had decided not to collect data through interviews, partly because they are time consuming and cannot be analyzed efficiently, but also partly lest individuals lose their sense of anonymity, no matter how much we might assure them that their responses would remain anonymous. We had also decided not to use behavioral data—that is, direct observation of what participants do in their relationships—because, though probably the most useful, these data are also the hardest to collect, especially since the mere act of observing behavior can change that behavior. Couples in a relationship are unlikely to act exactly the same way when being observed as when alone. Moreover, it is sometimes difficult to know what to make of behavioral data. A caress, for example, may mean one thing to one person but an entirely different thing to another.

In analyzing the data from this study, we sought to answer five main questions: First, whom do people love, and how much? Second, how well can you predict how much you love certain people from how much you love other people? Third, how are liking and loving related? Fourth, what is the structure of love? And finally, can you predict satisfaction in relationships from the kinds of variables considered in this study? Now, for our results.

WHOM DO WE LOVE, AND HOW MUCH?

The answers to our first question, concerning the relative amounts of liking and loving one had for particular people in one's life, differed for men and women. On the average, men loved their lover (or spouse) the most, their best friend of the same sex second, their father third, their mother fourth, and their sibling closest in age the least. Women loved their lover and best friend of the same sex the most and about equally; next their mother; then their father; and least, their sibling closest in age. Thus, lovers fared well for both men and women; but women loved their best friend of the same sex about as much as their lover, whereas men loved their lover more than their best friend of the same sex. Mothers and fathers ranked after the best friend of the same sex for both men and women, and ratings for mother and father were about the same. One thing both men and women agreed upon: they reserved their lowest ratings for their sibling closest in age, thereby indicating that it was their sibling that they loved the least of all the people rated in the study.

A striking difference emerged between the men and the women in respect to liking. The pattern of liking ratings for men was about the same as that of loving, with the lover at the top, the best friend of the same sex second, the mother and father next, and the sibling closest in age at the bottom. Both the mother and the father were liked less than they were loved, and the liking rating for the mother actually did not differ significantly from that of the sibling closest in age. Women, on the other hand, indicated that they liked their best friend of the same sex more than their lover; next came the mother, with the father and the sibling at the bottom. Males consistently showed a slight preference for the father over the mother, whereas females showed a slight preference for the mother over the father. For the females, liking for the father did not differ significantly from liking for the sibling closest in age.

Why might women like their best friend of the same sex at least as well as their lover? A plausible hypothesis is based on a possible difference between men's and women's conceptions of friendship. Men tend to have friendships through shared activities, with relatively little intimacy and one-to-one communication. Women are likely to be intimate with their friends and to emphasize one-to-one communication, which men seem less willing and able to strive for. In a close relationship, a woman often feels frustrated in her attempts to achieve emotional intimacy and communication with her lover or spouse and thus may seek it elsewhere—for example, with another woman. As she increasingly confides in this woman friend and becomes closer to her, she may ultimately like this friend more than the lover or spouse. The lesson is all too familiar: men need to be more receptive to women's needs for intimacy and communication, and women more sensitive to a socialization pattern whereby men are brought up to avoid intimacy and close communication.

Jeff learned this lesson the hard way. All his friends and colleagues view him as a wonderful person. He contributes time, money, and boundless energy to a variety of humane causes. Deeply caring about people at an abstract level, he has trouble bringing this caring into his personal life. When it comes to that life, he is like a closed book with its covers glued shut. Despite his global concerns for so many people, at a personal level he seems to have much less to give than at a societal one. His wife eventually tired of hearing from many people what a wonderful person her husband was: it didn't show in his personal relationship with her, which was almost devoid of intimacy. She left him. He is now alone, still doing for others what he seems to be unable to do for himself in his own personal relationships.

In respect to same-sex identification with parents, men generally displayed more liking and loving of their father; women preferred their mother—in contrast to the oedipal conflict early in life, when young boys generally prefer their mother, and young girls, their father. Freud, of course, explained that children must go through oedipal conflict in order first to develop attraction for members of the opposite sex and then to realize that their ultimate partner will not be their opposite-sex parent, who already belongs to someone else. This rejection—which occurs between the ages of five and seven and is essential to the young child's development—may be painful and make him or her angry at being forced in effect to give up all hope of having the opposite-sex parent exclusively. This resentment may continue at some level even into adulthood, and hence explain the preference of women for their mothers and of men for their fathers.

It was probably hardly surprising that siblings closest in age did not fare well in these ratings, whereas lovers fared particularly well. This finding probably reflects the long-term effects of sibling rivalry, which tends to be greatest between siblings who are closest in age and thus often have to compete with each other for certain resources, including parental affection. This competition, which is often imposed on the siblings by others, may undermine the closeness of the siblings and strain their relationship.

Of course, the participants' ratings may somehow be biased. For example, men might give lower ratings than do women, or ratings of siblings might be lower because participants do not feel as much sense of internal obligation to give siblings high ratings. We have no basis to believe that such biases were exhibited, but they always remain a possibility. The plausibility and interpretability of our results led us to believe that any biases were probably small.

PREDICTIONS FROM FAMILY TIES

According to one line of reasoning, the closer the lover's family, the better he or she is likely to be as a partner in a close relationship. The reasoning is that for a person to be successful in love, he or she needs good role models; that close family relationships provide these; and hence that a happy, loving family is auspicious. An alternative hypothesis, however, predicts just the opposite: that people from close families are less likely to become highly involved in loving in a new relationship because, having "used up" their love on their family, they do not have much love left to give to another. According to this hypothesis, closeness in the family of origin provides a bad prognosis for a new relationship. The lover just is not much needed.

Our data did not bear out either of these hypotheses. We can predict, to some degree, love for one member of the family of origin from love for another member of that family. In other words, families do appear to be, on the whole, more or less loving and more or less close. While ratings on the Loving and Liking Scales for one family member generally are in line with ratings for other family members, this correlation does not apply outside of the family of origin. In other words, knowing how much your lover loves her mother provides some prediction of how much she loves her father and siblings but none at all of how much she will love you. Thus, love within the family of origin is no indication of a person's ability to love another.

The Relation between Liking and Loving

We found a close relation between liking and loving, as measured by the Rubin scales. The relation was least close for the best friend of the same sex but quite high for the other rated individuals. Thus, it appears that loving and liking are not two truly separate and distinct entities, but may be related in a fundamental way—an issue I discuss in chapter 4.

The Structure of Love

In addressing the major question posed by our study— what is the nature of love?—we first used the technique of *factor analysis* to analyze the data. Factor analysis considers the underlying structure of a set of data. In breaking down our data, we found a clear general factor—one, moreover, that was the same for all of the loving relationships: mother, father, lover, sibling, and best friend of the same sex. In other words, although degrees of love differed from one relationship to another, at least some element of the structure of love did not differ. We labeled this general factor *interpersonal communication, sharing, and support*. These elements appeared to be at the heart of all of the loving relationships. Central to this factor, and hence to loving relationships, were—according to our data—sharing interests, ideas, and information, growing personally through the relationship, discovering new interests together, understanding each other well, making the other feel needed, receiving help from the other, helping the other to grow personally, and sharing deeply personal feelings.

Having determined that there is a general factor in loving relationships, we used the statistical technique of *cluster analysis* to find out whether it could be broken down into more basic elements. Once again, the results were clear. The general factor proved to be separable into meaningful clusters, such as compatibility, sharing, mutual support, and personal growth, as I will discuss in detail in chapter 2. For now, the main conclusion is that, although love may feel like a single thing, it is not: when one experiences love, one experiences a large set of feelings, desires, and thoughts that together lead a person to conclude that he or she "loves somebody." Thus, the data were consistent with Thomson's rather than Spearman's model and, of course, did not at all bear out Thurstone's model.

After one of my talks to an audience that happened to

be composed largely of retired people, a woman came up to me and told me of an experience that bore out the importance of not relying too much on one's global feelings in a relationship. Years before, having lost that global feeling, she considered her marriage just about dead. She would not even consider leaving it, however, because of her children and because she had grown up believing that a marriage is something you enter into, and then stay with, for better or worse. Eventually her mother-in-law died, and afterward, the woman found that her relationship with her husband changed dramatically. The global feeling came back. And she realized she had lost it because she had viewed herself as in competition with her mother-in-law. She had felt her husband paid more attention to his mother than to her, and so long as she felt that way, she could never fully love him. The loss of global feeling had not been global in its origin; rather, it had hinged upon one particular problem in her relationship with her husband. Had she realized what it was, she might have been able to do something about it.

PREDICTION OF SATISFACTION

To determine whether the kinds of measures used in our study would predict satisfaction in a relationship with a lover, we used the statistical technique of *stepwise multiple regression*, in which a single variable—in this case, satisfaction with the relationship with one's lover—is predicted by successively weighting statistically a set of other variables—here love-scale scores and personality variables.

Surprisingly, scores on the Rubin Liking Scale were a better predictor of satisfaction within a relationship than were those on the Rubin Loving Scale. This result, I believe, is important, because in intimate relationships, one is often much more aware of how much one loves than of how much one likes another person. While intimate relationships may be built on love, they need liking to thrive from day to day. Many relationships fail not because the people do not love each other, but because they do not particularly like each other and cannot get along. For an intimate relationship to work over the long term, both loving and liking are very important. Our results suggest that on a day-to-day basis, liking may be more important than loving. We found, though, that personality variables enter in as well.

Depressed and anxious people tended to be less satisfied in their relationships, although it is impossible to say whether the lower satisfaction was due to depression and anxiety, whether depression and anxiety were due to lesser satisfaction in the relationship, or whether both factors were due to some third variable. Relationships with depressed or anxious people tend to be difficult, for a variety of reasons. First, the significant other may feel responsible for the person's depression or anxiety. Even if you know intellectually that you are not responsible, it is hard to shrug off what can become an increasing burden of guilt over the other's unhappiness. Second, the significant other is likely to feel some compulsion to make the depressed or anxious person feel better, whether or not the other feels responsible for that person's state of mind. But the significant other is likely to find that there is little he or she can do to relieve chronic depression or anxiety and, as a result, feels frustrated and ineffectual. Over time, as the distressed person continues to be unresponsive to the significant other's attempts to cheer him or her up, the significant other may become angry. Finally, depression and anxiety can be contagious, with the result that where a relationship started off with one chronically depressed or anxious person, it may end with two such persons.

Many of us know from experience how difficult it can be to live with a chronically depressed person. Often the endings to such relationships are unhappy—but not always, as in Stuart's case. His lover seemed always to be depressed. She had sought psychotherapy, but to no avail. Stuart himself had become depressed, because he felt he was to blame for her depression, and suspected she felt the same way. The cycle of depression in one person instigating depression in the other was unraveling the relationship. The story has a happy ending. Stuart's lover sought medical help for a physical ailment. The ailment was difficult to diagnose, but when it was diagnosed, it turned out that the woman's depression was a psychological symptom of a particular illness she had. When she started taking medication for the illness, the depression largely (although not totally) subsided. And Stuart felt better not only because his lover was no longer depressed, but because he no longer felt responsible for her depression.

People who rated themselves as complementary with their lover—in other words, different in ways that rendered them compatible—were generally more satisfied in their relationships. This result supports the complementarity theory of relationships, which I shall discuss in chapter 7. Although, in general, people hit it off better if they are similar to each other, there is one area of interpersonal relationships where complementarity is particularly important—that is, complementarity with respect to needs. If one member in a relationship needs a lot of nurturance, then the relationship is likely to succeed only if the other member is truly nurturing. If both people need nurturance, but neither is capable of giving much, the relationship is likely to fail. Similarly, if one of the couple needs to feel dominating, it helps if the other seeks to be dominated. Two dominators are not likely to work things out together over a long period. One potential problem for relationships is that needs can change over time. For example, one may be used to being the nurturant and giving person in a relationship, and then decide it is time to take a little. If the other has little or nothing to give, the relationship may enter a period of distress. Also, some women who may have grown up accustomed to being dominated, and enter into their relationship willing to be dominated, decide at some point that they have had enough: The relationship will run into trouble unless such a woman's partner can modify his need to dominate.

Finally, men (but not women) who rated themselves as high in physical attractiveness were happier in their relationship than were men who rated themselves low in physical attractiveness. This last result suggests that men's physical attractiveness seems to be important to their satisfaction in relating to others. Women are generally happy to be physically attractive, but their attractiveness does not in itself bring them happiness in relating to another.

Thus, our study indicated that there was a strong likelihood of being able to predict satisfaction in loving relationships. In a follow-up study in 1985, Michael Barnes and I sought more systematically to investigate this issue by studying the role of real and ideal others in such relationships.

The Elusive Ideal

While romantic relationships typically involve two flesh-and-blood individuals—the self and another—two other elusive but nevertheless intrusive individuals may also be involved—each partner's ideal other. If each real participant in the relationship corresponds perfectly to the other's ideal, then the elusive ideal others may never intrude. However, if, as is often the case, one or the other individual differs significantly from the ideal other, the silent partners to the relationship may enter into, and possibly interfere with, the relationship in various ways. You may find yourself compared unfavorably with the ideal other, or have the feeling that the object of your partner's affections is not really you but an ideal other he or she has created. In either case, your happiness and satisfaction with the relationship may be significantly affected by a mere figment of the imagination—whether it is a "Hollywood" version of perfection or an expectation based on a person's present and past experiences and circumstances.

Consider two men, Bob and Ted, both of whom love their wives equally. Does that mean they are equally happy? Suppose Ted sets a high ideal for a loving relationship, whereas Bob does not: Ted simply expects more of a loving relationship than Bob does. For a given amount of love, then, Bob may actually be happier than Ted, because the amount of love he receives meets his expectations, whereas it does not meet Ted's. The difference between Bob's and Ted's relative levels of satisfaction may be understood in terms of a concept introduced by John Thibaut and Harold Kelley called the comparison level (CL): that is, what a person expects from a relationship, given past experience.[5] Your CL depends not only on outcomes that you have experienced or seen others experiencing but also upon the extent to which these outcomes have made an impression on you.[6]

According to Thibaut and Kelley, your happiness in a relationship will depend upon the degree to which your relationship falls above or below your CL. Suppose, though, that we slightly modify and expand the notion of the CL. First, we define the comparison level for present purposes as representing not the average level of love you have experienced in past relationships, but rather as your realistic ideal for present and future relationships—in other words, the ideal possible for your life. Second, let us expand the notion of a comparison level to include not only your ideal for how you would like to feel about the other individual, but also your ideal for how you would like your partner to feel about you. In this way, we are now in a position to explore more fully the antecedents of satisfaction in close relationships. For each member of a couple, we can then look at how each individual actually feels about the other, how each ideally would like to feel about the other, how each perceives the other to feel about him or her, and how each ideally would like the other to feel about him or her.

To explore these issues, Michael Barnes and I administered the Rubin scales, the Levinger scale, and another set of questions to twenty-four heterosexual couples involved in romantic relationships (Yale undergraduate and graduate students).[7] Participants in the study provided four different ratings for each of the items on the Rubin and the Levinger scales. These ratings were for how you feel about the other, how you believe the other feels about you, how you would wish to feel about an ideal other, and how you would wish an ideal other to feel about you. These four ratings from each member of each couple enabled us to compute many different kinds of scores on the questionnaire: In analyzing the data provided by these couples, we found that *both* absolute levels of experienced love and comparison levels of experienced love relative to ideal levels of love are very highly predictive of satisfaction in romantic relationships. Three scores entered into predicted satisfaction: first, a rating of how you feel about the other; second, a rating of how you would like the ideal other to feel about you; and last, the difference between the ratings of how the other was thought to feel about you and how you would ideally like the other to feel about you. The last could be expressed as the difference between what you want from the other and what you see yourself as getting.

Several interesting findings emerged. We first considered whether and how much ideal others matter for satisfaction in a romantic relationship. Indeed, feelings about ideal others in the abstract seem to matter, but they matter substantially less than do feelings about actual others. What matters is not so much how you feel about your ideal other, but the difference between how you feel about your ideal other as opposed to how you feel about your real other. In other words, what matters is not just what you want (ideally), but the difference between what you want and what you feel you get.

In considering whether your view of how the other feels about you matters for satisfaction in romantic relationships, and whether it matters as much as do your own feelings toward the other, we found that your views of the other's feelings toward you do matter for satisfaction as much as do your feelings toward the other. In other words, what you believe the other to feel about you matters just as much as how you feel about the other. This finding leaves an important question unanswered: To what extent are the other person's actual feelings important as opposed to your perception of those feelings?

Our data clearly indicated that the perceived rather than the actual differences best predict satisfaction. In fact, after you take into account the way you think the other person feels, how that person actually feels makes no difference to your satisfaction in the romantic relationship: that is, it is your perception of the other person's feelings rather than his or her actual feelings that matter for your satisfaction. Moreover, in our study, the actual correspondence between the ratings of a couple in a relationship is much lower than the perceived correspondence, or how each perceives the other as feeling. In other words, there is actually less agreement between the way you and your partner feel than each of you thinks there is. These findings support the notion that the partner to whom one relates is, in some sense, at least as much one's conception of the other, as it is that other as he or she exists in reality.

A former couple illustrate this point. They lived together reasonably happily for many years, but then things started getting rough. The husband acted in ways the wife could not understand. At the wife's urging, they sat down and talked about how things were going. The wife was dumbfounded by what she learned in the conversation. She discovered that her husband's feelings for her were very different from what she had thought them to be all along. The wife had a career, and discovered that her husband had resented her career all along, and had little respect for what she was doing. He had viewed himself as put upon, and as tolerating a life style that he had never wanted and still did not like. All that time, she had thought her husband had respected and even loved her the more for having a career that was important to her. After this conversation, the relationship could never again be the same, because the wife now knew that her husband was not supporting her but was rather, in his own words, "putting up" with her. The couple soon split up.

We can now see the dark side of the study's results: one often continues a relationship on the basis of essentially false information. Because our perceptions of others' feelings are often inaccurate, we may delude ourselves into being either more or less happy than we probably should be, based on the feelings of our partner. Over the long term, we may build a relationship on delusions. Sooner or later, something may happen to shatter these delusions —and then we may be in trouble. Or if the delusions are in the direction of experiencing less love than we are receiving, we may always feel unloved, regardless of what others feel for us. If we are that way, we tend to be unhappy, and to make others unhappy because of our inability to feel others' love.

An acquaintance of mine grew up in a family where there was little love. He never learned how to give love or to receive it. He eventually married a woman who loved him deeply, despite the little love she received from him. But he never could feel her love, no matter how much she offered him. Ironically, he was the one in the relationship who keenly felt unloved, and eventually he left, hoping to find love in another relationship. He probably will not find it, because he will not know it when he sees it.

Which of the variables we studied best predicted satisfaction? The single most powerful predictor of relationship satisfaction is the difference between how you think the other feels about you and how you would like an ideal other to feel about you. The best way to predict satisfaction in a love relationship with the least amount of effort would be to find out the difference between what a person wants from the other and what the person thinks he or she is getting. It is possible to receive too much as well as too little. Unhappy individuals do not always want more than they see themselves getting. Sometimes they want less. They want to keep a certain distance while their partner wants to get closer.

What do you do in a relationship where you want more closeness than your partner does? Most people in this dilemma try to bring the partner closer—and usually discover that this strategy is ineffective. As you try to draw the partner in closer, he or she reacts by pulling away. When you see the partner withdraw, you may try a different strategy. But by this time, the partner is aware that you are trying to draw him or her in, and your new strategy is likely to make him or her withdraw even further. The result often is that the more you try to bring the partner closer, the more he or she pulls away. Each person wants a certain distance or closeness, and strives to achieve it. The problem becomes more complex because often the person who wants less involvement is the one who most controls the relationship. That person has the resource the other person wants: love. As a result, relationships often break apart when the less involved person finds that there is no way that he or she can successfully maintain the relationship with the lesser level of involvement. That person often leaves the relationship altogether.

It is not always the less involved person who decides to leave. My conversations with many people who have been in asymmetrical relationships have persuaded me that it is just as often that the more involved person decides to leave. One of these people, Sarah, explained why. She left a man who, she was convinced, was phobic of commitment, at least with her. She felt, quite simply, that she was wasting her time. She was never going to get what she wanted from the man; and although it was painful to terminate the relationship, the alternative—a relationship that perpetually stood still—seemed even worse.

If you desire a higher level of involvement from the other person, the best strategy, paradoxically, is to become less involved yourself. If you are able to bring your level of involvement to a point lower than that of your partner, you may actually find that he or she will come closer to you, rather than pull away. Thus, to achieve greater closeness, you may actually have to start by looking for some distance. Relationships work because of a balance between intimacy and independence, and can fail when the balance tips too far one way or the other. To get a relationship to work, therefore, you need to know not only how to draw another person close to you (what we usually think of when we think about relationships), but also how to give the other the space he or she needs.

Another finding of the study was that in most relationships people's feelings for each other are perceived to be more or less symmetrical. Furthermore, the more asymmetrical or unequal the feelings are felt to be, the less satisfied are the participants in the relationship. This result suggests that it is important to seek at least some symmetry. In asymmetrical relationships, the more involved person is constantly frustrated with his or her inability to bring the other person closer, whereas the less involved person is continually frustrated by the repeated attempts of the more involved person to "draw" him or her in. The relationship will be happier if it is more symmetrical, even if it means the more involved person becomes less involved, at least for a while.

Finally, our study revealed a difference between the ratings of men and women. Greater involvement in the relationship by men led to satisfaction for women, whereas greater involvement on the part of women did not lead to satisfaction for men. This finding was consistent both with the cultural stereotype that, for the most part, it is women who want greater closeness, as well as with the results described earlier whereby women, but not men, often strive for greater intimacy in their close relationships.

From these findings we can conclude, first, that in evaluating your relationship with another, it is important to take into account that person's ideal as well as his or her feelings toward you. A partner who sets impossibly high ideals may never be happy with you, regardless of what you do. Similarly, if you tend to set impossibly high ideals, you may find yourself consistently unhappy. For example, I know a man who, though in his late thirties, has never married, in part because he sets such a high standard for his ideal that no one woman ever matches up to it. But having too low a standard for the ideal can be unfortunate as well, leading you to settle too quickly, and then to be disappointed with the relationship that you have chosen. By not waiting for a better partner, you may get a lot less than you bargained for or feel that you deserve. People with low self-esteem are especially likely to settle too early and for less than they actually want. Thus, the goal is to set a *realistic* ideal and then to seek it in your life.

The Role of Science in Understanding Love

You have now had a taste of how one scientist studies love. Clearly, I believe that there is a role for science in understanding love, but not an exclusive role. Science will not help us understand love's evolution through the history of civilization: that is the role of historical inquiry. Science will not let us experience through others the thrills and the tribulations of love, and to learn about love in doing so: that is the role of literature and the arts. Science will not enlighten us regarding the metaphysical properties of love or the ethical issues that surround it: that is the role of philosophy. And science will not provide for us any first-hand encounters with love: that is the role of life experience. But science can help us understand both the psychological bases and dimensions of love, and why we love in the ways we do. Scientific inquiry does not replace other forms of inquiry about love, but neither do other forms of inquiry about love obviate the need for science. Love can be explored in a wide variety of complementary ways. Although there are occasional turf wars over the "right" way to study love, no one right way exists. We need to concentrate on the notion rather than on the methodology for studying it, and a variety of methodologies converge to illuminate the notion in all its richness. If one were to "major in love," whether in college or in one's own independent study, one would probably want to take courses or do independent readings not only in psychology and sociology, but also in history, literature, the arts, and philosophy. No one discipline could possibly provide a complete understanding of love—or of anything else! And beyond any courses one might take or readings one might do, one would want to add a heavy dose of life experience to complete the major. I, for one, would be most suspicious of what anyone had to say about love if he or she had never experienced it first-hand! Science, then, can give us some answers, but by no means all of them.

In speaking of the science of love, I refer only to a segment of that field in its broadest definition. My own tradition in the field is that of social psychology, which seeks to understand the internal, psychological bases of social relations, including love. Another, historically older tradition within psychology is clinical psychology, represented by the work of Sigmund Freud, Theodore Reik, and others (see chapter 4). Whereas I seek to test my theories primarily through experiments that make heavy use of questionnaires, and only secondarily through the anecdotal evidence I have sprinkled throughout this book, clinical psychologists rely heavily on their experiences with clients in therapy as a basis for testing their theories. Perhaps for this reason, their theories take a different cast from my own and that of other social psychologists, with more emphasis on the atypical and abnormal than in social-psychological theories.

Other scientific traditions in the study of love and related phenomena go outside the boundaries of psychology. For example, Diane Vaughan, whose work is described in chapter 7, is a sociologist; and the emphasis in her research, as in the research of other sociologists, is on how social institutions affect individual and group behavior, and how such behavior affects the institutions. I believe Vaughan's work is a particularly good example of how sociological and psychological work can complement each other, dealing with different aspects of the same or related phenomena. Yet another tradition is that of biology, which is especially prominent in research on sexual behavior. Researchers in this field examine passion, but from a point of view almost totally different from my own: they examine a variety of sexual responses and the physiological mechanisms that mediate them. And, of course, anthropologists and anthropologically oriented psychologists may choose to concentrate on the evolutionary issues that underlie the development of love, or on the role of culture in defining what is meant by love. These different kinds of scientific research all contribute in their own ways toward our understanding of love.

The Ingredients of Love

I FIRST fell in love in the first grade. The girl, whom I will call Irene, was a classmate of mine and lived right up the block. She and I spent a lot of time together, playing (the usual childhood games, like hide and seek, tag, and house), walking to school, and helping each other out in any way we could. Irene and I had a modest plan: to become king and queen of the world, and to have everyone else in the world as our subjects. Irene eventually moved away, and that was the end of both our friendship and our kingdom: I never saw her again. But it seems clear in retrospect that she and I had at least one critical element of love: We were close friends and shared with each other intimacies we shared with no one else. We communicated well with each other and always felt comforted in each other's presence. Although we may not have had all the ingredients of love, we certainly had one of the most important: we cared about each other and supported each other. In short, we had an emotionally intimate relationship.

34

The Ingredients of Love

I next fell in love with Patti, who sat in front of me in tenth-grade biology class. The very first day I laid eyes on her, I fell madly in love. I spent whole classes just staring at her—but I never told her how I felt about her. My lack of communication was not for lack of feelings. I thought about Patti almost constantly and, for a year of my life, about little else. I did my schoolwork on automatic pilot. When I would talk to other people, I would be, at most, half there, because I was secretly thinking about Patti. I would go home at the end of the day and pine away thinking about her. The months went by, but I couldn't move myself to express my feelings toward her; indeed, I acted coldly toward her, because I was afraid of giving myself away (which I probably did, anyway). I was crushed when, right after New Year's Day, I saw her clandestinely reading a handwritten letter, and her best friend told me that Patti had met a boy at a New Year's Eve party and fallen in love with him. To make matters worse, the boy was captain of one of the school's athletic teams, and I wasn't even on a team. Eventually, I got over my obsession with Patti, and we even became somewhat friendly, though I discovered that I liked her decidedly less than I had loved her.

The feeling I had for Patti was a second ingredient of love: passion. And whereas the intimacy I felt with Irene was mutual, as intimacy almost has to be, the passion I felt for Patti was one-sided, as passion often is. In retrospect, of course, I would call my love for Patti infatuation, since it developed without my even knowing her and continued in the absence of any real mutual relationship between us. But infatuation is fueled more vigorously by doubts and uncertainties than by knowledge of what a person is like. Eventually, Patti went away to college, and I never saw her again.

The third time I fell in love was with Cindy, whom I met relatively soon after I met Patti. My relationship with Cindy was everything my relationship with Patti was not, and vice versa. In a word, my relationship with Cindy was "sensible." We had relatively similar backgrounds and upbringings; we both did well in school and were career oriented; and in a nutshell, we were what people would call a good match. Our relationship had neither the deep intimacy of my relationship with Irene nor the overwhelming passion of my one-sided relationship with Patti, but it did have something that the other two relationships had lacked. Cindy and I believed we loved each other, and relatively quickly committed ourselves to each other. We worked out a system whereby we would call each other every night and see each other regularly. We were viewed as an "item" by others, and viewed ourselves that way as well. Our relationship was pretty much exclusive; and as time went on and our commitment to each other increased, the time we spent with others decreased. Our commitment continued to grow; eventually, though, it declined, and we later split up. It is always hard to say why particular couples split up; but in our case I believe that, with the waning of passion over time, we had not developed sufficient intimacy to fuel our commitment to each other.

Paramount in each of these relationships of mine was one of the three ingredients, or components, of love: intimacy (with Irene), passion (for Patti), and commitment (to Cindy).[1] I believe that love can be understood as a triangle (which should not be confused with a "love triangle" of three people) of which each point is one of these three components: intimacy (the top point of the triangle), passion (the left-hand point), and decision/commitment (the right-hand point)[2] (see figure 2.1).

The Ingredients of Love

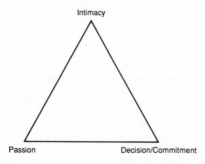

Figure 2.1 *The triangle of love. The assignment of components to vertices is one of convenience; it is essentially arbitrary.*

A substantial body of evidence, which I shall cite throughout the book, suggests that the components of intimacy, passion, and commitment play a key role in love over and above other attributes. Even before I collected the first bit of data to test my theory, I had several reasons for choosing these three components as the building blocks for it.

First, many of the other aspects of love prove, on close examination, to be either parts or manifestations of these three components. Communication, for example, is a building block of intimacy, as is caring or compassion. Were one to subdivide intimacy and passion and commitment into their own subparts, the theory would eventually contain so many elements as to become unwieldy. There is no one, solely correct fineness of division. But a division into three components works well in several ways, as I hope to show in this chapter and beyond.

Second, my review of the literature on couples in the United States, as well as in other lands, suggested that, whereas some elements of love are fairly time-bound or culture-specific, the three I propose are general across time and place. The three components are not equally weighted in all cultures, but each component receives at least some weight in virtually any time or place.

Third, the three components do appear to be distinct, although, of course, they are related. You can have any one without either or both of the others. In contrast, other potential building blocks for a theory of love—for example, nurturance and caring—tend to be difficult to separate, logically as well as psychologically.

Fourth, as I will show in chapter 4, many other accounts of love seem to boil down to something similar to my own account, or a subset of it. If we take away differences in language and tone, the spirit of many other theories converges with mine.

Finally, and perhaps most important, the theory works —as I hope to demonstrate in the remainder of this chapter and throughout the book.

✳ *Intimacy*

In the context of the triangular theory, intimacy refers to those feelings in a relationship that promote closeness, bondedness, and connectedness. My research with Susan Grajek (as described in the previous chapter) indicates that intimacy includes at least ten elements:

1. *Desiring to promote the welfare of the loved one.* The lover looks out for the partner and seeks to promote his or her welfare. One may promote the other's welfare at the expense of one's own—but in the expectation that the other will reciprocate when the time comes.

2. *Experiencing happiness with the loved one.* The lover enjoys being with his or her partner. When they do things

together, they have a good time and build a store of memories upon which they can draw in hard times. Furthermore, good times shared will spill over into the relationship and make it better.

3. *Holding the loved one in high regard.* The lover thinks highly of and respects his or her partner. Although the lover may recognize flaws in the partner, this recognition does not detract from the overall esteem in which the partner is held.

4. *Being able to count on the loved one in times of need.* The lover feels that the partner is there when needed. When the chips are down, the lover can call on the partner and expect that he or she will come through.

5. *Having mutual understanding with the loved one.* The lovers understand each other. They know each other's strengths and weaknesses and how to respond to each other in a way that shows genuine empathy for the loved one's emotional states. Each knows where the other is "coming from."

6. *Sharing oneself and one's possessions with the loved one.* One is willing to give of oneself and one's time, as well as one's things, to the loved one. Although all things need not be joint property, the lovers share their property as the need arises. And, most important, they share themselves.

7. *Receiving emotional support from the loved one.* The lover feels bolstered and even renewed by the loved one, especially in times of need.

8. *Giving emotional support to the loved one.* The lover supports the loved one by empathizing with, and emotionally supporting, him or her in times of need.

9. *Communicating intimately with the loved one.* The lover can communicate deeply and honestly with the loved one, sharing innermost feelings.

10. *Valuing the loved one.* The lover feels the great importance of the partner in the scheme of life.

These are only some of the possible feelings one can experience through the intimacy of love; moreover, it is not necessary to experience all of these feelings in order to experience intimacy. To the contrary, our research indicates that you experience intimacy when you sample a sufficient number of these feelings, with that number probably differing from one person and one situation to another. You do not usually experience the feelings independently, but often as one overall feeling.

What makes for intimacy? Different psychologists say similar things, albeit in different ways. For Harold Kelley and his colleagues, intimacy results from strong, frequent, and diverse interconnections between people.[3] The intimate couple, then, have strong ties and interact frequently in a variety of ways. Lillian Rubin lists as the qualities of friendship what I view here as some of the keys to intimacy: trust, honesty, respect, commitment, safety, support, generosity, loyalty, mutuality, constancy, understanding, and acceptance.[4]

Intimacy probably starts in self-disclosure. To be intimate with someone, you need to break down the walls that separate one person from another. It is well known that self-disclosure begets self-disclosure: if you want to get to know what someone else is like, let him or her learn about you.[5] But self-disclosure is often easier in same-sex friendships than in loving relationships, probably because people see themselves as having more to lose by self-disclosure in a loving relationship.[6] And odd as it may sound, there is actually evidence that spouses may be less symmetrical in self-disclosure than are strangers, again probably because the costs of self-disclosure can be so high in love.[7]

One theorist has tried to put together the various findings on self-disclosure by suggesting that there is a curvilinear relationship between reciprocity and self-disclosure.[8] The idea is that the rewards of reciprocity in self-disclosure increase up to a certain point; but when a couple become very intimate, the costs of self-disclosure become so great that it often will decrease, at least for one, if not both, partners.

Many of us have had the experience of confiding a deep, dark secret to someone, only to get burned for having done so. I once had a friend to whom I confided what I considered to be an intimate secret. In talking to a friend of my friend, I became painfully aware of the fact that this person, who was no friend of mine, knew every detail. Needless to say, I never confided in the so-called friend again, and was for a while hesitant to confide in anyone.

Intimacy, then, is a foundation of love, but a foundation that develops slowly, through fits and starts, and is difficult to achieve. Moreover, once it starts to be attained, it may, paradoxically, start to go away because of the threat it poses. It poses a threat in terms not only of the dangers of self-disclosure but of the danger one starts to feel to one's existence as a separate, autonomous being. Few people want to be "consumed" by a relationship, yet many people start to feel as if they are being consumed when they get too close to another human being. The result is a balancing act between intimacy and autonomy which goes on throughout the lives of most couples, a balancing act in which a completely stable equilibrium is often never achieved. But this in itself is not necessarily bad: the swinging back and forth of the intimacy pendulum provides some of the excitement that keeps many relationships alive.

Passion

The passion component of love includes what Elaine Hatfield and William Walster refer to as a "state of intense longing *for union* with the other."[9] Passion is largely the expression of desires and needs—such as for self-esteem, nurturance, affiliation, dominance, submission, and sexual fulfillment. The strengths of these various needs vary across persons, situations, and kinds of loving relationship. For example, sexual fulfillment is likely to be a strong need in romantic relationships but not in filial ones. These needs manifest themselves through psychological and physiological arousal, which are often inseparable from each other.

Passion in love tends to interact strongly with intimacy, and often they fuel each other. For example, intimacy in a relationship may be largely a function of the extent to which the relationship meets a person's need for passion. Conversely, passion may be aroused by intimacy. In some close relationships with members of the opposite sex, for example, the passion component develops almost immediately; and intimacy, only after a while. Passion may have drawn the individuals into the relationship in the first place, but intimacy helps sustain the closeness in the relationship. In other close relationships, however, passion, especially as it applies to physical attraction, develops only after intimacy. Two close friends of the opposite sex may find themselves eventually developing a physical attraction <u>for each other once they have achieved a certain emotional intimacy</u>.

Sometimes intimacy and passion work against each other. For example, in a relationship with a prostitute, a man may seek to maximize fulfillment of the need for passion while purposefully minimizing intimacy. An inverse relation between intimacy and passion can be a function of the person as well as of the situation: some people find that the attainment of emotional closeness and intimacy actually interferes with sexual fulfillment, or that passionate involvement is detrimental to emotional intimacy. The point, quite simply, is that although the interaction between intimacy and passion will vary across people and across situations, these two components of love will almost certainly interact in close relationships in one way or another.

<u>Most people, when they think of passion, view it</u> as <u>sexual. But any form of psychophysiological arousal can generate the experience of passion</u>. For example, an individual with a high need for affiliation may experience passion toward an individual who provides him or her with a unique opportunity to affiliate. For example, Debbie grew up in a broken home, with no extended family to speak of, and two parents who were constantly at war with each other and eventually divorced when she was an adolescent. Debbie felt as though she never had a family, and when she met Arthur, her passion was kindled. What he had to offer was not great sex but a large, warm, closely knit family that welcomed Debbie with open arms. Arthur was Debbie's ticket to the sense of belongingness she had never experienced but had always craved,

and his ability to bring belongingness into her life aroused her passion for him. As time went on, though, she found that an extended family did not a marriage make, and eventually divorced Arthur. She is still close to his family, however.

For other people, the need for submission can be the ticket to passion. Connie's father was happy with nothing less than the complete subjugation of her mother, physical as well as psychological. For Connie, as well as for other women who grew up in Connie's working-class milieu, being loved may be tantamount to being submissive or even subjugated. To some extent, the stimuli that ignite passion constitute a learned response. Thus, Connie learned to be dominated in body as well as mind. Social workers are often frustrated when, after months spent getting a battered woman to leave her husband, the woman ultimately goes back to the batterer. To some observers, her return may seem incomprehensible; to others, it may seem like a financial decision. But often it is neither. Such a woman has had the misfortune to identify abuse with being loved and, in going back to the abuse, is returning to what is, for her, love as she has learned it.

These patterns of response have been established through years of observation and sometimes first-hand experience, which cannot be easily undone by a social worker or anyone else in a few months. Probably the strangest learning mechanism for the buildup of passionate response is the mechanism of *intermittent reinforcement*, the periodic, sometimes random rewarding of a particular response to a stimulus. If you try to accomplish something, and sometimes are rewarded for your efforts and sometimes not, you are being intermittently reinforced.

The Ingredients of Love

Oddly enough, intermittent reinforcement is even more powerful at developing or sustaining a given pattern of behavior than is continuous reinforcement. You are more likely to lose interest in or desire for something, and to become bored, if you are always rewarded when you seek it than if you are sometimes rewarded, but sometimes not. Put another way, sometimes the fun is in wanting something rather than in getting it. And if you are never rewarded for a given pattern of behavior, you are likely to give up on it ("extinguish," as learning theorists would say), if only because of the total frustration you experience when you act in that particular way.

Passion thrives on the intermittent reinforcement that is intense at least in the early stages of a relationship. When you want someone, sometimes you feel as if you are getting closer to him or her, and sometimes you feel you are not—an alternation that keeps the passion aroused. Thus, the little boy may, in seeking out his mother, feel for a while that he is making progress in getting her; but then, as I mentioned in chapter 1, must come to terms with the fact that he can never have her in just the way he wants. Those passionate feelings do not entirely disappear, however, but go into a latent state, waiting to be rekindled, usually years later, by a female peer who, more often than not, resembles the mother in significant ways. The stimulus that rekindles the passion is similar to the stimulus of the past—the mother. And the pattern of intermittent reinforcement starts again, except this time one has some hope of getting the object of desire. But if the getting or the keeping is too easy, and continuous reinforcement replaces the intermittent kind, the man may, ironically, lose interest in what he has been seeking. The same principles apply for women, but with respect to the father.

Decision and Commitment

The decision/commitment component of love consists of two aspects—one short-term and one long-term. The short-term aspect is the decision to love a certain other, whereas the long-term one is the commitment to maintain that love. These two aspects of the decision/commitment component of love do not necessarily occur together. The decision to love does not necessarily imply a commitment to that love. Oddly enough, the reverse is also possible, where there is a commitment to a relationship in which you did not make the decision, as in arranged marriages. Some people are committed to loving another without ever having admitted their love. Most often, however, a decision precedes the commitment both temporally and logically. Indeed, the institution of marriage represents a legalization of the commitment to a decision to love another throughout life.

While the decision/commitment component of love may lack the "heat" or "charge" of intimacy and passion, loving relationships almost inevitably have their ups and downs, and in the latter, the decision/commitment component is what keeps a relationship together. This component can be essential for getting through hard times and for returning to better ones. In ignoring it or separating it from love, you may be missing exactly that component of a loving relationship that enables you to get through the hard times as well as the easy ones. Sometimes, you may have to trust your commitment to carry you through to the better times you hope are ahead.

The decision/commitment component of love interacts with both intimacy and passion. For most people, it results from the combination of intimate involvement and passionate arousal; however, intimate involvement or passionate arousal can follow from commitment, as in certain arranged marriages or in close relationships in which you do not have a choice of partners. For example, you do not get to choose your mother, father, siblings, aunts, uncles, or cousins. In these close relationships, you may find that whatever intimacy or passion you experience results from your cognitive commitment to the relationship, rather than the other way around. Thus, love can start off as a decision.

The expert in the study of commitment is the UCLA psychologist Harold Kelley, who believes that love and commitment overlap, but that you can have one without the other.[10] He gives as an example the Michelle Triola–Lee Marvin lawsuit, in which Triola sued the actor Marvin for "palimony." Although they had lived together for some time, they had never been married. And, however they may have loved each other, permanent commitment was clearly not in Marvin's mind.

For Kelley, commitment is the extent to which a person is likely to stick with something or someone and see it (or him or her) through to the finish. A person who is committed to something is expected to persist until the goal underlying the commitment is achieved. A problem for contemporary relationships is that two members of a couple may have different ideas about what it means to stick with someone to the end or to the realization of a goal. These differences, moreover, may never be articulated. One person, for example, may see the "end" as that point where the relationship is no longer working, whereas the other may see the end as the ending of one of the couple's lives. In a time of changing values and notions of commitment, it is becoming increasingly common for couples to find themselves in disagreement about the exact nature and duration of their commitment to each other. When marital commitments were always and automatically assumed to be for life, divorce was clearly frowned upon. Today, divorce is clearly more acceptable than it was even fifteen years ago, in part because many people have different ideas about how durable and lasting the marital commitment need be.

Difficulties in mismatches between notions of commitment cannot always be worked out by discussing mutual definitions of it, because these may change over time and differently for the two members of a couple. Both may intend a life-long commitment at the time of marriage, for example; but one of them may have a change of mind —or heart—over time. Moreover, as Kelley points out, it is important to distinguish between commitment to a person and commitment to a relationship. While two people may both be committed to each other, one may see the commitment as extending to the person and to a relationship with that person, but not necessarily to the type of relationship the couple have had up to a certain point. This person may wish to alter the kind of relationship they have. For example, one may be committed to one's husband and to having a relationship with that husband, but not to the kind of submissive role one has taken in the past with respect to him.

Properties of the Components of Love

The three components of love have different properties (see table 2.1). For example, intimacy and commitment seem to be relatively stable in close relationships, whereas passion tends to be relatively unstable and can fluctuate unpredictably. You have some degree of conscious control over your feelings of intimacy (if you are aware of them), a high degree of control over the commitment of the decision/commitment component that you invest in the relationship (again, assuming awareness), but little control over the amount of passionate arousal you experience as a result of being with or even looking at another person. You are usually aware and conscious of passion, but awareness of the intimacy and decision/commitment components can be highly variable. Sometimes you experience warm feelings of intimacy without being aware of them or able to label them. Similarly, you are often not certain of how committed you are to a relationship until people or events intervene to challenge that commitment.

The importance of each of the three components of love varies, on the average, according to whether a loving relationship is short-term or long-term. In short-term involvements, and especially romantic ones, passion tends to play a large part, whereas intimacy may play only a moderate part, and decision/commitment may play hardly any part at all. In contrast, in a long-term close relationship, intimacy and decision/commitment typically must play relatively large parts. In such a relation-

TABLE 2.1
Properties of the Triangle

Properties	Intimacy	Passion	Decision/ Commitment
Stability	moderately high	low	moderately high
Conscious controllability	moderate	low	high
Experiential salience	variable	high	variable
Typical importance in short-term relationships	moderate	high	low
Typical importance in long-term relationships	high	moderate	high
Commonality across loving relationships	high	low	moderate
Psychophysiological involvement	moderate	high	low
Susceptibility to conscious awareness	moderately low	high	moderately high

ship, passion typically plays only a moderate part, and its role may decline somewhat over time.

The three components of love also differ in their presence in various loving relationships. Intimacy appears to be at the core of many loving relationships, whether that relationship is with parent, sibling, lover, or close friend. Passion tends to be limited to certain kinds of loving relationship, especially romantic ones; whereas decision/commitment can be highly variable across different loving relationships. For example, commitment tends to be high in love for one's children, but relatively low in love for friends who come and go throughout the span of a life.

The three components also differ in the amount of psychophysiological involvement they offer. Passion is highly dependent on psychophysiological involvement, whereas decision/commitment appears to involve little psychophysiological response. Intimacy involves an intermediate amount of psychophysiological involvement.

In sum, the three components of love have somewhat different properties, which tend to highlight some of the ways they function in the experiences of love as they occur in various close relationships.

Kinds of Loving

How do people love, and what are some examples of ways in which they love? A summary of the various kinds of love captured by the triangular theory is shown in table 2.2.

TABLE 2.2
Taxonomy of Kinds of Love

Kind of Love	Intimacy	Passion	Decision/ Commitment
Non-love	−	−	−
Liking	+	−	−
Infatuated love	−	+	−
Empty love	−	−	+
Romantic love	+	+	−
Companionate love	+	−	+
Fatuous love	−	+	+
Consummate love	+	+	+

Note: + = component present; − = component absent. These kinds of love represent idealized cases based on the triangular theory. Most loving relationships will fit between categories, because the components of love occur in varying degrees, rather than being simply present or absent.

INTIMACY ALONE: LIKING

Joe was intensely jealous. He had thought he and Stephanie were "a couple." But Stephanie seemed to be spending almost as much time with Alex as she was spending with Joe. Joe was afraid she was two-timing him. Finally, he confronted her.

"I just can't stand this any more."

"Huh? What can't you stand?"

"Your relationship with Alex. If you prefer him to me, that's fine. Just say the word, and I'll be on my way. But you seem to want us both, and I just won't stand for it any longer."

"I don't know what you're talking about. Alex is no competition for you—none at all. What in the world makes you think he is?"

"But you're spending as much time with him as you are with me, not to mention what you may be doing with that time."

"Joe, you're off, you're way off. Alex is a good friend. I do like his company. I like doing things with him. I like talking to him. But I don't love him, and I never will. I don't plan to spend my life with him. He's a friend, and nothing more, but nothing less either."

"Oh, I see." But Joe didn't really see that Stephanie's relationship with Alex was a friendship, and nothing more.

Liking results when you experience only the intimacy component of love without passion or decision/commitment. The term *liking* is used here in a nontrivial sense, to describe not merely the feelings you have toward casual acquaintances and passers-by, but rather the set of feelings you experience in relationships that can truly be characterized as friendships. You feel closeness, bondedness, and warmth toward the other, without feelings of intense passion or long-term commitment. Stated another way, you feel emotionally close to the friend, but the friend does not arouse your passion or make you feel that you want to spend the rest of your life with him or her.

It is possible for friendships to have elements of passionate arousal or long-term commitment, but such friendships go beyond mere liking. You can use the absence test to distinguish mere liking from love that goes beyond liking. If a typical friend whom you like goes away, even for an extended period of time, you may miss him or her but do not tend to dwell on the loss. You can pick up the friendship some years later, often in a different form, without even having thought much about the friendship during the intervening years. When a close relationship goes beyond liking, however, you actively miss the other person and tend to dwell on or be preoccupied with his or her absence. The absence has a substantial and fairly long-term effect on your life. When the absence of the other arouses strong feelings of intimacy, passion, or commitment, the relationship has gone beyond liking.

Passion Alone: Infatuated Love

Tom met Lisa at work. One look at her was enough to change his life: he fell madly in love with her. Instead of concentrating on his work, which he hated, he would think about Lisa. She was aware of this, but did not much care for Tom. When he tried to start a conversation with her, she moved on as quickly as possible. Tom's staring and his awkwardness in talking to her made her feel uncomfortable. He, on the other hand, could think of little else besides Lisa, and his work began to suffer as the time he should have been devoting to it went instead to thinking about Lisa. He was a man obsessed. The obsession might have gone on indefinitely but Lisa moved away. Tom never saw Lisa again, and after several unanswered love letters, he finally gave up on her.

Tom's "love at first sight" is infatuated love or, simply, infatuation. It results from the experiencing of passionate arousal without the intimacy and decision/commitment components of love. Infatuation is usually obvious, although it tends to be somewhat easier for others to spot than for the person who is experiencing it. An infatuation can arise almost instantaneously and dissipate as quickly. Infatuations generally manifest a high degree of psychophysiological arousal and bodily symptoms such as increased heartbeat or even palpitations of the heart, increased hormonal secretions, and erection of genitals (penis or clitoris). Infatuation is essentially what the love researcher Dorothy Tennov calls "limerence" and, like it, can be quite lasting.[11]

DECISION/COMMITMENT ALONE: EMPTY LOVE

John and Mary had been married for twenty years, for fifteen of which Mary had been thinking about getting a divorce, but could never get herself to go through with it. Because she did not work outside the home, she was afraid she would be unable to make a living; besides, life alone might be worse than with John. And life with John was not bad. Basically, he left her alone. He was almost never home; and when he was, he pretty much stuck to doing his work. Whatever passion they might once have had was long since gone—Mary had long felt that John had found other women; and even the little intimacy they had once had had vanished. At this point, they hardly ever even talked. Mary often wondered whether John would leave, and sometimes wished he would. But he seemed content to have her wash his clothes, prepare his meals, keep house, and do all the things that she had long ago been taught a wife should do. Mary often felt that her life would be completely empty were it not for her children.

Mary's kind of love emanates from the decision that you love another and are committed to that love even without having the intimacy or the passion associated with some loves. It is the love sometimes found in stagnant relationships that have been going on for years but that have lost both their original mutual emotional involvement and physical attraction. Unless the commitment to the love is very strong, such love can be close to none at all. Although in our society we see empty love generally as the final or near-final stage of a long-term relationship, in other societies empty love may be the first stage of a long-term relationship. As I have said, in societies where marriages are arranged, the marital partners start with the commitment to love each other, or to try to do so, and not much more. Here, *empty* denotes a relationship that may come to be filled with passion and intimacy, and thus marks a beginning rather than an end.

INTIMACY + PASSION: ROMANTIC LOVE

Susan and Ralph met in their junior year of college. Their relationship started off as a good friendship, but rapidly turned into a deeply involved romantic love affair. They spent as much time together as possible, and enjoyed practically every minute of it. But Susan and Ralph were not ready to commit themselves permanently to the relationship: both felt they were too young to make any long-term decisions, and that until they at least knew where they would go after college, it was impossible to tell even how much they could be together. Ralph was admitted to graduate study at UCLA and decided to go there. Susan, an engineer, had applied to the California Institute of Technology and was accepted, but without financial aid. She was also accepted by the Massachusetts Institute of Technology with a large fellowship. The difference in financial packages left her with little choice but to go to Massachusetts. When she went out east, neither she nor Ralph had much confidence that their relationship would survive the distance; and in fact, after a year of occasional commutes and not so occasional strains, it ended.

Ralph and Susan's relationship combines the intimacy and passion components of love. In essence, it is liking with an added element: namely, the arousal brought about by physical attraction. Therefore, in this type of love, the man and woman are not only drawn physically to each other but are also bonded emotionally. This is the view of romantic love found in classic works of literature, such as *Romeo and Juliet*. Elaine Hatfield and William Walster, however, argue that romantic love does not differ from infatuation.[12]

INTIMACY + COMMITMENT: COMPANIONATE LOVE

In their twenty years of marrige, Sam and Sara had been through some rough times. They had seen many of their friends through divorces, Sam through several jobs, and Sara through an illness that at one point had seemed as though it might be fatal. Both had friends, but there was no doubt in either of their minds that they were each other's best friend. When the going got rough, each of them knew he or she could count on the other. Neither Sam nor Sara felt any great passion in their relationship, but they had never sought out others, because they both believed they had what mattered most to them: the ability to say or do anything they might want without fear of attack or reprisal. Although they each knew there were probably limits to their regard for each other, they had never sought to test these limits, because they were happy to live within them.

Sam and Sara's kind of love evolves from a combination of the intimacy and decision/commitment components of love. It is essentially a long-term, committed friendship, the kind that frequently occurs in marriages in which physical attraction (a major source of passion) has waned. This view of companionate love—captured in the title of Steve Duck's *Friends for Life*[13]—is also essentially the same as that of Ellen Berscheid and Elaine Walster.[14]

PASSION + COMMITMENT: FATUOUS LOVE

When Tim and Diana met at a resort in the Bahamas, they were each on the rebound. Tim's fiancée had abruptly broken off their engagement and essentially eloped with the man who had been Tim's close colleague. Moreover, Tim had just lost his job. Diana was recently divorced, the victim of the "other woman." Each felt desperate for love, and when they met each other, they immediately saw themselves as a match made in heaven. Indeed, it was as though someone had watched over them, seen their plight, and brought them together in their time of need. The manager of the resort, always on the lookout for vacation romances as good publicity, offered to marry them at the resort and to throw a lavish reception at no charge, other than cooperation in promotional materials. After thinking it over, Tim and Diana agreed. They knew they were right for each other, and because neither was particularly well off at the moment, the possibility of a free wedding was appealing. Regrettably, the marriage proved to be a disaster once Tim and Diana returned from their vacation. Although he was great fun to be with, Tim had never been one for taking employment seriously, whereas Diana expected him to get a job and support her. Tim, in turn, was shocked to learn that Diana did not expect to work, thus disappointing his expectations of receiving at least some financial support from her in order to further his aspiration to become a poet.

Fatuous love, as in the case of Tim and Diana, results

from the combination of passion and decision/commitment without intimacy, which takes time to develop. It is the kind of love we sometimes associate with Hollywood, or with a whirlwind courtship, in which a couple meet one day, get engaged two weeks later, and marry the next month. This love is fatuous in the sense that the couple commit themselves to one another on the basis of passion without the stabilizing element of intimate involvement. Since passion can develop almost instantaneously, and intimacy cannot, relationships based on fatuous love are not likely to last.

INTIMACY + PASSION + COMMITMENT: CONSUMMATE LOVE

Harry and Edith seemed to all their friends to be the perfect couple. And what made them distinctive from many such "perfect couples" is that they pretty much fulfilled the notion. They felt close to each other, they continued to have great sex after fifteen years, and they could not imagine themselves happy over the long term with anyone else. Harry had had a few flings, none of them serious, and eventually told Edith about them, unaware of the fact that she already knew about them because he was so transparent. Edith, on the other hand, had had no extramarital affairs. But they had weathered their few storms, and each was delighted with the relationship and with each other.

Consummate, or complete, love like Edith and Harry's results from the combination of the three components in equal measure. It is a love toward which many of us strive, especially in romantic relationships. Attaining consummate love is analogous, in at least one respect, to meeting your goal in a weight-reduction program: reaching your ideal weight is often easier than maintaining it. Attaining consummate love is no guarantee that it will last; indeed, one may become aware of the loss only after it is far gone. Consummate love, like other things of value, must be guarded carefully.

I do not believe that all aspects of consummate love are necessarily difficult either to develop or to maintain. For example, love for one's children often carries with it the deep emotional involvement of the intimacy component, the satisfaction of motivational needs (such as nurturance, self-esteem, self-actualization) of the passion component, and the firm commitment of the decision/commitment component. For many but not all parents, formation and maintenance of this love is no problem. Perhaps the bonding between parents and children at birth renders this love relatively easier to maintain, or perhaps evolutionary forces are at work to ensure that parent-child bonding survives at least those formative years in which the child must depend heavily on the parent's love and support. Whichever of these possibilities holds (and it may be more than one), whether consummate love is easy or hard to form and maintain depends on the relationship and the situation.

THE ABSENCE OF THE COMPONENTS: NON-LOVE

Jack saw his colleague Myra at work almost every day. They interacted well in their professional relationship, but neither was particularly fond of the other. Neither felt particularly comfortable talking to the other about personal matters; and after a few tries, they decided to limit their conversations to business.

Non-love, as in the relationship of Jack and Myra, refers simply to the absence of all three components of love. Non-love characterizes many personal relationships, which are simply casual interactions that do not partake of love or even liking.

Time Course of the Components of Love

Each of the three components of love has a different course, and the changes in each over time almost inevitably result in changes in the nature of a loving relationship.

INTIMACY

Bill and Brenda had what for both of them was an ideal courtship. They shared the same interests and values and felt they could confide in each other. When they married, they felt they had every reason to expect a successful marriage. And it wasn't bad. But as time went on, they had less and less to say to each other, and sometimes found themselves manufacturing small talk to keep themselves occupied. Bill worked hard, but didn't believe in bringing his work home with him and so didn't talk to Brenda about it. Brenda was involved in various clubs and group activities, but Bill didn't seem very interested in hearing about them. Their sexual relationship continued to be good, but they felt themselves drifting away from each other. It wasn't any one thing—just a slow, seemingly inexorable drift. What had started as an intimate relationship became rather distant, and eventually Brenda remarked that she felt that they were living in parallel rather than together. At that point, they sought marital counseling, which succeeded in bringing them back together as they realized that their lack of communication and mutual support had become essentially a bad habit, but one that could be broken with effort on both their parts.

The course of the intimacy component of love, as I present it here, is based on Ellen Berscheid's theory of emotion in close relationships, which is itself based on George Mandler's more general theory of emotion.[15] According to Berscheid, emotion in close relationships is experienced only as the result of interruption of stereotypical interactions between partners, or what might be referred to as *scripts*.[16] In other words, if an expected action is performed, it will not cause you to feel any particular emotion; but if your partner fails to perform an expected action or performs an unexpected action, you are most likely to feel some emotion in respect to it. As two people get to know each other, they form increasing numbers of these scripts. Early in a relationship, each person will be highly uncertain about what the other will feel, say, or do, because neither has yet become able to predict the other. In general, there will be frequent interruptions and disruptions of the relationship as the two people get to know each other. As time goes on, the frequency of interruptions is likely to decrease, because the partners are getting to know each other better, becoming more predictable to each other, and becoming dependent on each other for expected behavior. According to Berscheid's theory, as the interruption decreases, so will the experienced emotion. Eventually a partner may experience little or no emotion at all. This course of emotion in close relationships may have led Kenneth Livingston to refer to love as a *process of uncertainty reduction.*[17]

The decrease in experienced intimacy in a close relationship, especially a romantic one, has both a positive and a negative side. The positive side is that the decrease in experienced intimacy is the result of an increase in interpersonal bonding: in other words, it results from the relationship's becoming closer. The couple are so connected with each other that the one doesn't recognize the other is there, just as the air we breathe can be taken for granted, despite its necessity to life. Thus, the relationship might be viewed as having a large amount of hidden intimacy. The negative side is that the lack of observable intimacy often makes it difficult to distinguish the close relationship from no relationship at all. This situation is represented in figure 2.2, which shows both hidden and experienced levels of intimacy as a function of the time course of the relationship. The failed or failing relationship will differ from the successful relationship in terms primarily of the hidden intimacy rather than of the experienced or observable intimacy.

Fortunately, there are ways of distinguishing a live relationship from one that is dying or dead. The most obvious way is to generate some interruption (unpredicted action or change in behavior) in order to activate intimacy. For example, the lover's going away, even for a brief period, can help you ascertain how much feeling you still have for him or her. Or, changing established routines, as on a joint vacation, can be useful in assessing the state of intimacy in a relationship.

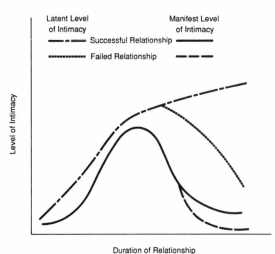

Figure 2.2 *The course of intimacy as a function
of duration of relationship.*

Sometimes it is only through extreme intervention, whether intentional or unintentional, that one learns how much intimacy one has or has had in a relationship. For example, when a partner dies, the survivor is often surprised, as are others, by his or her intense grief and distress. According to Berscheid, even couples who argue and never seem to get along can have considerable intimacy invested in the relationship, whatever the nature of that intimacy may be.[18] The death of a spouse is one of the surest ways of discovering how much you have invested in the relationship. Not that you should knock off your partner to see how you really feel about him or her, but just imagining never seeing your partner again could spark some of the hidden intimacy. Similarly, couples who divorce are often surprised by the amount of regret, or at least emotion, they experience afterward. Often they had no idea of the amount of intimacy they had in the relationship until they forcibly ended it. Indeed, the divorce may have stemmed in part from a partner's unawareness of his or her own and the other's intimate investment. Therefore, according to this view of the course of intimacy in close relationships, it is essential that couples experience minor interruptions so that they can recapture awareness of their intimate involvement before they create such a major interruption as divorce.

PASSION

When Rick met Sally, he felt passionate love for the first time. He had had other relationships and a string of casual affairs, but the relationship with Sally was different: he had never before felt truly passionate toward and engrossed by a woman. Sally, in turn, viewed the relationship as her salvation. She had just finished the second of two disastrous relationships, and this one was as different as could be. Rick and Sally saw each other every day and made love every time they got together. Over time, the relationship continued to be rewarding, but both of them felt the passion dwindling. And they both worried: What happened to the passion they had felt toward each other? Where had it gone, and how could it be restored? However much they tried, it wouldn't come back, and they felt a keen disappointment at the loss of what had once seemed so valuable to them.

The course run by the passion component in close relationships is different from that of the intimacy component. The view I present here is based on Richard Solomon's opponent-process theory of acquired motivation.[19]

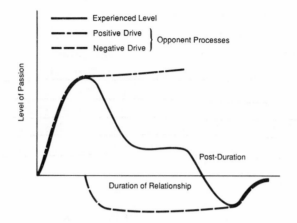

Figure 2.3 *The course of passion as a function of duration of relationship.*

According to Solomon's theory, experienced motivation (wanting or craving) for a person or an object is a function of two underlying opponent processes: the first, positive process, is quick to develop but also quick to fade; the second, negative or opponent process, is slow to develop and also slow to fade. The result of the two processes working in conjunction is a motivational course somewhat like that depicted in figure 2.3.

The passion component appears to draw heavily on psychological and bodily arousal. Moreover, its course closely resembles that predicted by Solomon's theory. Thus, this theory provides a good description of the time course of the passion component, or at least its motivational aspects.

According to the theory as used here, you can experience a surge in passion almost immediately upon meeting another person to whom you are attracted, whether physically or otherwise. This passionate arousal increases quickly but also peaks fairly rapidly. At the peak of

The Ingredients of Love

arousal, a negative force begins to work literally in opposition to the passion. At this point, the passion you experience begins to decrease; and under the influence of the negative force, you will gradually reach a more or less stable state of *habituation* of feeling in respect to the person or the object. Now both the positive and the negative (opponent) forces are in equilibrium. Should you lose the person (or the object), you do not merely go back to baseline—that is, the null level of passionate arousal you felt before encountering person or object; rather, you are likely to sink into depression, remorse, and extreme discomfort. This retrogression results from the loss of the positive passionate force (the person or object is gone) but the continuance of the negative force (the effects of the absence continue to be felt). It is only gradually that the effects of the negative force, which is slow to disappear, begin to moderate and you eventually return to the state where you originally started.

It is useful to think of the motivational model in terms of an addiction. Indeed, the similarity of the passion component of love to the motivational aspect of an addiction has led Stanton Peele to refer to love as an addiction.[20] In respect, for example, to addictive substances such as drugs, cigarettes, or coffee, one initially has no particular motivation toward or need for the addictive substance. When one starts to use the addictive substance, one feels a ''high'' as a result and is then likely to use more of the substance. With increased use, however, one starts to habituate: a given amount of the substance no longer has the same effect nor does it produce the same high it once did. Eventually one is so habituated as to need to continue the use of the substance merely to prevent withdrawal, with its resulting symptoms of depression, irritability, and craving for the substance. Should one cease use of the substance, there will be a difficult withdrawal period in which one experiences a variety of unpleasant psychological and somatic symptoms. After the withdrawal period has ended, one eventually returns to one's normal state.

DECISION AND COMMITMENT

Jeanne and Jim were nothing if not committed to each other: nothing took priority over their relationship. They married after an engagement of four years. Their marriage had the usual up-and-down swings, with some rocky times because Jim's job required frequent moves to enable him to climb the corporate ladder. But they got through it all, and when Jim turned sixty, they decided they were ready for their second honeymoon. While on the honeymoon, they realized that even when they had married, they had not realized just how committed they could be to each other. Commitment was no longer confessions of everlasting love or assurances that their relationship was forever. It was being together and staying together through the hard times as well as the easy ones, and reaffirming to each other and to themselves that, through it all, their relationship always had come first and always would.

The course of the decision/commitment component of love in a close relationship depends in large part on the success of that relationship (and vice versa). Generally, this level starts at zero, before you meet the person, and then increases. Usually, if the relationship is to become a long one, the increase in commitment in the decision/commitment component will be gradual at first and then speed up. If the relationship continues over the long term,

The Ingredients of Love

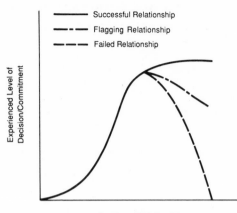

Figure 2.4 *The course of decision/commitment as a function of duration of relationship.*

the commitment will generally level off, yielding an S-shaped curve. If the relationship begins to flag, the commitment will begin to decline; and if the relationship fails, commitment may disappear entirely.

As always, the smoothness of the hypothetical curve does not take into account the tribulations of many relationships. Even the most successful relationship has its ups and downs. Figure 2.4 shows an idealized curve of decision/commitment over the duration of a relationship, without the bumps that almost inevitably occur along the way.

To conclude, the respective curves representing degrees of intimacy, passion, and decision/commitment show somewhat different forms—differences that can be even greater than shown here because of individual differences in close relationships. Because of the different trajectories of the components of love over time, relationships will change over time. By means of the geometry of the triangle of love, I shall in the next section explore the changes that occur in a relationship over time.

The Geometry of the Love Triangle

Allen and Wendy knew they loved each other. They also knew they had a problem. For Allen, true love was based on physical passion. After a series of unsatisfactory relationships, he had come to the conclusion that if a couple were good in bed, they could get through pretty much everything. For Wendy, closeness had to come first. She just couldn't go to bed with Allen if they were having an argument or feeling distant from each other. But her attitude frustrated Allen, because he believed that there was scarcely a problem that a couple couldn't work out in bed, if only given the chance. At the same time, Wendy felt frustrated with Allen: solutions to problems had to come before going to bed; they couldn't come out of going to bed, because then they were not really solutions at all, but rather avoidance of the problems. Eventually, Allen and Wendy split up, unable to resolve this fundamental difference between them.

In proceeding thus far as though there is only one type of love triangle, I have been oversimplifying. Now it is time to extend the triangular theory to take into account the great complexity of love in close relationships. In the preceding vignette, it is clear that Allen and Wendy had

The Ingredients of Love

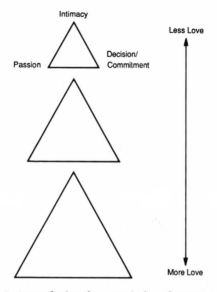

Figure 2.5 *Area of triangle as an index of amount of love.*

different ideas of what the shape of the love triangle should be.

The geometry of the love triangle depends upon two factors: amount of love and balance of love.

AMOUNT OF LOVE: AREA OF THE TRIANGLE

Figure 2.5 shows three triangles differing only in area. These differences in area represent differences in amounts of love experienced in three hypothetical relationships: the larger the triangle, the greater the amount of experienced love. It is actually possible to specify coordinates for the three components of love, with higher absolute values of coordinates representing greater amounts of each of the three hypothetical constructs.

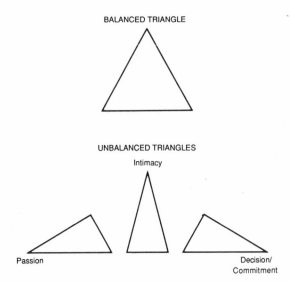

Figure 2.6 *Shape of triangle as a function of kind of love.*

BALANCE OF LOVE: SHAPE OF THE TRIANGLE

Figure 2.6 shows four distinct triangles that are dissimilar in shape. The equilateral triangle at the top represents balanced love, in which all three components of love are roughly equally matched. The second, a scalene triangle (no two sides of equal length) pointing to the left side, represents a relationship in which passion is emphasized over the other components of love. In this relationship, physical attraction is likely to play a larger part than do intimacy and decision/commitment. The third, an isosceles triangle (two sides equal in length), represents a relationship in which intimacy plays a large part and passion and decision/commitment play smaller parts. This triangle represents a relationship in which the two lovers are good friends and close to each other, but the physical aspects and commitment to the future are marginal. The

fourth, a scalene triangle pointing to the right side, represents a relationship in which the decision/commitment
component rules over intimacy and passion. This triangle
represents a highly committed relationship in which intimacy and physical attraction have waned or were never
present in the first place.

By varying both the area and the shape of the triangle
of love, one can represent a wide variety of relationships
and, particularly, the course of a close relationship over
time. The triangle is, of course, only a gross representa-
tion of the subtleties of love in a relationship. As mentioned earlier, the intimacy component in a loving relationship is not a single feeling but rather a union of many
different feelings. Similarly, many different sources of
passion may enter into love in a close relationship, and a
variety of conditions in the decision/commitment component yield the decision to love someone and the decision
to remain committed to that love. Hence, a detailed diagnosis of the state of a relationship would necessitate
going beyond looking only at the area and the shape of
the triangle. Moreover, there is much more than love to
making a relationship work. For example, such factors as
financial security, views on how to bring up children,
possible external supports in raising children, and parental involvement can contribute to making or breaking a
relationship.

My feeling for Irene, my first-grade companion, could
be described as "puppy love." Most of us know couples
who build a relationship on little more than their friendship with each other. They emphasize intimacy. For
some, friendship may be all they are looking for, but
other couples may be frustrated in their inability to attain
anything more. Richard and Martha, for example, recently split up. For years, each was the other's best friend.

They got along beautifully, never seemed to fight, and did lots of things together. They were the couple everyone was betting on, the one people were sure would not split up. After they did split up, I talked to both of them. Martha, the one who decided to leave, still describes Richard as her best friend. But her frustration with the relationship, she told me, was that she and Richard were "more like roommates than lovers." She wanted a friend, but she also wanted more, and felt that no matter how she tried, she couldn't get it from Richard. The relationship was warm, she said, but never, ever hot. There was no passion between them. Richard's characterization of the relationship was similar to Martha's. But he was in great pain over her, to him, unexpected and unjustified decision to leave. He believed they had what love is in a long-term relationship: sure, there may be intense passion early on, but, according to Richard, that passion is quickly replaced by friendship. Thus each member of the couple defined differently what it means to love in a long-term relationship—a difference Martha found irreconcilable.

Relationships involving little more than passion are by no means rare. Sometimes the passion is requited, and it can happen within as well as outside of a marriage. Jason and Bernadette are a case in point. Married for three years, they fight constantly, and cheat in their fights, hitting "below the belt" with great regularity. (Ironically, Jason is a consultant whose job it is to create harmony within large organizations.) If Jason and Bernadette like each other, they hide it well from the outside world and even from one another. I have asked each of them what holds them together. "Sex," Jason says, "the best sex I've ever had by far, and I've had a lot of it." According to Jason, he and Bernadette even fight when they make love, and he likes it that way. For him, anyway, it adds to the excitement. "Romance," says Bernadette. "We don't get along, but we're madly in love with each other, and it's been that way for three years. It was even that way when we were going out. We've never gotten along, but it's like magnetism: we're the opposite poles that attract."

Many couples stay together because of a conscious commitment—sometimes a direct one with respect to each other, but other times an indirect one. In the latter case, the partners may be committed actually to the institution of marriage, to keeping an intact family for the sake of the children, to keeping financial solvency, or to any of a host of other things. There are, for example, many couples like Jerry and Susan. Susan describes herself as feeling nothing at all for Jerry. Once she loved him, but no more. She has entertained the idea of leaving, but in all likelihood never will. Why does she stay? "For the kids," she says (they have two), "and because I have no money and no marketable skills. I could try to slug it out in court, but I'd lose; he's as much as told me that if I ever leave him I won't get a dime. I believe him. I just can't take the chance. Maybe I'd do it if I were the only one involved, but I'm not. I can't risk my kids." For Susan, what is left is commitment to a life she feels she can have only if she stays with Jerry.

The sizes and shapes of triangles may be translated into the day-to-day events that shape and are shaped by relationships. Relationships where people are differentially involved—different sizes of triangles—often fail because the less involved partner feels as if he or she cannot provide what the more involved partner wants, whereas the more involved partner feels as if the less-involved partner is always holding back and preventing the relationship from realizing its full potential.

If each partner has a triangle of a different shape, the result can be equally devastating. If one partner is frustrated owing to lack of intimacy, and the other owing to lack of passion, it is unlikely there will be any meeting of the minds—or of anything else—when the couple attempt to make the relationship work. Each wants what the other does not have to offer, and the couple is likely to go around and around, trying to make work a relationship that is failing because of the different "love triangles" each partner desires.

The Multiple Triangles of Love

Gene, at the age of thirty-six, was reasonably happy and eager to get married. But although he had met several women over the years, he did not feel that any of them were quite right for him. He viewed himself as having high standards, and none of the women he had met could quite measure up to them. Gene could not see himself entering into a permanent relationship with a woman he felt was not what he really wanted. And none of the women he had met were really what he wanted. Early on in some of his relationships, he had thought he had found what he was looking for, only to become disappointed once he got to know the women better. Discouraged, he wondered whether he would ever find the woman of his dreams. Friends suggested that he set more reasonable standards, but he did not view his standards as unreasonable. A marriage that represented a compromise could hardly be a marriage at all for him, because he would always wonder whether waiting just a little bit longer might not find him the woman he had always been looking for.

<u>Love involves not just a single triangle but, rather, a great number of triangles, only some of which are of major theoretical and practical interest.</u> The main triangles are real versus ideal, self-perceived versus other-perceived, and feelings versus actions.

REAL VERSUS IDEAL TRIANGLES

There is, in a close relationship, not only the triangle representing your love for the other but also one representing an ideal other in that relationship. This ideal may be based in part on experience in previous relationships of the same kind—Thibaut and Kelley's comparison level (as discussed on pages 23–24)—and, in part, on expectations of what the close relationship can be.[21] Expectations of a relationship's potential may or may not be grounded in reality. Figure 2.7 represents four of the possible relations between real and ideal triangles. The first panel shows real and ideal triangles as coincident: in other words, the actual relationship corresponds essentially perfectly to the ideal for that relationship. The second panel shows underinvolvement: the person's triangle in the actual relationship shows lower levels of the three components than the person ideally would like. The third panel shows overinvolvement: levels of the three components are greater than one would like. The fourth triangle shows misinvolvement: here levels of intimacy and passion are less than what one ideally might desire, but the

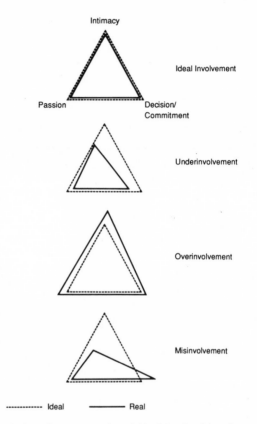

Figure 2.7 *Relations between real and ideal levels of involvement.*

level of decision/commitment is greater than that desired. Note that whereas the second and third triangles involve mismatches primarily in area, the fourth triangle involves mismatch primarily in shape. Of course, it is possible to have mismatches in both area and shape or in neither, as in the first triangle.

Our research suggests that the overlapping area between the real and the ideal triangles is associated with satisfaction in close relationships, whereas the nonoverlapping area between the two triangles is associated with

The Ingredients of Love

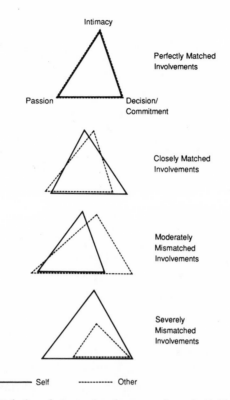

Figure 2.8 *Relations between involvement of two individuals in a relationship.*

dissatisfaction.[22] In other words, once again, you are happier when the level of involvement is close to what you want, neither more nor less.

SELF-PERCEIVED VERSUS OTHER-PERCEIVED TRIANGLES

Finally, it is possible to distinguish between self-perceived (the way you see things) and other-perceived (the way your partner sees things) triangles. In a loving relationship, you have a triangle that represents your love for the other. However, there is no guarantee that this triangle of the way you feel will be experienced by the other in the same way it is experienced by you. Since your partner in a loving relationship may not perceive your level of the three components of love in the same way you perceive your involvement, there can be discrepancies between one triangle as experienced by the self and as experienced by the other. Figure 2.8 shows two possible levels of discrepancy—one minor and one major—between self- and other-perceived triangles.

FEELINGS VERSUS ACTION TRIANGLES

Craig had assured Lucy that she was everything to him, that his life would mean nothing without her. At first, she was very pleased with his assurances. She wanted a man who put her as his top priority in his life. But over time, the assurances began to wear thin: because although Craig said that Lucy was the most important thing in his life, she did not feel that he acted that way. He traveled a great deal, and when he was around, he always seemed to have things to do that took precedence over Lucy. Craig and Lucy talked about her perception, and he assured her that he understood why she would feel as she did—but also that she was misconstruing his actions, because it was she who came first. At the same time, though, he did have other responsibilities and could not very well just let them be unfulfilled. Eventually, Lucy decided to leave the relationship: unable to reconcile Craig's actions with his words, she decided that actions speak louder than words.

The case of Lucy and Craig shows how feelings and actions can diverge. There can be any number of sources of the discrepancy between the way one person feels toward another and the way the other perceives that feeling. But almost certainly one of the most powerful sources is the failure to express one's love fully in action. It is one thing to feel a certain way but another thing altogether to express these feelings, and often the feelings fail to be communicated because of one's inability or unwillingness to show one's feelings of love. Another source of discrepancy is the fact that certain actions performed by a person as demonstrating love may not be perceived by the other as such, or may go unnoticed altogether. This discrepancy may be due to different backgrounds or upbringings, through which individuals come to understand behavior to mean certain things. This situation is most evident in couples who come from different cultural or religious backgrounds where the scheme of a close relationship may be particular. In other words, an action performed by one individual as loving according to his or her upbringing may be seen by the other as cold or meaningless. Consider, for example, physical affection. For some people, physical affection is a crucial ingredient o´ romantic love; for others, it is not.

Each of the three components of love is expressed through particular actions. For example, you might express intimacy by communicating inner feelings; promoting the other's well-being; sharing your possessions, time, and self; expressing empathy for the other; and offering emotional and material support to the other. Some ways of expressing passion include kissing, hugging, gazing, touching, and making love. Some ways of expressing decision/commitment include pledging fidelity, staying in a relationship through hard times, engagement, and marriage. Of course, the actions that express a particular component of love can differ somewhat from one person to another, from one relationship to another, and from one situation to another.

Nevertheless, it is important to consider love as it is expressed through action, because action has so many effects on a relationship. In the first place, actions can affect the level of the three components. According to self-perception theory, one's feelings and thoughts can be affected by one's actions just as one's actions can be affected by one's feelings and thoughts.[23] In other words, the way people act shapes the way they feel and think, possibly as much as the way they feel and think shapes the way they act. Second, certain actions lead to other actions. In other words, acting in certain ways tends to produce acting in related ways and, thus, to build up a network of actions. Expressing your love through action can lead to further expression of this love through action, whereas failure of self-expression can lead to further failure of this kind. Third, the way you act is likely to affect the way the other feels and thinks about you. In other words, your actions can be expected to have an effect on the other's triangle of love for you. Fourth, and finally, your actions will almost inevitably have an effect on the other's actions, thereby leading to a mutually reinforcing series of paired action sequences.

Thus, a theory of love involves not only partners in a relationship but also how they express their love. Without expression, even the greatest of loves can die.

The triangular theory may be most useful in demonstrating that relationships are dynamic. "Happily ever after" need not be a fairy tale; but if it is to be a reality, it must be happiness based upon different configurations of mutual feelings at different times in a relationship. Couples who expect the passion to last forever, or the intimacy to remain unchanged, are in for a big disappointment. Relationships are constructions that decay over time if they are not maintained and even improved. A relationship cannot take care of itself, any more than a building can. Rather, we must take responsibility for making our relationships the best they can be, and constantly work to understand, build, and rebuild them.

Looking at Love: Applying the Triangular Theory

THE TRIANGULAR THEORY accounts for many of the major findings of love research. Having dealt in chapter 2 with the various combinations of intimacy, passion, and decision/commitment, as well as the role of comparison levels and of action, I shall now show how the triangular theory can account for still other characteristics of love relationships. I will apply the theory to findings of others as well as of myself, in order to emphasize the broad applicability of the theory.

Some Earlier Findings on Love

Research clearly shows that, on a first date, physical attractiveness is almost all that matters for satisfaction.[1] The triangular theory explains why: the passion component of love sets in before the others. As a result, after a first date, one may have relatively little basis—other than passion criteria, such as physical attractiveness—for judging a partner as suitable for a loving relationship.

LOVE AS ADDICTION

According to the triangular theory, the passion component of love acts like an addiction.[2] The course of acquired motivations described earlier—habituation, increased use, dependency—applies at least as well to dependency on things such as drugs and alcohol as to dependency on other people.[3] Even though these other dependencies are physiological whereas dependency on another person is psychological, substance dependencies actually have a major psychological component. Hence, readdiction is likely, even after the physiological dependency has been conquered. Moreover, dependencies on other people probably acquire physiological as well as psychological properties. (Indeed, some psychologists maintain that psychological states always have physiological bases.) When you are jilted by a lover, the reaction can be both psychological and physiological, including symptoms such as irritability, loss of appetite, depression, and inability to concentrate.

Ignoring the addictive property of passionate love—and the likelihood of recidivism once things are over—can be perilous, as Brenda found out. She was the "other woman" in a married man's life for three years, and then decided to end the affair. Although the man repeatedly talked about leaving his wife, something kept "coming up" just when he was supposed to take the final step. Brenda told the man, Lee, that she was determined to terminate her relationship with him. He implored her for one more chance, and this time he actually left his wife. Unfortunately, the story he told his wife was very different from what he told Brenda. He told his wife he needed space and time alone—a common enough request in the California community in which they all were living. He never even mentioned Brenda—not because he didn't care but because he simply didn't know what he wanted. Disingenuously, he decided to play ball in two courts. Brenda, in the meantime, was ecstatic. She and Lee did not move in together, but they did start making plans for the future. This went on for about six months. Then, suddenly, Lee decided that he just couldn't be happy without his wife and family and abruptly moved back, this time terminating the relationship with Brenda. I believe that Lee did love Brenda, but he was addicted to his wife and also cared greatly about his children, even though he had stopped feeling close to his wife long before.

THE "HARD-TO-GET" THEORY

One of the most common observations in everyday life —that people want what they cannot have—holds for relationships, too: one is attracted to the man or woman who is "hard to get." But it is not quite that simple. For example, Elaine Hatfield and her colleagues found that people tend to be attracted not to those who are hard to get, in general, but to those who are hard for *others* to get but relatively easier to get for themselves.[4] I know many who bear out this finding: they want a woman to be not just attracted, but uniquely attracted, to them. The supreme flattery for such a man is hearing that he is the one the woman has been waiting for. Many women surely say this partly because they know the man wants to hear it.

Looking at Love: Applying the Triangular Theory

There is, though, an irony in all this. After basking in the glory of being "unique," some of these men come to feel their freedom being threatened and to worry about being rushed into a commitment. They begin to withdraw, and the relationship ends. What works in the short term may backfire in the long term. Larry, for example, repeats this pattern again and again. At forty, he is still single and—double irony—a nationally respected marriage counselor.

Of course, the Hatfield study may apply far more broadly than to love alone. Taking all one can of what others cannot get may well be a general human quality. If one gets a promotion at work, someone else doesn't. If one makes a shrewd investment, someone else loses out.

In the psychological literature, *reactance theory* seeks to explain why some people want what they have difficulty getting.[5] In effect, they react against perceived threats to their freedom of choice. According to this theory, people tend to rebel when their freedom of choice is taken away from them (that is, they react against the restriction of their freedom). Thus, things you may once not have wanted when they were readily available to you, you may want after they are no longer available to you. Ray provides a good example of this theory at work. For the sixteen years he and his wife lived together, he seemed to have little time for or interest in her. But after she left and was no longer available to him, Ray got interested in her very quickly.

Reactance theory has an interesting implication for why couples who live together before marriage are no more likely to stay together after marriage than are couples who do not first live together, and in Sweden at least, the couples actually are more likely later to divorce. When a couple live together without marriage, there may be ties of all kinds, but each member of the couple knows that the other could walk out, legally, at any time and without any notice. There may be psychological commitments, but there is no legal one; and either member of the couple who dispenses with the psychological commitment is always free to leave. Marriage can generate a state of reactance, especially among those who are used to their freedom, and it is likely that those who choose to live together without marriage may be particularly concerned with retaining some additional sense of autonomy.

The triangular theory attributes reactance largely to the passion component of love. To experience reactance, one must have difficulty attaining a desired goal (for example, attaining a lover) and believe that the desired goal is within one's grasp. The difficulty intensifies passion and usually leads to renewed attempts to attain the goal. After a certain point, these attempts can start to feed on themselves and to persist, even in the absence of a realistic chance of attaining the goal.

LIKE ATTRACTS LIKE

One of the most common findings in the literature on interpersonal attraction is that people are more likely to form relationships with and later to marry people who are similar to themselves, and to be happier in relationships with such people.[6] In the triangular theory, great similarity in each of the three components of love will lead to triangles that are more overlapping in area than not. Hence, so far as the partners have similar backgrounds, attitudes about life, and attitudes about the particular relationship, the couple are more likely to be happy in their relationship.

Looking at Love: Applying the Triangular Theory

The effects of similarity are of at least three kinds, two of which show up early in a relationship; the other does not typically show up until much later.

The first kind of similarity to show up is usually in the activities each member of a couple enjoys. If you are an outdoor type, and the other will only leave the house under duress, the mismatch will show itself fast. Couples can determine fairly rapidly whether they are matched in terms of the activities they enjoy.

The second kind of similarity is in basic beliefs and values—the couple's views on religion, politics, children, monogamy, sharing of possessions, money, and so on. Here, while similarities and dissimilarities show up quickly, what may *not* do so is how important each of these beliefs and values is to each member of the couple. Often a person does not even know how important beliefs and values are until they are challenged or even threatened. Thus, the pair may agree to disagree on religious issues, but then find themselves forced to confront the difference when children arrive on the scene, and issues of holiday celebrations and religious training come to the fore. Or the couple may disagree politically, and find the difference amusing, until one member of the couple becomes actively involved in a political movement the other finds distasteful. Or differences in views on how to spend money, and how much to save, may suddenly become important when, for the first time, a couple who have been well off find their finances tight. The point, quite simply, is that disagreements in beliefs and values can lose their charm when external circumstances, in some cases beyond the couple's control, force them to confront just how much a given belief or value means to each.

The third kind of similarity is by far the hardest to detect, and its effects may long remain latent. Oddly enough, to the extent that the partners are similar with respect to this third issue, they will not even be aware that it exists, but to the extent that they are dissimilar, it can become an issue of major importance. This third source of similarity (or dissimilarity) is in tacit assumptions about the way the world, and a relationship, should be. Because these presuppositions are tacit, they are almost never really spoken about, and most people are unaware that they even exist. But they are there, waiting to be called up at what may be the most unexpected times. For example, a man or a woman may believe that it is fine for a woman to work—and hold that belief right up to the time the first child is born. But then the woman's place is in the home with the child. I want to underscore the fact that this belief may be held by either a man or a woman. To some, this belief may sound old-fashioned; to others, it may seem the simple reality of what is best for the child. But regardless of which point of view one holds, there may be real trouble if the couple cannot reach agreement. Another related example is how much should be sacrificed by either member of the couple for a career. What if one spouse's company wants that person to move? How much time or energy should be sacrificed in the interests of a promotion, increase in wages, or increase in renown? Again, this kind of issue is hard to confront in advance because most people are only vaguely aware of how they feel about it. Thus, presuppositions can greatly influence a relationship, and it is to a couple's advantage to try to make explicit the implicit.

THE "MERE EXPOSURE" EFFECT

One of the odder findings in the literature is what Robert Zajonc has called the *mere exposure effect*.[7] It has been found that mere exposure to another individual can foster liking, although it is much less clear whether it fosters loving. This finding fits in with the triangular theory. Whereas mere exposure is not likely to generate physical attraction in and of itself, it is likely to generate at least some elements of emotional connectedness. It is difficult to be with a person over an extended time and not form some emotional bond. And it is the emotional bond that is responsible for intimacy, and thus for liking in the triangular theory. Hence, the exposure effect is likely to promote liking, but not passionate or necessarily committed love.

The mere exposure effect applies to almost anything—foods, for example. Many people do not like coffee when they first encounter it—or various forms of alcohol—but gradually acquire a taste for it. Similarly, one may only gradually come to like certain kinds of music.

A potential peril of the mere exposure effect is in various sorts of extramarital relationships that start off as cross-gender friendships and are never intended to be anything more. The husband or wife may genuinely have all of the best intentions, and then find those intentions becoming shakier and shakier as the mere exposure effect runs its course. Thus, Peter, an engineer, developed a friendship with a woman colleague, Sherry. They worked together on several projects, and it was only natural that their relationship might change, given both their proximity and their common interests. The story of Peter and Sherry is an oft-told tale. What started as a collegial relationship developed into a good friendship, and what developed into a friendship was on the road to becoming what for both of them could have been an extramarital affair. This particular case, though, didn't go that way. Sherry confronted Peter with what she perceived to be happening, and both decided it would be too much of a risk for them to become romantically involved. They continued to be friends, and are friends to this day, despite the fact that Sherry was promoted and eventually transferred elsewhere.

MAINTAINING A RELATIONSHIP

Once a relationship is established, it goes through a certain course. Among various ideas about this course, some theorists have proposed stage models of the development and, in some cases, dissolution of relationships.[8] The triangular theory predicts that a relationship will generally fluctuate in quality over time, owing to the different courses over time of the three components of love (see chapter 2).

One frequent finding, both in people's experience and in the literature on interpersonal attraction, is that it is difficult to maintain romantic love over a long period.[9] This aspect of the course of relationships is predicted by the rapid rise but also the relatively rapid fall of the passion component in close relationships. Romance can wane relatively rapidly. However, the rate at which passion declines will depend on the relative strengths of the positive and negative forces in the opponent-process account of motivation, and the relative strengths of these two forces are likely to differ with the particular individuals involved. For example, one's general need for sexual fulfillment may last long beyond the need for sexual fulfillment from any particular person. The needs that lead many of us to feel unconditional love for our children also seem to be remarkably persistent, for reasons that are not altogether clear. In general, relationships will go through different stages as a function of the courses of the three components; and although there will be differences among people, relationships, and situations in the exact shapes of the respective curves of intimacy, passion, and commitment, there will always be changes in the nature of the relationship with changes over time in the three components of love.

Consider an analogy. Most of us know at least several people who have tried to stop smoking. Some of them succeeded; others failed. Of those who succeeded, some found it easier to stop than others. The ease with which people quit is only moderately related to the strength and longevity of the habit (the positive force behind their smoking), because people differ in the counter force (opponent process) they can bring to bear against the smoking. Similarly, people differ in how easily they can get over (as well as form) relationships as a function of the relative strength of whatever has kept them in a relationship versus the strength of the force they can muster to get over it.

One aspect of development in virtually all successful relationships is what Irwin Altman and Dalmas Taylor refer to as _social penetration_—the increasing depth and breadth of relationships as people get to know each other over time.[10] In the triangular theory, social penetration, which is one's piercing through successive layers of outer façade in a person, has its most immediate effects on the intimacy component of a relationship. Indeed, the results of the Sternberg-Grajek study suggest that ability to communicate effectively is a sine qua non of a successful loving relationship.[11] In traditional conceptions of sex roles, women tend to stress intimacy and social penetration more in their lives than do men.

Of course, "good communication" is a cliché of our culture and may sound too self-evident to bear discussion.

If so, you might ask yourself how good communication is in your own relationship, and if it is less than satisfactory —as in the large majority of relationships—why is that so?

The reason, I believe, lies in what I refer to as *metastasis of communicational breakdown*. When communication starts to deteriorate, it metastasizes like a cancer; and if there is no therapeutic intervention, eventually the cancer can consume the whole relationship. In my experience, despite what people know about the importance of good communication, this breakdown is more the rule than the exception.

Sooner or later, something will happen in your life, and probably already has happened, that you would feel uncomfortable talking about to your partner. It can be absolutely anything—an incident on the job or with another person, or just a feeling you experience. Perhaps once or twice before something similar happened, and you tried to talk to your partner—but, to your consternation, an argument ensued. So this time you say nothing, and you receive what is called *negative reinforcement*, the absence (or discontinuation) of punishment. This time there is no argument, no fight; and indeed, there cannot be, because your partner does not know that there is even anything to argue about. So you are reinforced for your silence, and reinforcement tends to result in the repetition of the behavior (in this case, silence). And each time, you are negatively reinforced. Gradually, the silence extends to more domains, and soon you can find yourself like many couples—with nothing to talk about. The way to fight this metastasis is never to let it start in the first place or, if it has started, to fight it off right away. You may well take a short-term loss. There may be an argument. Or better, the two of you may learn how to deal with a difficult issue. But in most cases, you will achieve a long-term gain.

But what goes wrong in the first place? Why do relationships so often start to go downhill? First, consider the intimacy component of love. If, in accordance with Berscheid's theory, emotion in close relationships is felt when there is some disruption of the expected interaction between two people, the worst enemy of the intimacy component of love is stagnation.[12] Although people want some predictability from a loving relationship, too much predictability will probably undermine the intimacy experienced in a close relationship. Hence, it is necessary to introduce some elements of change and variation—to keep the relationship alive and growing. Obviously, change and growth may take place in different ways: for some people, the elements of change are provided by vacations; for others, through experimenting with new behavioral patterns in the relationship. The means of growth and change must be individualized to the relationship, but the need for these two elements in experiencing intimacy is probably common across long-term relationships.

Separation, whether intentional or not, is almost certainly one of the stronger tests of a relationship. Paul, a university professor, was thinking of leaving his wife. He decided to take a sabbatical instead, and to spend part of it away from home as a test of the relationship. He never put it this way to his wife, but rather emphasized what a fine professional opportunity it was for him. She could not go, because of her own job and because they had mutually decided not to disrupt their children's schooling. When the sabbatical was about to start, he was itching to get away. But just three weeks into the semester he

THE TRIANGLE OF LOVE

was ready to throw in the towel and go back. He hated living alone, and the romantic adventures he had been anticipating did not come to pass. Now, five years later, the man is back with his family. Of course, the story is supposed to end with his being happy ever after. Alas, he complains as much as he ever did. But he never talks about leaving as a serious option. He is a man who, simply, likes to complain.

On the other hand, a woman living abroad, Emily, took a prolonged business trip back to the United States for much the same reason that Paul took his sabbatical. Emily liked what she saw, and is still here; her husband is still there.

Second, consider the passion component of love. In some sense, this component is probably the most difficult to sustain, because it is least subject to conscious control and most subject to rapid decline. It is well known from conditioning theory, as mentioned before, that intermittent reinforcement (that is, occasional reward) is probably the best maintainer of behavior that results from acquired motivation (that is, a motivation you pick up during the course of your life rather than being born with it). However, intermittent reinforcement in the context of a long-term close relationship can take on a sinister character. The administration of intermittent reinforcement can become manipulative, as in withholding love making from your partner as a disciplinary strategy. Perhaps the best way to maximize the passion component of love over the long term is, first, to analyze the needs the relationship is fulfilling and to do what you can to make sure that these needs continue to be fulfilled; and, second, to analyze what needs the relationship is not fulfilling and to try to develop the relationship so that it can meet these needs as well.

Looking at Love: Applying the Triangular Theory

Attempting to use the intermittent-reinforcement principle deliberately can backfire. Jake liked to keep his wife "on her toes," as he put it, by constantly keeping her off-guard. He would be the most mercurial of characters, unpredictable in his reactions to what his wife did. The very same behavior that one time would win his gratitude would the next time earn her a figurative slap in the face. Jake referred to himself as a "Marxian" in relationships (though not in politics): you've got to keep a revolution going to keep the relationship alive. His wife left him for a political liberal who is utterly predictable, and very conservative with respect to relationships. I don't know whether she is happy today. Jake is not.

Third, consider the decision/commitment component of love, in which intervention is easiest because it is most subject to conscious control. The best way to maintain commitment in a relationship is probably both to maintain the importance of the relationship and to maximize the happiness you achieve through the relationship. Doing these things entails working on the intimacy and passion components of love, and especially expressing these components as well as your commitment to the relationship through action. Further, you may need to talk it out with your partner so that you both are sure what certain actions mean to each of you and so that you can have a better understanding of your partner's actions toward you. Many of the arguments people have with their partners result from them and their partners defining situations in different ways. For example, a spouse may like to receive lavish presents from the other: what that spouse interprets as a symbol of caring the other spouse may interpret as misuse of hard-earned monetary resources.

The Triangular Love Scale

The triangular theory of love has at least two practical applications—diagnostic and therapeutic. For the first I have developed a scale to measure each of the three components, which allows couples to gain a better sense of where each partner stands in a loving relationship. Then the scale can, in pointing out the specific differences between the loves of two members of a couple, be therapeutic by helping to pinpoint the areas where change is necessary and suggesting the kinds of action that might effect change. Thus, a couple may be brought closer together or at least to the point where they can understand and respect their differences. Both of these applications depend on the scale to measure the components of love.

Table 3.1 displays a questionnaire I have used to measure love—the Sternberg Triangular Love Scale. In one of my studies, I sought to validate this new scale and simultaneously to validate the triangular theory. Participants in the study were 101 adults from the New Haven area, comprising 50 men and 51 women, who answered an advertisement in a local newspaper. To be eligible for participation, the participants had to be over eighteen, describe themselves as primarily heterosexual, and either be married or currently involved in a close relationship with someone. They also could not have participated in one of our earlier experiments. The range in age of participants was from eighteen to seventy-one, with an average age of thirty-one. Lengths of close relationships ranged from 1 to 42 years, with an average of 6.3 years.

Participants in the study provided some demographic

TABLE 3.1
The Sternberg Triangular Love Scale

INSTRUCTIONS

The blanks represent the person with whom you are in a relationship. Rate each statement on a 1-to-9 scale, where 1 = "not at all," 5 = "moderately," and 9 = "extremely." Use intermediate points on the scale to indicate intermediate levels of feelings.

---

1. I am actively supportive of ____'s well-being.
2. I have a warm relationship with ____.
3. I am able to count on ____ in times of need.
4. ____ is able to count on me in times of need.
5. I am willing to share myself and my possessions with ____.
6. I receive considerable emotional support from ____.
7. I give considerable emotional support to ____.
8. I communicate well with ____.
9. I value ____ greatly in my life.
10. I feel close to ____.
11. I have a comfortable relationship with ____.
12. I feel that I really understand ____.
13. I feel that ____ really understands me.
14. I feel that I really can trust ____.
15. I share deeply personal information about myself with ____.
16. Just seeing ____ excites me.
17. I find myself thinking about ____ frequently during the day.
18. My relationship with ____ is very romantic.
19. I find ____ to be very personally attractive.
20. I idealize ____.
21. I cannot imagine another person making me as happy as ____ does.
22. I would rather be with ____ than with anyone else.
23. There is nothing more important to me than my relationship with ____.
24. I especially like physical contact with ____.
25. There is something almost "magical" about my relationship with ____.
26. I adore ____.
27. I cannot imagine life without ____.
28. My relationship with ____ is passionate.
29. When I see romantic movies and read romantic books I think of ____.
30. I fantasize about ____.
31. I know that I care about ____.
32. I am committed to maintaining my relationship with ____.
33. Because of my commitment to ____, I would not let other people come between us.
34. I have confidence in the stability of my relationship with ____.

TABLE 3.1 *(continued)*

---

35. I could not let anything get in the way of my commitment to ____.
36. I expect my love for ____ to last for the rest of my life.
37. I will always feel a strong responsibility for ____.
38. I view my commitment to ____ as a solid one.
39. I cannot imagine ending my relationship with ____.
40. I am certain of my love for ____.
41. I view my relationship with ____ as permanent.
42. I view my relationship with ____ as a good decision.
43. I feel a sense of responsibility toward ____.
44. I plan to continue in my relationship with ____.
45. Even when ____ is hard to deal with, I remain committed to our relationship.

Items 1 to 15 are for measuring the intimacy component; 16 to 30, for the passion component; and 31 to 45, for the decision/commitment component. In order to obtain your score, add up your ratings for each of the component subscales and divide by 15. This will give you an average rating for each item. (In the scale as it is used outside the context of this book, the scale items appear in a random order, rather than clustered by component, as they are here.)

information about themselves, and then filled out a satisfaction questionnaire, which asked them to evaluate on a scale of 1 ("not at all") to 9 ("extremely") how satisfying, happy, rewarding, close, important, good, personally inspiring, emotionally intimate, passionate, and committed the close relationship was in which he or she was involved. Participants also filled out the Sternberg Triangular Love Scale (table 3.1) as well as the Rubin Liking and Loving Scales.

The subjects rated each statement on the scales twice: once on how characteristic it was of their relationship (how things actually were going); and then on how important they felt the statement to be (in their own mind) to making a relationship ideal.

Average scores for characteristicness ratings were 7.39 for intimacy, 6.51 for passion, and 7.20 for commitment. The typical high scores were 8.6, 8.2, and 8.7 for inti-

Looking at Love: Applying the Triangular Theory

macy, passion, and commitment, respectively. The corresponding low scores were 6.2, 4.9, and 5.7. The high scores represent approximately the top 15 percent of scores; and the low scores, the bottom 15 percent. The lower average score for passion compared with intimacy and commitment may be a reflection of the average length of the relationships—6.3 years—passion being the hardest component to maintain. The average scores for importance ratings were slightly higher than for characteristicness—8.18, 6.75, and 7.64 for intimacy, passion, and commitment, respectively. The high scores were 9.0, 8.0, and 8.8 for intimacy, passion, and commitment, respectively. The corresponding low scores were 7.4, 5.4, and 6.5. The overall satisfaction score was 7.02, with a high score of 8.4 and a low of 5.6. In comparison, the Rubin Liking and Loving Scales had an average of 6.87 and 6.79 in characteristicness, but were rated slightly lower in importance (6.32 and 6.75, respectively).

Gender differences were not significant although on the average women were older than men (thirty-two versus thirty years old) and had been in their relationship longer (6.8 versus 5.7 years). Women also tended to be slightly more satisfied in their relationship (7.2 versus 6.8). Although women tended to rate characteristicness higher than men, the reverse was true for importance ratings. For this group of subjects, then, the disparity between characteristicness and importance is *greater* for men than for women. It is also interesting to note that the greatest overall disparity between characteristicness and importance is found in intimacy (for both sexes), followed by commitment (for men only).

I used the statistical technique of factor analysis in order to determine whether the underlying structure of the questionnaire was what we expected. In other words, while the theory identifies intimacy, passion, and decision/commitment as major components of love, there is no guarantee that these three components are the only ones, or that the ratings people give when filling out the questionnaire will be in accord with the structure suggested by the theory. Factor analysis provides a way of determining whether the questionnaire does indeed measure these three components, or something else. The factor analyses of both the characteristicness and importance ratings revealed three factors, which corresponded to commitment, passion, and intimacy (the order indicates the strength of the factors). The large majority of items measured what they were supposed to. Although the items worked well generally, some (fifteen out of forty-five) did not fit into the pattern predicted by the triangular theory.

Consider another question about the Triangular Love Scale. To what extent do the items within a given component subscale, on the average, measure that component? Each of the components is supposed to be relatively coherent and distinct from the others. A measure called *internal-consistency reliability* indicates the extent to which each item on a given subscale measures a single attribute. The internal-consistency reliabilities of the three component subscales were all very high, indicating that the items are measuring distinct attributes.

In respect to the extent to which ratings for one component predict ratings on another, the overall correlations for characteristicness ratings were highest between intimacy and commitment, and commitment and passion, and slightly lower between passion and intimacy. Commitment seems to predict well levels of both intimacy and passion; intimacy, on the other hand, does less well in predicting passion, particularly for importance ratings.

Finally, consider the question of how my Triangular Love Scale corresponds to the Rubin Loving and Liking Scales, and how well each of these relate to satisfaction as measured by the satisfaction scale. Intimacy, commitment, and passion scores correlate well with the Rubin scales overall, and higher with the Loving than with the Liking Scale. Passion correlates slightly better than the other two components, especially with the Loving Scale. In predicting satisfaction in close relationships, intimacy and passion scores correlate the best, followed by commitment and then the Liking and Loving Scales. Intimacy, in particular, predicted satisfaction best in terms of happiness, closeness, rewardingness, and goodness of the relationship. In general, then, the Triangular Love Scale predicted overall satisfaction better than the two Rubin scales.

In sum, these and other, more technical data provided quite good support for the triangular theory of love. The theory is not only intuitively plausible but makes sense in terms of the empirical data. We can therefore use the theory and the scale with some confidence in understanding love in close relationships, recognizing that neither this nor any other theory will answer all possible questions about love.

Refining the Triangular Theory

Love scales developed by myself and other psychological researchers reveal certain aspects of love, but what does love really mean to people? Probably the most straightforward way to find out is to ask them—as, indeed, Michael Barnes and I did in a study of people's conceptions of love. First, we asked some adults from the New Haven area (excluding college students) what kinds of behavior they believe characterize romantic love. Unlike the approach in the studies reported elsewhere in this book, we asked the subjects themselves to provide the items, rather than responding to preformulated ones, in an attempt to avoid biasing the results in favor of any theory, including the triangular theory. After breaking down a long list of items into 140 distinct behaviors, we asked 114 New Haven area adults—again, excluding students—to rate each behavior on a 1-to-9 scale with respect to the importance of each to their concept of romantic love. Using the statistical technique of factor analysis, we found four basic dimensions underlying people's notions.

The first dimension looked pretty much like the intimacy component of the triangular theory. Some of the core behaviors, in order of importance, were:

1. Feeling loved by your partner.
2. Feeling certain that your partner would always be there for you when you needed him or her.
3. Believing in the excellence of the other and supporting each other when needed.
4. Making each other happy.
5. Having a partner who is considerate of and sensitive to your needs.
6. Trusting your partner completely.
7. Believing in each other.
8. Having a partner who is your best friend.
9. Feeling you can confide in your partner.
10. Liking what has grown between the two of you.

11. Living most fully and most rewardingly when you are with your partner.
12. Enjoying being very close to your partner emotionally.
13. Depending on your partner for understanding and support.
14. Feeling that the relationship has a good future.
15. Being confident that your partner is faithful to you.

The behaviors in this dimension emphasize communication, sharing, acceptance, and support—exactly the core of the intimacy component of the triangular theory. But people distinguish among different aspects of intimacy, because the second dimension, although similar to the first, appears to be a special aspect of intimacy: namely, having a partner who is good for you in particular. The behaviors at the core of this dimension are:

1. Having a partner who understands your feelings and personality.
2. Having a partner who stimulates you intellectually.
3. Having a partner who brings out your strengths and helps your weaknesses.
4. Having a partner who is observant of your needs.
5. Liking the way you feel around your partner.
6. Having a partner who lets you have your own time.
7. Working together to make ends meet.
8. Having a partner who has compassion.

9. Feeling at ease, happy, and comfortable together.
10. Receiving constant feelings of security through his or her care.
11. Being honest with your partner.
12. Having a partner who has a good sense of humor and who can laugh at himself or herself.

To skip the third dimension for a moment, the fourth is even more special: it is having a partner and relationship that is truly special. The core behaviors are:

1. Thinking your partner is special.
2. Respecting your partner.
3. Having a partner who makes you feel special.
4. Being needed by your partner.
5. Having a partner who is gentle and kind.
6. Having a partner who tries to make you happy.
7. Trying to make your partner happy.
8. Treating each other as special.

These findings suggest some refinements in the triangular theory. These three dimensions seem to refer not so much to different kinds as to different levels of intimacy. The generalized aspects of the first dimension of intimacy apply to any intimate relationship, while the second deals with aspects that are good particularly for the person. And the third goes still further—to those aspects of intimacy that make the relationship special and perhaps unique. This dimension deals especially with the things that make a truly close couple feel together in their apartness from the rest of the world. In talking about the bonds that make a couple intimate, therefore, we distinguish among at least three levels of intimacy: from those that are good for *anyone* in an intimate relationship, to those that are especially good for the *individual person*, to those that make the *two partners in a couple* unique.

The third dimension, which I passed over in order to discuss in sequence the levels of intimacy, is a dimension of passion, particularly sexual passion, and includes these core behaviors:

1. Having a partner who is good sexually.
2. Being sexually attracted to your partner.
3. Wanting to be with your partner more than anyone else.
4. Having a partner who stimulates you sexually.
5. Being close to your partner sexually.
6. Experiencing love making that is very emotional.

Does the absence of a commitment dimension from our analysis doom the triangular theory? No, for *romantic* love, according to the theory, consists of intimacy and passion but not necessarily commitment (consummate love includes all three).

One troubling generalization emerges from all three dimensions: conceptions of love hinge much more on what a partner can do for one than on what one can do for a partner. Such a "consumer" orientation to relationships is bound to lead to repeated disappointments, making it impossible to sustain a strong and mutually supportive reciprocal relationship. You need to find someone who not only has a lot to offer you, but also stands to benefit unusually well from what you have to give, and whose receipt of it makes you feel good about the relationship and about yourself. In a relationship, one needs to look at oneself as a "producer" as well as a "consumer."

A second important generalization is that one person in a relationship may not want the same level of intimacy his or her partner wants. For example, you may seek only the first level, but your partner may seek all three, or vice versa. A common frustration in relationships is the desire of one partner for the relationship to be extra special, whereas the other partner desires a less close, possibly more mundane relationship. It is important, therefore, to strike a balance between what you want and what the other person has to give.

Liking versus Loving

Mike and Louise had been dating for about three months. Both of them seemed happy in the relationship, but their friends saw trouble. Louise just seemed a lot more involved than Mike. One night she confessed her love and told Mike about her plans for their future together. Mike was dumbfounded. He hadn't made any plans, and didn't want them. He told Louise that he liked her, but didn't love her and didn't think he ever could. Mike broke off the relationship the next day.

This vignette illustrates something most of us are aware of, sometimes painfully: liking and loving are not the same. *Liking*, according to *Webster's New World Dictionary*, is a "fondness" or "affection" for another; whereas *loving*, or *love*, is "a strong affection for or attachment or devotion to a person or persons," or "a strong, usually passionate, affection for a person of the opposite sex."[1] But these definitions only scratch the surface of what

I. Quantitative - Difference View

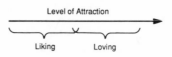

Level of Attraction

Liking   Loving

II. Qualitative - Difference View

A. Liking and Loving as Distinct

Liking   Loving

B. Liking and Loving as Overlapping

Liking   Loving

C. Liking as a Kind of Loving

Loving

Liking

Figure 4.1 *Alternative models of the relationship between liking and loving.*

liking and loving are all about, and give us very little idea of how they are related. Various psychologists have had different ideas about liking and loving and their relationship (see figure 4.1), and these ideas will be the focus of this chapter.

Loving as "More" than Liking

Some scholars view liking and loving as quantitatively different: love is more of whatever constitutes liking. The research literature points to *interpersonal attraction* as the common ingredient. According to Ellen Berscheid and Elaine Hatfield, two leading psychologists, interpersonal attraction is an individual's tendency or predisposition to evaluate positively another person or a symbol of that person.[2] A symbol can be anything that reminds you of the person or somehow evokes him or her in your mind. Attraction has three components: cognitive (thoughts), affective (feelings), and behavioral (actions).

How does liking, according to this view, become loving? Or, for that matter, how does loving sometimes "backslide" into liking? There are several schools of thought on this issue: reinforcement theory, social exchange theory, equity theory, and the cognitive-consistency theories. I shall consider first the oldest of these theories—reinforcement—which dates back to the turn of the century.

REINFORCEMENT THEORY

Suppose you are introduced to someone who immediately compliments you on something that matters to you: it might be your looks, or your brains, or your brawn, or whatever. Chances are you will like that person the more for the compliment. In psychological terms, you have been reinforced by the person, who has increased your attraction to him or her. Unfortunately, there is an obverse to reinforcement—punishment. It often happens in relationships that someone does something that really hurts you. That action—whether intentional or wholly inadvertent—increases your aversion to the person. This result, too, follows from reinforcement theory. The sad part is that the aversion may not go away, even after you forgive the person (if you do!). Most reinforcements and punishments in interpersonal relationships are *conditioned emotional responses* over which one has relatively little conscious control. Thus, seeing someone evokes a certain response, even though you may not want to have that response.

For example, Jill had gone through a bitter divorce from her husband, Bill, who acted cruelly. For him, divorce meant getting the most you could for yourself, even at the other person's expense. After it was all over, Bill wanted to let bygones be bygones and to be friends with Jill. But although she could forgive him, she couldn't forget. Every time she saw him, she felt a knot starting to form in her stomach. Bill couldn't understand that he had, in effect, become an aversive stimulus, one that Jill now tried to avoid at all cost.

Reinforcement theory, though it sometimes oversimplifies a situation, often provides the simplest and most elegant explanation of what goes on in interpersonal relationships.

The basic principles of reinforcement, while apparently obvious, actually have nonobvious implications. A person, for example, who has a low opinion of herself will find reinforcing beliefs that concur with her own. Ironically, she may be most reinforced when someone expresses a low rather than a high opinion of her, because the low opinion concurs with hers. That is exactly what happened with a graduate student who, suspicious of anyone who complimented her, suspected such a person of having an ulterior motive. Being with her was very frustrating, clearly putting one in a "no win" situation.

Consider a second implication of reinforcement theory —a powerful one for why things can go wrong in a relationship. We know that people, on the average, react more strongly to negative comments than to positive ones. In letters of recommendation, for example, negative comments generally carry far more weight than do positive ones. In relationships, too, punishments often carry more weight than do rewards. Over time, then, your partner can come to have more ability to punish you than to reinforce you positively. The buildup of negatives may therefore well exceed the buildup of positives, and relationships may seem less and less attractive over time.

Two of the earliest reinforcement theorists of attraction were Albert and Bernice Lott.[3] According to them, attraction is a positive attitude toward another; liking is response in anticipation of a goal; and a liked person is someone who acts as a secondary or indirect reinforcer. In other words, one finds attributes of the liked person to be primarily reinforcing; and because the liked person continuously possesses these attributes, that very person becomes secondarily reinforcing.

According to the Lotts, liking for a person will result when one experiences reward in the presence of that person (thereby enabling him or her to become a secondary reinforcer). Conditioning can play a role in the development of liking. An interesting implication of this view is that you can come to like someone not because of who the person is, but because you happen to experience positive reinforcements in his or her presence. Similarly, you can come to dislike people who are associated with unpleasant circumstances (shooting the messenger who brings the bad news, for instance). The Lotts have done considerable research to show that one comes to like people who only incidentally are associated with positive reinforcement. For example, the Lotts found that children who were systematically rewarded by their teacher came to like their classmates more than did children who were either ignored or punished by their teacher.[4] On the opposite side of the coin, William Griffitt and Russell Veitch found that people tend to dislike strangers met in a hot, crowded room, regardless of their actual personalities.[5]

This principle shows why it is a mistake, in relationships, to keep putting off for tomorrow (or the next day or the next) the fun you could have today. It is very easy to put a relationship on the back burner while you attend to other things. The problem is that if you don't do together things that you enjoy, there is no fun to rub off onto the relationship. In fact, if you do little together, or things that are essentially boring, you can quickly find yourself bored with each other.

A fairly typical professional couple, Louis and Ann, are both concerned about their professional advancement and understand each other in this regard, because they both want the same thing—to come out on top in their work. It seems always that if one of them is not temporarily snowed under by work, the other is. They rarely have time to do things together, but have been expecting—for half a decade—that the "busy time will pass." By now they seem to have forgotten how to have fun together and enjoy each other, and are obviously using their work to avoid the fact that their relationship has become empty. They are a good example of how the process can change the product. They once saw professional advancement for each of them as their mutual goal to happiness.

But their absorption in the professional domain left them with little in the personal domain, and now they seem unable to recover what they lost.

A similar point of view has been expressed by Gerald Clore and Donn Byrne,[6] who believe that a rewarding experience in the presence of a person creates a positive emotional response that in turn leads to liking that person. Their view derives, in part, out of Byrne's extensive research, which indicates that a potent source of attraction is attitudinal similarity.[7] According to Byrne, attitudinal similarity leads to attraction because it provides one with independent evidence for the correctness and value of one's opinions. Byrne's findings suggest that it is the proportion, rather than the number of attitudes shared with another, that leads to attraction. According to his theory, attraction toward another person can be calculated as a function of the number of positive reinforcements associated with the other, divided by the total number of positive reinforcements and punishments associated with the other.

What does all this mean in practical terms? For one thing, it helps explain why newcomers can threaten old relationships. When you have known someone for a long time, you are likely to know many of their attitudes, and almost inevitably, there will be a fair number that you do not share. In the case of someone newly met, you will learn initially only a few of that person's attitudes: it takes a while to learn any substantial number of them. If initially a few of the other person's attitudes are inconsistent with your own, you are likely to be rapidly turned off, even though these are only a small portion of the person's entire set of attitudes.

However, suppose in meeting a new person, you find you agree with the attitudes you learn about initially.

Although the number of agreements may be small, because you don't yet know much about the new person, the proportion of agreements will be high. *Voilà!* You are attracted. The new attraction may not last, however. If the initial attitudes you learn about are mostly ones you agree with, there is a good chance you are getting a biased sample, and that as you get to know more of that person's attitudes, the disagreements will be greater than you thought.

According to Donn Byrne's view, doing pleasant things with a person can increase one's liking for that person, even if he or she is not particularly pleasant. Of course, many different kinds of things can be positively reinforcing. Sharon Brehm considers three major categories of reward: intrinsic characteristics of a person, such as beauty, sense of humor, and intelligence; behavior of the person toward one, such as providing sexual attention or consolation in times of stress; and access to desired external resources granted by the other person, such as prestige, money, and other people.[8] Edna Foa and Uriel Foa have also proposed a resource theory according to which external resources can be characterized as being of six kinds: love, services, goods, money, information, and status.[9]

People often make one or both of two wrong assumptions in relationships. The first is that the other person values what one does: if you think love is important, you assume he or she does; or if you think money is important, you assume he or she does. In truth, one should assume nothing. Find out what the other person values. Ask the person, and also watch what kinds of reward (and punishment) he or she most responds to. The second wrong assumption is that the other person does—or should—value what one has a lot of. But especially when you travel outside your own immediate circle of friends and colleagues, you may find that people don't respond, because their values are different from yours.

In my first talk to a group of business executives, my introducer went through a long string of academic credentials. Looking at the audience, I could see that I had lost them before I had even started. Their assumption was that anyone of interest could come only from outside the "ivory tower." Not only did they not value the credentials, but they were suspicious of them. Now, when I am introduced to business groups, I have my introducer stress my practical, business-related experience, and skip the list of academic credentials.

This principle works at the individual level as well. When, for example, at a party, a man tried to impress a woman with hints of his financial well-being, she promptly excused herself and would not talk to him for the rest of the evening. The man made the mistake of assuming the woman valued what he did, rather than first finding out what she did, in fact, value.

SOCIAL EXCHANGE THEORY

A looser application of the reinforcement approach is expressed in George Homans's social exchange theory, which has been influenced by theories of economic exchange as well as by B. F. Skinner's theory of operant conditioning.[10] According to Homans, people seek to maximize rewards and minimize punishments. People will therefore be attracted more to those who provide more rewards and fewer punishments. At the same time, the learning principle of satiation holds that the more of something a person has, the less valuable further increases in it will be. Just as a thousand dollars means less to a millionaire than to a pauper, being liked by someone is less valuable to a person who is almost universally well liked than to a person who is generally not well liked. The economic principle of supply and demand also applies to social relationships: People are willing to pay more for scarce resources than for abundant ones. Hence, one may be more willing to give up a lot to obtain the attentions of another if that person is unique in the attentions or resources he or she has to offer than if those attentions or resources are readily available from others.

Homans's theory has several important implications for interpersonal relationships. The first is that people want most to be rewarded in their areas of insecurity. Jane, for example, is an extremely attractive professional woman, who is forever being complimented on her looks. The man she is more likely to respond to is not the one who compliments her on her appearance but the one who instead compliments her on her professional work, an arena she is insecure about. Incidentally, what matters here is not how good the person really is in any objective sense, but how the person feels about himself or herself.

A second implication of Homans's theory may be summed up in an old adage: in the country of the blind, the one-eyed man is king. When in a competitive situation, whether at work or in personal life, people tend to stress what they are good at. Homans's theory points out that this stress isn't quite right. What one needs to stress is what one is particularly good at that others are not. In other words, what distinguishes you from the rest? George, a doctor, uses this principle very well. When he meets someone at a party of doctors, he doesn't even bother to play up his medical expertise. His view—right or wrong—is first that the women he meets will assume that all the doctors at a gathering are good, and any differences are insignificant; and second, that women who meet doctors are concerned more about their being "grungy" and tight-fisted and egotistical and possibly "workaholic" than about their professional competence. George, therefore, stresses his personal qualities—what he thinks will set him apart from other men in the minds of the women he meets.

EQUITY THEORY

Equity theory derives indirectly from reinforcement theory, but more directly from social exchange theory. According to Elaine Walster, William Walster, and Ellen Berscheid, probably the leading developers of equity theory as it applies to interpersonal relationships, equity theory can be understood in terms of just four propositions.[11] First, individuals try to maximize their outcomes (that is, the rewards minus the punishments received). Second, a group of people can maximize their collective reward by developing an agreed-upon system for fairly apportioning available rewards and costs among group members. Third, when one finds oneself in an inequitable relationship, one becomes distressed, the amount of distress being proportional to the inequity experienced. Finally, one will attempt to eliminate that distress by restoring equity to the relationship: the greater the experienced inequity, the greater the effort to restore equity.

In the present context, people will be more attracted to those with whom they have a more equitable relationship. They are attracted to people who take in proportion to what they give. The results of the many experiments that have been conducted to test equity theory, and to explore its implications, generally support it.[12] Among the interesting implications is that victims tend to fare better if, in communicating with someone who has hurt or exploited them, they minimize the amount of harm they say they have endured. Otherwise, the exploiter may conclude that they have endured so much harm that equity cannot possibly be restored, and then may convince himself or herself that the victims actually deserved the harm done them. Exploited groups, of course, are often made to feel as though they deserve the treatment they are getting—a surprising implication of equity theory; in order to "restore" equity, the aggressors convince themselves that the exploited groups are, in fact, being treated equitably.

Equity theory has important implications for relationships. The first and simplest is that, over the long term, it is important that both members of a couple feel that their rewards (and punishments) from the relationship are approximately equal. Over the short term, there will always be inequities—one person, for example, making sacrifices for the sake of the other's work. But what starts to destroy a relationship is when it is always the same person making the sacrifices. Sometimes one member of the couple may think, say, that his or her career is the more important. The two members of the couple may even agree on this, for financial or other reasons. But if the one who makes the sacrifices for the other's career is not recompensed in some other way, the debts will build up, and sooner or later both members of the couple will pay. One couple I know of have managed to work out a reasonably creative solution to the problem of moves. The husband is in a large, high-tech firm that tends to transfer its employees a lot. The couple's agreement is that they move to another locale for the man, but the woman gets her pick of house and neighborhood. Each has veto power, so that if the woman absolutely does not want to move again they don't move; and if the man can't stand the house or the neighborhood, they look for something else. Neither has ever used the veto power, but having it gives each of them a safety valve that seems necessary for the relationship to keep working.

Another implication of equity theory is that when you feel wronged by your partner, continually throwing that wrong in the partner's face is likely to backfire. The partner who feels that no matter what he or she does, equity cannot be restored, may decide to give up on the whole thing. Eric and Davida had been married for seven years when Davida had an affair. Eric found out. The affair had been just a fling, but he used it as a weapon, bringing it up every time he and Davida had a fight. After a while, Eric brought it up any time he wanted to make a point with her. Davida tried—unsuccessfully—to get him to cut it out. He wouldn't. She left him, feeling unable to restore equity no matter what she did.

COGNITIVE-CONSISTENCY THEORIES

Equity theory is, in a sense, a bridge between reinforcement theories, on the one hand, and cognitive-consistency theories, on the other. According to cognitive-consistency theories, individuals strive to keep their cognitions psychologically (although not necessarily logically) consistent. When inconsistencies in cognitions arise, people strive to restore consistency.

Cognitive-consistency theories arose as a response to problems with reinforcement theories. In their classic experiment on cognitive dissonance, Leon Festinger and J. Merrill Carlsmith showed that one can come to like a task more the *less* one is paid for doing it.[13] In an interpersonal context, if you find yourself doing for someone things that, in themselves, are not rewarding, you are likely to come to the conclusion that you must like that person, because you could not be doing the things for their own sake. By interpreting the situation in this way, you achieve cognitive consistency.

An alternative interpretation is provided by Daryl Bem's self-perception theory, according to which one decides what one is like by observing one's own behavior. Thus, doing something unrewarding on a person's behalf, one can conclude that that action must reflect one's liking of that person.[14] This result, of course, seems in direct opposition to reinforcement theory. Although cognitive-consistency theories were a reaction to inconsistencies in reinforcement theories, Berscheid has pointed out that reinforcement and cognitive-consistency theories have in common the assumption, often implicit, that the individual is engaged in a struggle for survival and well-being.[15] But the theories differ in the ways that they posit individuals seek to attain this well-being.

An interesting implication of cognitive-consistency theory is that it is probably not a good idea explicitly and extrinsically to reward someone every time that person does something. Indeed, extrinsically rewarding one with money or some other concrete token of thanks may undermine one's intrinsic motivation. My nine-year-old son, Seth, for example, mowed the lawn because he liked mowing and because it was a token of his feelings for me: if he did it, I didn't have to. Feeling guilty about having him mow the lawn (my mistake), I started paying him to do it. Seth then began to see himself mowing the lawn for the money. Now he will only do it for money. He no longer likes doing it, and no longer sees the mowing as a token of his affection for me. Of course, the same principle applies to children in school or adults at work. By giving out grades, promotions, or other rewards, we can undermine the intrinsic motivation people initially have for a task, and actually convince them that they are doing it only for the rewards.

In Fritz Heider's balance theory, liking is one of two kinds of relationship that can exist between persons;[16] he refers to it as a *sentiment relationship*. The other kind of relationship is a *unit relationship*—the perception that any two of three persons do or do not belong together. The unit is a matter of perception rather than of any "objective fact." According to Heider, relationships (whether sentiment or unit) are balanced when positive sentiments are felt toward individuals and objects with whom one perceives oneself to be in a unit relationship, and negative sentiments are felt toward those with whom one does not perceive oneself to be in a unit relationship. For any three entities (individuals or objects), an imbalance exists when there is an odd number of negative sentiment relationships. Thus, for example, if you dislike someone (negative sentiment) who is liked (positive sentiment) by someone you like (positive sentiment), then there is an imbalance, which you will try to correct either by coming to like more the person you had disliked, or by coming to dislike more the person you had liked. A related theory is that of Theodore Newcomb, according to which people strive for symmetry in their relations.[17] To some extent, Newcomb's theory might be viewed as a generalization to groups of Heider's theory: when imbalance exists within a large group, one or more members of the group will attempt to reduce the imbalance within the group by changing people's perceptions of each other.

Heider's balance theory explains why, in a relationship, each of a couple's friends can be important to the way the relationship goes. Suppose you don't like your partner's friends but do like your partner. According to balance theory, this situation puts you into a state of disequilibrium, or imbalance. You can stay in this state of imbalance. But the chances are that you will try to achieve balance. One way to achieve balance is to try to like your partner's friends more, which is likely to be the first thing you try. But another way is to start liking your partner less. You thereby achieve balance, but at the expense of the relationship.

Probably the best known of the cognitive-consistency theories is Leon Festinger's theory of cognitive dissonance.[18] According to this theory, cognitions are dissonant when they are psychologically incompatible or seemingly contradictory. When dissonance arises, people feel pressure to eliminate or at least reduce it. An experimental test of this theory yielded a result also consistent with equity theory: Keith Davis and Ned Jones found that one who is induced to make another person suffer for reasons that have nothing to do with one's feelings for the other person will come to dislike that person in order to reduce the dissonance resulting from harming someone whom one does not dislike.[19] In another well-known experiment applying the theory of dissonance, Elliot Aronson and Judson Mills found that experiencing a severe initiation to join a group encouraged women to report liking that group considerably more than if they experienced a mild initiation or no initiation.[20] Here, the effect seemed to result from a justification of effort: if a woman worked so hard to join the group, then, she reasoned, the group certainly must be a worthwhile one with which to be affiliated.

I have seen dissonance theory at work in interpersonal relations on the job. For example, Irwin found himself in the uncomfortable position of having to fire a subordinate who was also a personal friend. For years, he had only spoken well of the subordinate personally, although he had doubts about his professional competence. Now, though, he began to attack the subordinate personally as well, in effect seeking justification for what he had to do in a way that was unfair to the subordinate. Of course, the same can happen outside the workplace. I found myself talking to a man I hardly knew about how he was going to tell his wife he had had an affair. He was committed to telling her. He didn't expect her to take it well. But as he talked, he began to say more and more negative things about her, apparently intent on convincing himself that she was so inadequate that he had truly deserved to have the affair. It was clear that none of this had occurred to him in advance, and was unlikely to, because he was, by his own statement, basically happy with his marital relationship. But he had to put down his wife in order to justify to himself what he did.

LIMITATIONS OF THE QUANTITATIVE VIEWS

Quantitative views of the relationship between liking and loving are probably less accepted now than in times past (again, with the caveat that the theories discussed were usually not directly addressed to the issue of how liking and loving are related). There are several reasons why these views are less in fashion.

First, they tend to address some other construct directly—such as interpersonal attraction or types of relationship—rather than the constructs of liking and loving. These latter constructs, especially loving, are treated at best as secondary matters and often seem to be neglected entirely.

Second, the relations between the primary and the secondary constructs sometimes seem to get lost. Does greater reinforcement always lead to more liking, or can we actually come sometimes to resent the people who have a great deal of power to reinforce (or punish) us? And isn't it true that loving relationships often seem, on their face, to be less rather than more reinforcing than liking relationships? Lovers' quarrels and confrontations are often much more punishing than conflicts among friends.

Third, as Elliot Aronson has pointed out in his gain-loss theory of attraction, it is extremely difficult at times to specify just what constitutes a reward in a given relationship.[21] One man's meat can be another man's poison: for example, the particular cosmetics a woman wears may be a reward to one man and a punishment to another. Aronson and his colleagues have presented some strong evidence for the difficulty of pinpointing just what constitutes a reward. Aronson, along with Ben Willerman and Joanne Floyd, discovered that when a person of average competence commits a social blunder, we like the person less than before, but when a person of superior competence commits a social blunder, we like the person more.[22] According to the gain-loss theory, we like most, not people who merely reward us most, but rather people whose rewards for us start out relatively lower but increase over time. Conversely, we like least people who start out by rewarding us a great deal, but whose rewards then decrease consistently over time. In short, the question of what constitutes a reinforcement cannot be answered in a simple or straightforward way.

Finally, it is a lot clearer how the reinforcement-based theories apply to liking than to loving. Personal experience and research do seem to indicate that liking can be understood, at least in part, in terms of proportions of rewards. But love does not seem to work this way at all. There are many instances of passionate love where the lover receives little but punishment.[23] Of course, one could somehow define these punishments as rewarding, but then we end up with the problem pointed out by Aronson: the definition of *reward* becomes too flexible for the concept to be of much use.

It would seem, then, that the theories holding that liking and loving are a matter of degree are best understood as applying only to one or more aspects of liking and loving, and not to either construct in its entirety. For example, the theories seem to apply to issues of exchange better than to intimacy in communication. Moreover, the aspects may not be a major part of liking and especially of loving. The next class of theories—in large part a reaction to the quantitative theories—consider liking and loving to be qualitatively distinct rather than quantitatively continuous entities.

Liking and Loving as "Qualitatively" Distinct

For the reasons I have noted, some theorists of liking and loving became disenchanted with reinforcement theories in general and with reinforcement-based theories of liking and loving in particular. Other theorists never believed that liking and loving were on a continuum. The latter include clinical, as well as two-component, interruption, evolutionary, and attachment theorists.

CLINICAL THEORIES

Most clinical theorists hold that there is a discontinuity between liking and loving, but have had more to say about loving than about liking (Freud,) for example, viewed love in terms of sublimated sexuality. Since we want sexual relations more frequently, with more people, and in more places than society in general or other people in particular will allow, love is a way of sublimating— bringing to a higher plain—our sexual desires. It rechannels at least some of these desires in a socially acceptable way.

Adult love also helps to rechannel the frustration stemming from childhood when boys and girls are disappointed to find that their desire for the parent of the opposite sex (the Oedipus and the Electra complexes, respectively) cannot be fulfilled. After this painful discovery, which usually occurs around the age of six, children enter a latency period, in which their desire for a member of the opposite sex becomes dormant. Hurt by the perceived rejection by the opposite-sex parent, the child simply represses all his or her sexual desires. During the latency period, many boys want to have as little to do with girls as possible, and vice versa.

Theodore Reik, on the other hand, viewed love as arising out of dissatisfaction with oneself and one's lot in life.[24] People seek out love when life is disappointing and when one needs someone else to fill the void within. One seeks salvation in love, much as some people do in religion, hoping to find in another the perfection one cannot find in oneself. At first, one may well think that salvation is at hand. Early in a relationship, the other person may indeed seem to be just what you are looking for, and your being in love is tantamount to being saved—from the world and often from yourself. But eventually disillusionment is almost certain to set in. You discover two facts. First, the other person has flaws: you cannot maintain the illusion of perfection in the face of ever more evidence that he or she is not, in fact, perfect. Second, no other human can save you, not even the love of your life. Perhaps you can save yourself, but one cannot expect or even ask this of another. You now have either to adjust to a new kind of love or else forever live with the disappointment of knowing that you cannot find salvation through love of another. Of course, some people take a third course: they try to find someone else to save them and once again re-enter the cycle of high hopes followed by disappointment.

While, on the one hand, people may know at an intellectual level that no one can "save" another through love, they may, on the other hand, find it hard to convince themselves of it at an emotional level.

According to Melanie Klein, who holds a view related ✳ to Reik's, love arises from one's dependency upon others for the satisfaction of one's needs.[25] Some degree of dependence is healthy, and people who cannot allow themselves to be at all dependent are likely to be unhappy. Gordon, for example, a successful lawyer, is highly dependent on others in his professional life, drawing on associates in his firm for the preparation of case material and on secretaries for all his word processing. But he never lets himself become truly dependent on anyone in his personal life. If he doesn't like the way someone is acting, he can put that person out of his life on a moment's notice, and never let himself be bothered by him or her. Mere acquaintances see Gordon as a very strong person indeed. But the opposite is true. He has felt rejected by almost every significant person in his life. His father died when he was only eight. His mother entered into a whirlwind social life and was too busy to have anything to do with him, especially after she remarried. His two wives both left him. He perceives himself as so vulnerable that the only way he can protect himself is by shutting other people out entirely. He won't let them hurt him any more, at the expense of being unable to get close to them.

Abraham Maslow's "D-love," or "deficiency love," is also of the kind noted by Reik and Klein, arising from the need for security and belonging.[26] Indeed, the term *deficiency* provides an apt characterization of most of these theories, in that they view love as arising from some lack or feeling of something missing within the person. Maslow's "B-love," or "being love," arises out of a person's higher emotional needs, especially the desire for self-actualization and actualization of another.[27] This kind of love represents for Maslow the highest kind of personal fulfillment.

Psychological theories are products of their time. Thus, Sigmund Freud's theory is often thought to reflect the Victorian times of which he was a product; and Maslow's seems to be a good match to the 1960s, the "me era," during which self-actualization was seen by many as the attainment of the highest level of emotional well-being. Reading Maslow on being love, I wonder whether any couple has ever had the kind of completely secure, placid, and untroubled love he describes. I doubt it, and suspect anyone who did have it would quickly become bored. Full self-actualization for oneself and another may be a fine goal, but I suspect that most of the pleasure is getting there, and that anyone who ever reached the tranquil, self-sufficient state Maslow describes would generate problems to stir things up.

Erich Fromm, living in roughly the same era as Maslow, viewed love as arising from care, responsibility, respect, and knowledge of another.[28] I am sometimes accused of making love sound too cold, too rational, too sensible. But if any theorists fit that description, I think Maslow with his B-love, and Fromm with his notions of the art of loving, come close. It is easy to speculate on the sources of Fromm's theory: he was caught up in and much affected by the fascist madness in the Second World War. For him, love was an escape from that madness; caring, responsibility, respect, and trust all seemed to be missing from that world.

Recently, Dorothy Tennov has introduced the concept of limerence, or intrusive thoughts about, acute longing for, and intense dependency on another.[29] Tennov seems to be talking about what Hatfield and Walster would refer to as romantic love: a state of intense absorption in another whereby lovers long for their partners and for ecstasy and complete fulfillment through them.[30] This is certainly the kind of love that Stanton Peele views as being addictive, and that Denis de Rougemont and many other observers have seen as requiring obstacles and impediments in order to survive.[31] Tennov's *Love and Limerence* (1979), is, I believe, a classic, insufficiently appreciated by love researchers, in part because it was written for a popular audience. It shows through scores of interviews the experiences and anguish of those who have been involved in obsessive, passionate, but unrequited love. Indeed, frustration seems to be necessary for the experience of limerence to maintain itself. (Tennov planned to follow up her book with another based on further, tighter research, but illness prevented her from continuing this research at her accustomed pace.)

✳ Kenneth Livingston, another clinical love researcher, refers to love as a process of uncertainty reduction: once the uncertainties are removed, and there are no obstacles to the consummation of romantic love, it seems to dissipate.[32] Livingston's view, I believe, contains an important message. In order for love to thrive, there has to be at least some mystery—some degree of doubt about what will happen when. It is no coincidence that the great seducers and seductresses of history have maintained an air of mystery. They have known intuitively what scientists have learned through research: that for love to endure, you must always feel that you are learning new things about and doing new things with your lover, that the relationship has not gone stale.

✳ A very different, but also clinically based view is that of Scott Peck, who would not view passion as even truly being love.[33] Rather, he views love as largely a decision, and then a commitment to that decision. After the initial strong physical attraction of a romance, a couple must settle down to the day-to-day living that makes them a team; and when hard times come, as inevitably they will, it is the commitment of each to the decision to love the other that gets the couple through. While Peck is no doubt right in stressing the importance of commitment, I think he does too little justice to the intimacy and especially passion that feed into commitment. When times get hard, commitment helps, but so do intimacy and passion.

THE TWO-COMPONENT THEORY OF PASSIONATE LOVE

Elaine Walster and Ellen Berscheid, like the clinical theorists, have argued that love, or at least passionate love, is qualitatively distinct from liking (or companion-ate love, which Walster and Berscheid view as a durable form of liking in a long-term close relationship).[34] These theorists draw upon Stanley Schachter and Jerome Singer's theory of emotion, according to which the emotions human beings feel depend largely upon how one labels, in a situationally appropriate way, the arousal one experiences.[35] (The Schachter-Singer theory itself draws upon the earlier James-Lange theory of emotion.)[36] Thus, arousal experienced in the presence of a threatening stimulus will be felt as fear, whereas that same arousal experienced in the presence of a loved one will be felt as desire.

According to these theorists, then, the objective physiological experience of seeing a poisonous snake slithering toward you and getting ready to strike is essentially the same as the objective experience of seeing an extremely attractive member of the opposite sex walking toward you with stars in his or her eyes. What differs is the interpretation you assign to each of these events and, hence, the subjective psychological experience you undergo. The difference in psychological experience clearly has survival value, in that your best move in the case of the snake is certainly in the opposite direction; whereas for the attractive member of the opposite sex, there is at least some ambiguity with respect to the direction in which you ought to move.

AN "INTERRUPTION" THEORY OF EMOTION IN LOVE

Recently Ellen Berscheid has proposed a new theory of emotion in close relationships based upon George Mandler's theory of emotion.[37] According to Berscheid, one feels emotion in a close relationship to the extent that interruption of some kind in the relationship (for example, discovering a spouse is having an extramarital affair) causes interruption of the attainment of one's own goals or desires for that relationship (for example, the desire for sexual exclusivity in marriage). Early on in a relationship, when there is much uncertainty, the amount of interruption is probably substantial. As time goes on, and the uncertainty decreases, so does the amount of interruption, and so we are less susceptible to feeling emotion in a close relationship. To the extent that romantic love is dependent upon one's experiencing emotion—and almost certainly it is, to some extent—romantic love is difficult to maintain over the long term.

Note that Berscheid's view is similar to Livingston's. To keep a relationship alive, you need some sprinkling of uncertainty or hardship. I know of a couple who strove hard to get everything they wanted. They were fantastically successful, achieving their main life goals in their middle thirties. Their friends were envious—right up to when the couple split up. They had reached a point where they just didn't know what to do with themselves or how to keep their life interesting, and I suspect that their solution to the problem was to split up to generate some interest in their lives. That they did, although by battling through a bitter divorce rather than by finding things to achieve in common. They achieved, eventually, by working against each other, the fight against boredom they could not achieve by working together.

AN EVOLUTIONARY THEORY OF LOVE

The theory of evolution was first applied, of course, to biological species. A fundamental question addressed by that theory was how human beings come to be. The evolutionary account is that through a process of natural selection, species that were able to adapt to the environment survived, and species that were not able to adapt met their demise. Over time, selective forces favored some species over others. New species evolved through essentially random mutations, most of which hindered the ability of the mutants to adapt. But every once in a great while, a favorable mutation would occur, giving the mutant an advantage over existing species. Eventually humans evolved and were favorably endowed for adaptation to the environment.

Attempts were made in the nineteenth century to apply the theory of evolution to the social as well as the biological realm, but "social Darwinism" proved to be little more than an apology for the existing social order. With little to contribute, the movement faded.

In the past decade or so, a new attempt has been made to use evolutionary theory in the social realm under the rubric of *sociobiology*. A proponent of this point of view, the psychologist Glenn Wilson, has proposed an evolutionary account of loving and liking that uses a sociobiological framework to understand each construct, but especially loving.[38] Sociobiology is essentially the study of the biological evolution of social behavior. Wilson suggests that adult love is an outgrowth of at least three main instincts which, in the view of sociobiologists, are a part of human life just as they are a part of the lives of other species.[39]

The first instinct is the need of the infant to be protected by either its parents or substitutes for them. Wilson suggests that the evolutionary function of attachment is primarily protection from predators; and that, indeed, people—whether children or adults—tend most to seek attachments when they are somehow threatened from the outside. We see this tendency in wars, for example, when besieged nations seek allies; or in people who, threatened by legal action, seek lawyers or other advocates; or in families when, if one member is somehow besieged, the family rallies around him or her, even if, in the past, they have not been particularly close. Tragedy can bring together couples as well as families, although great stress can also tear a couple or a family apart.

Wilson suggests a close analogy between the attachment John Bowlby has studied in infants and the attachment that can be observed in adult lovers.[40] Bowlby observed the tendency of the infant to seek out—to attach to—the mother as a sort of security and as a haven from distress. Wilson believes that, as children, humans are imprinted by their parents; and that later, as adults, they tend to seek lovers who resemble those parents in certain critical respects. He suggests that males are particularly susceptible to visual imprinting, so that they may even look for lovers who physically resemble the mother in significant ways. It is known that male rats, when imprinted with a particular smell of their mother at birth, years later will prefer female rats who smell as their mother did. And a male human often finds that, as he gets to know better the woman he has been attracted to, more similarities to his mother emerge.

The second basic instinct—in some respects, the flip side of the coin—is the parental protection instinct. One seeks not only to be protected by one's lover but to protect him or her as well. Thus, Wilson argues, men often are attracted to women who in certain ways resemble infants, such as in having big eyes and soft skin. These men describe their lovers as cute and cuddly, use diminutive nicknames, and often indulge in babytalk when being affectionate. Women, as well, often enjoy the "little boy" aspects of their boyfriends and husbands and use diminutive nicknames. The evolutionary function is the protection one gives to the other, and thereby to any children resulting from the relationship.

The third kind of instinct is sexual. Wilson suggests that sexual imprinting develops around the age of three or four, and that sexual orientation arises at that time. Generally, although not always, imprinting is on a member of the opposite sex.

Wilson believes that men are fundamentally polygynous "harem builders," whose natural inclination is to form short-term sexual liaisons. In choosing sexual partners, men tend to be less selective than women because they can rather easily spread their genes through sexual liaisons, and can continue to do so throughout much of their adult life. Women tend to be more selective because they have limited opportunities to spread their genes. They ovulate once a month, and only prior to menopause, and can be impregnated only once every year or so; whereas there is almost no limit to the number of women a man can impregnate, even within a short span of time. For women, given their limited opportunities, their best bet in terms of having the best possible children—genetically—is to be very careful about their choice of a man with whom to mate, and also about when they mate. Wilson notes that our current civilization is an exception among human civilizations in its tendency toward monogamy, and that two forces—a sense of morality and fairness, and stable living conditions for parents and children—propel us in this direction. For example, children have a more stable environment in a conventional home setting than when they are moved around with one parent from one lover to another.

The ultimate function of romantic love, from an evolutionary point of view, is to propagate the species, through sexual intercourse. Romantic love, Wilson points out, does not last long; and were it the only force keeping couples together, there would be trouble indeed in assuring that children are raised in a way that enables them to develop to their potential.[41] Companionate love, or just plain liking, often helps a couple stay together and bring up the children after romantic love has died. But Wilson emphasizes that he does not believe that long-term liaisons are, evolutionarily, the natural state for humans. Indeed, many couples do split up after their children are grown. The greater unconditionality of our love for our children makes evolutionary sense in terms of the greater need of the child than of the adult for the parent to remain in the early years. Indeed, for some parents at least, some of the unconditionality fades as the child gets older and no longer is as critically dependent on the parent.

Although Wilson does not map out the evolutionary functions of liking outside the heterosexual pair bond, it is clear that liking serves an evolutionary function quite different from that of loving, in that liking does not generally lead to procreation and, hence, to the continuation of one's genes. Within the heterosexual pair bond, however, liking can help keep a couple together and, thus, available to needy children after romantic love has faded.

Wilson's theory is a bold attempt to place love within the sociobiological framework. Obviously, it does not answer every question about love. At the same time, it provides answers that no other kind of theory of love has been able to address: for example, why love for young children seems to have a kind of unconditionality missing from other loves; and why we find babies cute, even when by some standards they might seem ugly. It is obviously of survival value to the species for people to find babies cute rather than ugly. While Wilson's theory has not yet caught on among love researchers, and is not widely cited or even widely known, I believe that it will eventually gain recognition.

In an interesting study of people's conceptions of love motivated by a sociobiological view of love, David Buss of the University of Michigan asked one hundred college students to "think of people you know of your own gender (sex) who have been or are currently in love. With these individuals in mind, write down five acts or behaviors that they have performed (or might perform) that reflect or exemplify their love." In a second study, forty students were asked to rate how central each of 115 "love acts" thus obtained is to the concept of love. Since in Buss's study, as in our own, laypersons rather than psychologists decided upon the behaviors to be rated, the behaviors obtained were "theory-free" with respect to psychologists' preconceptions of what should be listed or rated.[42]

People's ratings were on a seven-point scale. Consider the top fifteen love acts in terms of the ratings. Behaviors are listed in descending order of centrality:

1. She agreed to marry him.
2. She remained faithful to him when they were separated for more than a month.
3. He called her when she was feeling down.
4. He canceled his plans in order to be with her when she was upset.

139

5. She gave up going out with other men for him.
6. She listened devotedly to his problems.
7. He resisted the sexual opportunity he had with someone else.
8. He told her that he wanted to marry her.
9. She stuck up for him when someone tried to put him down.
10. She told him, "I love you."
11. He put up with her "bad days."
12. He told her that he wanted to have children with her.
13. He talked to her about marriage and the future.
14. She took care of him when he was sick.
15. She talked to him about her personal problems.

There are two main differences between the Buss studies and those Michael Barnes and I did (see chapter 3). First, our group was older, while Buss surveyed college students, who typically seem more concerned with getting engaged and married. A second, and more fundamental, difference concerns what the participants were actually rating. In our study, they were rating romantic love; whereas in Buss's study, they were rating "being in love," which seems likely, at least for many people, to come at least as close to the notion of consummate love as to the notion of romantic love. In any event, decision and commitment clearly play a larger role in Buss's data than in ours, a finding consistent with the notion that Buss's participants were rating consummate love. Decision/ commitment was expressed in certain statements, not all of which are illustrated in the previous partial listing: "She agreed to marry him," "She remained faithful to him when they were separated for more than a month," "She gave up going out with other men for him," "He talked to her about marriage and the future," and "She gave him a symbolic ring." Intimacy is reflected in such behavior as: "He called her when she was feeling down," "He canceled his plans in order to be with her when she was upset," "She listened devotedly to his problems," and "She talked to him about her personal problems." Passion is reflected in such behavior as: "She lost sleep thinking about him," "He gazed into her eyes," "She wrote him a poem," "He wrote her a love note," and "He made love to her."

While I have discussed Buss's data in terms of their implications for the triangular theory, Buss himself takes an evolutionary perspective on love. (Many of the behaviors relevant to the evolutionary framework did not, however, appear in the top fifteen list presented earlier but rather appeared lower down in the ratings.) Let me now consider Buss's data from an evolutionary perspective, similar to the one taken by Glenn Wilson. Buss is concerned with how love can be adaptive in fostering the propagation of the species, and cites eight proximal goals of love acts, all leading to increased reproductive success.

1. *Resource Display*. Reproductive success will increase to the extent that both the male and the female can find a mate with the most resources to offer. In many societies, a major resource of men is their financial success, which helps ensure the well-being of any offspring they father. A major resource of women is their attractiveness, which, research has shown, enhances the prestige of the man.

2. *Exclusivity: Fidelity and Mate Guarding*. In many species, the male and female guard each other from the sexual interest of third parties—again, for an evolutionary reason. The female has a vested interest in the male's not having children with other females, lest her own

offspring be deprived of some of the man's resources. The male has a vested interest in guarding the female because her getting pregnant by another male will delay her pregnancy by himself. Thus, fidelity fits into the evolutionary framework.

3. *Mutual Support and Protection.* Since offspring are dependent on their parents for nurturance and many kinds of support, they benefit if the parents support and protect each other.

4. *Commitment and Marriage.* To the question of why, with divorce rates so high, one should even bother with marriage, there is again an evolutionary answer. Children from stable homes are most likely to thrive. And, indeed, many couples stay together "for the sake of the children." Of course, a home with two parents can be more unstable and torn than one with a single parent, but marriage helps ensure that a parting of ways will not be whimsically undertaken. Indeed, almost all societies have customs and laws to make parting at least somewhat difficult.

5. *Sexual Intimacy.* Obviously, sexual intimacy is necessary for reproduction to take place.

6. *Reproduction.* Since, from an evolutionary point of view, the goal of sexual intimacy is the reproduction of the species, reproduction is a proximate goal of love acts.

7. *Resource sharing.* Resource sharing could be viewed as a form of mutual protection and support, in that it enhances the environment in which children are raised.

8. *Parental Investment.* Parental investment in children is needed for the children to thrive and, ultimately, be reproductively successful themselves.

Buss's theory and mine are basically compatible, but

my theory is concerned with the internal structure of love—what it is—whereas Buss's is concerned with the evolutionary function of love—why it is the way it is. When my first child was born, I watched the delivery, and had the closest thing I have ever had to a "conversion experience," having felt some ambivalence earlier on. I instantly felt a love and bond for the boy that I had never known it was in me to feel. I had the same experience again when my daughter was born seventeen months later. Understanding evolutionary theory helps me understand why I had those experiences, without detracting in the least from the feelings I had then and have now. And, indeed, I believe there is an important point here: understanding love does not undermine its emotional power but, rather, enhances it.

THE ATTACHMENT THEORY OF LOVE

"Exciting theory" Sternberg wrote

Glenn Wilson, as I noted, links romantic love to attachment and develops this link within an evolutionary framework.[43] Phillip Shaver and Cindy Hazan have greatly expanded upon this view of love as deriving from infantile attachment, and proposed a theory of romantic love as attachment.[44] Like Wilson, they borrow the attachment concept from Bowlby, but extend it by showing that styles of romantic love correspond to styles of attachment among infants for their mothers, as explained by the theory of attachment styles proposed by Mary Ainsworth.[45]

Ainsworth observed that infants, when separated from their mothers and placed in a strange situation with someone unknown to them, tended to react in one of three ways. Secure infants could tolerate brief separations and then would be happy when the mother came back; they seemed to have confidence that their mother *would* come back. Avoidant infants seemed to be relatively detached upon their mother's return; they seemed more distant from their mothers and less trusting of them. Anxious-ambivalent infants had great difficulty tolerating the separation and would cling to the mother upon her return.

According to Shaver and Hazan, romantic lovers tend to have one of the three different styles in a relationship. A person's style is a matter of individual differences, and derives in part from the kind of attachment one has had to one's mother when young. Secure lovers find it relatively easy to get close to others. They also find they can be comfortable in depending on others and in having others depend on them. They do not worry about being abandoned or about someone getting too close to them. Avoidant lovers are uncomfortable being close to others. They find it difficult to trust others completely and to allow themselves to depend on others. They get nervous when anyone gets too close, and often find that their partners in love want to become more intimate than they find comfortable. Anxious-ambivalent lovers find that others are reluctant to get as close as they would like. They often worry that their partners do not really love them or want to stay with them. They want to merge completely with another person—a desire that sometimes scares others away. In their research, Shaver and Hazan found that about 53 percent of their subjects were secure, 26 percent avoidant, and 20 percent anxious-ambivalent, proportions that correspond roughly to those of the three kinds of attachment relation in infants.

The attachment view can explain certain empirical

phenomena in terms of developmental theory. For example, the waning of passion can be interpreted as the development of increasingly secure attachment, with its associated reduction of uncertainty.[46] Tennov's construct of limerence is viewed largely as a function of style of attachment, and thus the Shaver-Hazan theory explains the individual differences in limerence proneness observed by Tennov.[47] In general, the attachment theory is an exciting development in the understanding of love.

LIMITATIONS OF THE QUALITATIVE-DIFFERENCE VIEWS

Whereas reinforcement and cognitive-consistency theories have a lot to say about liking but less about loving, the qualitative views have a lot to say about loving but less about liking. Further, they concentrate on what Hatfield and Walster refer to as "passionate love," not on "companionate love."[48] Another limitation is the weakness of the evidence supporting most of these theories, which have received little or no direct empirical testing. Finally, the theories seem to be as much oversimplifications of the mechanisms behind love as are the reinforcement and cognitive-consistency theories. Recent research suggests, for example, that psychophysiological arousal actually differs from one emotion to another.[49] Hence, it seems unlikely that love is merely one label for a set of psychophysiological responses that as well might be labeled fear, anger, or hate. Similarly, passionate love seems to be something more than an attempt to fill a gap in oneself, in that even people with high self-esteem can fall passionately in love. The following theories look at love as a more complex phenomenon and attempt to account for it in a more complex way.

Liking and Loving as Overlapping

Some theorists have viewed liking and loving as qualitatively distinct but nevertheless overlapping. Two such approaches are psychometric theory and the theory of bonds.

PSYCHOMETRIC THEORY

As I have described in chapter 1, one way to understand love is to do some preliminary research on what it is, to construct a scale to measure it, and then to define it—operationally—as what the scale measures. While this approach has been used, with mixed results, in studying intelligence, the results have been, if anything, better in the field of love, because the first person to take this "psychometric" approach seriously—Zick Rubin—is such a competent psychologist.

Rubin was a graduate student at the University of Michigan when he began his studies on how to measure love, and he continued them later at Harvard and then at Brandeis. He produced the first psychometrically based theory of liking and loving.[50] Rubin used factor analysis and related methods to derive two scales: the Liking Scale and the Loving Scale. Factor analysis, as noted earlier, is a statistical technique for discovering latent sources of individual differences among people which underlie their scores on some set of tests or test items.

First, Rubin constructed roughly eighty items measuring a variety of attitudes one person might express toward another. He then asked 198 undergraduates to respond to each item in terms of how they would feel toward a boyfriend or girlfriend, on the one hand, and toward a platonic friend of the opposite sex, on the other hand. Rubin used his factor analysis to select those items that were especially characteristic of loving or liking. Two thirteen-item scales resulted.

Rubin suggested that the items on the Loving Scale could be viewed as falling into three distinct clusters.[51] He thus proposed a three-component theory of love, although the components were not strictly based on an analysis of factors. Some items measure dependent need of the other (for example, "If I could never be with ____, I would feel miserable"). Others measure predisposition to help ("If ____ were feeling badly, my first duty would be to cheer him [her] up"). And still others measure exclusiveness and absorption ("I feel very possessive toward ____").

The Liking Scale contains items measuring attributes more akin to friendship. Rubin does not, however, propose a "componential" theory of liking analogous to his theory of love. Some examples of items on the Liking Scale are "I think that ____ is unusually well adjusted," "I have great confidence in ____'s good judgment," and "I think that ____ and I are quite similar to one another."

The Rubin scales have proven to be something of a psychometric tour de force, and Rubin has gone a long way toward validating both them and his theory. The scales are reliable, meaning that when a person takes the scales twice in succession, the scores tend to be similar each time.[52] They are also related to scores on a variety of external measures. For example, for those couples who count love highly in their marital choices, scores on the Loving Scale predict couples' ratings of the probability that they will eventually get married; but for couples who do not count love as a significant basis for marital choice, the scales do not predict marital choice well. Scores on the Loving Scale also predict how much two people in a close relationship will gaze at each other. Thus, when a couple are put in a waiting room and told someone will soon be with them to do an experiment, they are, unbeknownst to them, being watched by a hidden camera which records how much of the time the two partners spend gazing into each other's eyes. Higher loving-scale scores are associated with more gazing. Moreover, although men and women both love and like their romantic partners more than their friends, the difference between romantic partners and friends is greater for loving-scale than for liking-scale scores. In other words, the extent to which your feelings for your romantic partner exceed those for your friends is greater for loving than for liking.

Although the scale items are distinct, liking and loving are clearly overlapping entities in Rubin's theory, at least statistically. Rubin reported a moderate relation between the Loving and Liking Scales for men and a low-to-moderate relation for women.[53] In my work with Susan Grajek, we found considerably higher relations for both men and women.[54] Michael Barnes and I, using a college-student sample more restricted in range of types of relationship than the New Haven townspeople sample of Grajek and myself, found a moderate relation between the two scales.[55] In other words, the relation between liking and loving seems to be higher in a general population of subjects than in a population drawn from students in college.

A THEORY OF BONDS

After testing alternative psychometric theories of love, Grajek and I proposed a theory of love as a sampling of many overlapping bonds, as described earlier.[56] We based our theory upon Thomson's psychometric theory of intelligence.[57] According to Thomson, intelligence can be understood in terms of the mind's possessing an enormous number of bonds, including reflexes, habits, bits of knowledge, and the like. Performance on any one task would activate a large number of these bonds. Related tasks, such as those used in mental tests, would sample overlapping subsets of bonds. For example, all of the mental tests might require you to perceive stimuli, recall knowledge, and make inferences.

The theory of bonds provides a rather straightforward account of the overlapping nature of liking and loving: some, but not all, bonds are shared between the two experiences. For example, "experienced happiness with" and "high regard for" another are certainly characteristic of both liking and loving; but "passionate arousal" would be characteristic only of loving. Hence, the full development of this theory would require specification of all of the bonds involved in close relationships, particularly of those that apply to love, to liking, and to both. Our results, described in chapter 1, describe some of the bonds (for example, being able to count on the other person, and the other person's being able to count on you).

LIMITATIONS OF THE OVERLAPPING-ATTRIBUTE THEORIES

Since the theories of Rubin and of Grajek and myself were both psychometrically derived and tested, they have at least some empirical support. The particular strength of these theories is in their structural models of the nature of love. Yet these theories, like those discussed earlier, have limitations.

First, the love scales seem to do to love what intelligence tests do to intelligence: they leave it devitalized and bloodless. The relatively high correlation between liking and loving scales is not surprising, since the love scales seem to measure those aspects of love that are most akin to liking. They certainly do not fully measure the passionate aspects of love dealt with in the theories of Freud, Reik, Tennov, and other clinical psychologists discussed earlier.[58] Indeed, the Sternberg-Grajek results suggest that love is the same in kind from one close relationship to another, but certainly this finding seems like an oversimplification in respect to love in all its richness.

Second, the psychometric theories are weak on mechanism and especially development, as psychometric theories of other constructs tend to be as well. Although the theories specify in some detail the structure of the constructs under consideration (a strength of psychometric theories), they have little to say about the development of those constructs. Reinforcement and cognitive-consistency theories, and the two-component theory, in contrast, have quite a bit to say about the development of the constructs. Thus, the psychometric theories are not complete.

Third, and again in common with other psychometric theories, the psychometric theories of love have a certain ad-hoc quality. Because they are not only tested upon psychometric analysis but based upon it as well, the theories largely follow from the data, rather than the other way around. These theories probably come closest, of all the theories thus far considered, to being restatements of the data, in that factor analysis essentially reduces data from one form to another.

Finally, these theories, unlike many of those considered earlier, do not tie into more general theories of psychological functioning. The reinforcement, cognitive-consistency, two-component, attachment, and interruption theories are all special cases of general psychological theories. The theories of Rubin and of Sternberg and Grajek are not. Of course, there is no a-priori reason that a theory of liking and loving must be a special case of a general psychological theory. At the same time, it remains to be seen how the psychometric accounts of love can be tied into general theories of psychological functioning.

But, on the positive side, the psychometric approach to liking and loving shows that these can be measured, at least to a first approximation. Of course, no measure will be perfect or complete, but even a rough measure is an advance for the psychology of love, showing that what would seem to be unmeasurable is at least measurable in part. Second, since Rubin and others have shown that the study of love can be as scientific as any other aspect of psychology, the approach puts this study on a footing roughly equal to that of other areas of psychology. Finally, a measurement device opens the way for genuine assessment of the psychology of love as a basis for diagnosis and improvement of real relationships.

Liking as a Kind of Loving

The three theories described in the following section were partly intended to cure the ills of the psychometrically based theories. These three theories have all been tested through psychometric scales, but none derived utterly from psychometric analysis; rather, the psychometrics followed development of the theory. Moreover, the theories are broader than the psychometrically based theories in their conceptualization of the nature of love. The theories to be considered are Lee's colors of love, Davis's cluster theory, and my own triangular theory.

COLORS OF LOVE

John Lee used the metaphor of colors as the basis for his proposal for a typology of kinds of love.[59] One could imagine different kinds of love arrayed in a wheel, just like the color wheel. Lee derived the typology not only from the metaphor but from an examination of literature, both fiction and nonfiction, which he then verified on the basis of a task in which individuals were asked to sort into piles about fifteen hundred cards containing brief descriptions of love-related events, ideas, or emotions. The results of the sorting were then subjected to factor analysis, which generally supported the theory.

Lee's typology distinguishes among six major kinds of love: (1) *eros*, the love style characterized by the search for a beloved whose physical presentation of self embodies an image already held in the mind of the lover; (2) *ludus*, which is Ovid's term for playful or gamelike love; (3) *storge*, a style based on slowly developing affection and companionship; (4) *mania*, a love style characterized by obsession, jealousy, and great emotional intensity; (5) *agape*, or altruistic love, in which the lover views it as his or her duty to love without expectation of reciprocation; and (6) *pragma*, a practical style involving conscious consideration of the demographic and other objective characteristics of the loved one. Marcia Lasswell and Norman

Liking versus Loving

Lobsenz used Lee's theory as the basis for their construction of the Love Scale Questionnaire.[60] Some of the strongest validation for Lee's theory has come from recent work of Clyde Hendrick and Susan Hendrick, who have tested the theory with their own questionnaire, using factor-analytic methods.[61]

A given person does not necessarily display the same style in each of his or her relationships. Rather, different relationships may evoke different styles of loving. Moreover, people may switch from one style to another over time within a single relationship. It is useful to know and understand both your own and your partner's style of loving within a given relationship. For example, a ludic lover may well be playing the field while going out with you, and "forget" to mention it; while the manic lover is much less likely to play the field, but may well explode if you do. The storgic lover may develop into your best friend but is less likely to develop into your most intense romance. Such a romance is much more likely with an erotic lover. And if you become involved with an agapic lover, do not expect always to be at the center of his or her attention: the person who loves agapically tends to be very giving—and may well give of his or her selflessness to others beside yourself. Finally, if yours is a pragmatic lover, be prepared for a relationship based on practicalities that may even smack at times of a business deal.

Lee's theory is covered in this section because one of the styles of love, storge, is essentially a friendship love based on liking.[62] Storgic lovers are basically each other's best friends (or close to it); and hence, liking (obviously, in a nontrivial sense that goes beyond mere acquaintanceship) may be seen as one of the forms of love in Lee's theory.

A CLUSTER THEORY OF LIKING AND LOVING

Keith Davis has proposed that liking, as in a friendship, can be understood in terms of eight main elements: enjoyment, mutual assistance, respect, spontaneity, acceptance, trust, understanding, and confidence.[63] He proposes in addition, however, that loving is involved when two clusters of feelings are added to the friendship base: passion, which involves fascination with the other, sexual desire for the other, and exclusiveness of one's relationship with the other; and caring, which involves championing or being a primary advocate for the other, and giving the utmost of oneself to the other. Davis's data indicate that spouses or lovers do not differ much from close friends in terms of the base of friendship that he believes underlies both liking and loving relationships.[64] But they do differ considerably on most of the attributes that form the passion and caring clusters. Thus, Davis sees love as liking, plus a good bit more—namely, passion and caring.

Davis's theory has some practical implications for discerning when a friendship has become a loving relationship, or when a loving relationship has turned into a friendship. The things to monitor are the passion and the caring clusters. If you find your passion declining at the same time that you care less and less about your lover and your relationship with him or her, you may be losing your feelings of love. And if you are in a friendship, but find the attraction growing and your caring for your friend on a steady upswing, you may be on the road to love.

Liking versus Loving

The Triangular Theory of Liking and Loving

Also among these theories belongs the triangular theory of love, which holds that love can be understood in terms of three components that together can be viewed as forming the vertices of a triangle (see chapters 2 and 3).[65]

Limitations of the Theories of Liking as a Kind of Loving

These theories have several limitations. First, neither Davis's nor my theory has a large data base stemming from specific tests of the theory.[66] The data base for Lee's theory is only slightly larger.[67] Although both Davis and I draw upon past data that are consistent with our views, obviously such consistency tests are different from an extensive data base directly supporting it.

Second, the subset-set relationship proposed between liking and loving may be close, but not quite correct. There are probably aspects of liking in same-sex friendships, or even opposite-sex friendships, that do not appear in any of the kinds of loving relationships considered by the theories. For example, you might confide in a close friend about things that you would not feel comfortable confiding to a spouse, such as extramarital affairs or other things that could impinge upon and possibly be destructive in the relationship with the lover. Of course, one way of looking at this phenomenon is that certain aspects of intimacy can be greater with a same-sex friend. Another, however, is that there are in friendship aspects of liking that are different from aspects of liking in a love relationship.

Third, even these more nearly complete theories of love are probably incomplete with respect to the understanding they give us of the whole phenomenon of love. For example, many people feel that there is something about their love for their children that is different from their love for anyone else—perhaps the unconditionality of the love. The triangular theory might account for this difference in terms of greater commitment in such relationships, but this quantitative difference perhaps does not capture what to some feels like a qualitative difference. As noted earlier, this difference may have an evolutionary basis.

Integrating the Theories of Liking and Loving

The triangular theory of loving and liking, in knitting together aspects of past theories and the mechanisms underlying them, provides a sound basis for understanding the interrelations of those theories and their mechanisms. Table 4.1 summarizes how the triangular theory applies to each of the theories I have discussed.

Reinforcement principles appear to affect both the intimacy and the passion components of love, but the two components seem susceptible to different mechanisms. Liking—deriving from the intimacy component—seems to operate primarily under consistent reinforcement: one comes to like people who feed one a steady diet of reinforcement. The work of Byrne and others under the attraction paradigm suggests that one will like people as a function of the proportion of positive reinforcements one

TABLE 4.1

The Triangular Theory: Integrating Theories of Liking and Loving

Theory	Components of the Triangular Theory to Which It Most Applies		
	Intimacy	Passion	Commitment
Theories of Quantitative Difference			
Reinforcement Theories			
(Lott and Lott, Clore and Byrne)			
Consistent reinforcement	X		
Intermittent reinforcement		X	
Social Exchange Theories			
(Homans, Mills, and Clark)			
Exchange relationships	X		
Communal relationships		X	X
Equity Theory			
(Walster, Walster, and Berscheid)	X		
Cognitive-Consistency Theories			
(Heider, Festinger)	X		
Theories of Qualitative Difference:			
Liking and Loving as Distinct			
Clinical Theories			
Freud		X	
Reik		X	
Maslow			
D-love		X	
B-love	X	X	X
Fromm	X		X
Tennov		X	
Peele and Brodsky		X	
Peck			X
Two-Component Theory			
(Walster and Berscheid)			
Romantic love		X	
Companionate love	X		X
"Interruption" Theory			
(Berscheid)		X	
Evolutionary Theory			
(Wilson)			
Self-protection	X		X
Procreation		X	
Protection of children			X

TABLE 4.1 (*continued*)

Theory	Components of the Triangular Theory to Which It Most Applies		
	Intimacy	Passion	Commitment
Attachment Theory			
(Shaver and Hazen)	X	X	
Liking and Loving as Overlapping			
Multi-Component Psychometric			
Theory (Rubin)			
Liking	X		
Loving*	X	X	
Theory of Bonds			
(Sternberg and Grajek)*	X	X	
Liking as a Kind of Loving			
Colors of Love Theory			
(Lee)			
Eros		X	
Mania†		X	
Ludus‡	X	X	X
Storge	X		X
Agape‡	X	X	X
Pragma			
Cluster Theory			
(Davis)			
Liking	X		
Loving	X	X	
Triangular Theory			
(Sternberg)			
Non-love			
Liking	X		
Infatuated love		X	
Empty love			X
Romantic love	X	X	
Companionate love	X		X
Fatuous love		X	X
Consummate love	X	X	X

* Passion component de-emphasized relative to intimacy component.
† Passion gone berserk.
‡ Styles can apply to any component but are not equivalent to, or "captured by," those components.

receives from them.[68] Passionate or infatuated love—deriving primarily from the passion component—seems to operate primarily under intermittent (occasional) reinforcement. The evidence suggests that such love may survive *only* under intermittent reinforcement, when uncertainty reduction plays a key role in one's feelings for another.[69] Tennov's analysis suggests that limerence can survive only under conditions in which full development and consummation of love are withheld, and in which titillation of one kind or another continues over time.[70] Once the relationship is either allowed to develop or becomes an utter impossibility, limerence is extinguished.

Principles of social exchange and equity appear to apply most aptly to the intimacy component in liking relationships. We expect, more or less, a fair exchange from our friends. Judson Mills and Margaret Clark have distinguished between exchange and communal relationships: in the former, one basically expects reciprocity and equity principles to hold; whereas in the latter, one does not.[71] Friendships can be either exchange or communal relationships, depending on the level and type of involvement; whereas romantic loves are primarily communal. Infatuation—the presence of the passion component in the absence of the intimacy component—involves little equitable exchange. An individual experiencing limerence often receives a great deal of negative feedback from the object of the limerence, and will often persist as long as there is a slight hope of developing and ultimately consummating the relationship. Depending upon its level, commitment seems to be differentially susceptible to exchange. At lower and intermediate levels, we usually expect some commitment in exchange for our own commitment. In the absence of a return, partners may lower their commitment accordingly. At the highest levels—as in the love of a mother for a child—unconditional commitment may be relatively unsusceptible to exchange: the mother continues to love her child, regardless of the child's behavior.

Principles of cognitive-consistency theories seem most applicable to liking relationships and hence to the intimacy component of the triangular framework. These principles provide an alternative interpretation of roughly the same domain of phenomena as reinforcement theories were meant to deal with. While Fritz Heider's theory, for example, was intended to deal with liking relationships, and seems to work reasonably well in describing them,[72] in general we would not expect it to apply in most love relationships. There is no imbalance, for example, if Jane loves her boyfriend, Bill, and her sister, Mary, but Bill and Mary do not love each other. If, however, Bill and Mary do not like each other, imbalance and tension may well result as Mary criticizes Bill, and Bill, Mary.

The clinical and two-component theories of love seem primarily to deal with passion in loving relationships. Some of the clinical theorists, such as Reik, speak of seeking salvation, completion, or self-actualization through another.[73] Maslow's deficiency love seems to be essentially of a passionate nature, as does Freud's striving for an ideal.[74] Walster and Berscheid describe a kind of love that is highly based upon psychophysiological arousal, a primary characteristic of passion.[75] Moreover, according to Peele and Brodsky, love may be understood in part as an addiction, corresponding to the view of passion as an acquired motivation having many of the same properties as an addiction.[76] Of course, not all of the more clinically oriented theories deal only with passion. Peck's view of love is primarily based on the role of the commitment component in love, and Fromm's view seems to describe a companionate love that represents a combination of the intimacy and the commitment components.[77]

The sociobiologically based theory of Wilson draws upon evolutionary theory in attempting to understand loving and, to a lesser extent, liking.[78] Sociobiology serves the useful function of pointing out how different kinds of love may serve different evolutionary purposes. Love based primarily or solely upon passion serves a procreative function—ensuring reproduction of the species. Love (or liking) based primarily upon intimacy serves a protective function: members of a given species form pairs or bands to protect themselves against potentially hostile outsiders. Love based primarily, or at least in part, upon commitment serves the function of keeping parents, and especially the mother, with the child during the early years, when the child needs the parents in order to develop. Such love also, to some extent, binds the parents to each other, thereby increasing the probability that a child will have the additional protection and nurturance that two parents can potentially provide over a single one.

The attachment theory of Hazan and Shaver, as derived from the theories of Bowlby and especially of Ainsworth, seems to apply most to the form intimacy takes in a passionate adult relationship.[79] Thus, although the theory deals with the types of intimacy, it does so not for just any intimate relationship but rather only for those relationships in which some element of romance is involved, at least initially.

The psychometric theories of Rubin and of Grajek and myself seem primarily to deal with the intimacy component of love, and only lightly to deal with the issue of passion.[80] Commitment enters in little. The relatively high correlation between liking and loving scales presumably reflects this joint emphasis upon the single component of intimacy. Intimacy seems to be the component most easily susceptible to scaling on a unidimensional scale and, indeed, to be the most easily quantifiable component, perhaps because of the susceptibility of liking to more direct reinforcement principles.

The relation of Lee's theory to the present framework is complex. Eros would be regarded in the triangular theory as fairly close to infatuated love (passion), whereas mania would be regarded as infatuated love gone berserk. Ludus would be viewed not as a kind of love in and of itself, but rather as a style of interrelating that people can use in various loving relationships. For example, infatuated lovers, romantic lovers, and companionate lovers, as well as lovers of other kinds, are all capable of playing games with one another. Storge would be viewed as close to companionate love; agape, as a concomitant to the love characteristic of persons with an altruistic disposition in their personalities; and pragma, not as a kind of love at all, but rather as a pragmatic style of searching for a lover, as its name implies. Those who exhibit pragma may be searching for physical, financial, or other forms of comfort rather than for love.

Davis's theory is viewed as basing both liking and loving fundamentally on the intimacy component, a characteristic that is true to some extent of the triangular theory as well.[81] The addition of physical attraction in loving would be tantamount to the addition of the passion component of the triangular theory to the intimacy component of liking. Whereas the triangular theory views physical attraction as distinguishing infatuated or romantic love from liking, it would not distinguish caring from the liking involved in friendship, other than perhaps by there being more caring, on the average, in love. According to the triangular theory, caring is typically a part of the liking in a friendship; and indeed, Davis's own data may not clearly support his separation of the caring cluster from the liking involved in good friendships.

Despite their disagreements, these theories of liking, loving, and the relationship between them have a lot in common, and each of them highlights different aspects of liking and loving. You can use these theories in your own relationships by asking yourself the questions that each of the theories deals with best:

1. Are you being sufficiently reinforced in your relationship with your partner? Are you still getting the rewards that make a relationship worthwhile, or are you continuing the relationship on the basis of rewards you once got but are no longer getting? If so, can you restore some of the old rewards into your relationship, or introduce new ones?

2. Are you being intermittently reinforced? Are you having trouble getting over an old lover because he or she is intermittently reinforcing you, or are you being strung along by someone who is doling out just enough periodic reinforcement to keep you in the relationship?

3. What kinds of resource do you want from your partner, and what kinds are you actually getting? If you are not getting what you want, is it because your partner is unwilling to give it to you, does not have it to give, or does not know what you want because you are unable or unwilling to communicate your needs or desires?

4. Do you value what your partner values, and vice versa? Or do you have value conflicts that just won't lend themselves to resolution?

5. Is your relationship equitable, or is one partner usually on either the giving or the receiving end? If the

relationship is not equitable, what can be done to make it so?

6. Is there a justification of effort involved in your relationship? In other words, how much of your staying in it is because you want to justify the past investment you have put into it, rather than your enjoying it for what it still gives you?

7. Do you like your partner's friends? If not, how is your dislike of the friends affecting your relationship (if at all)?

8. Are you looking for salvation in your relationship, or other things that no one can really give you, except perhaps yourself?

9. Are there obsessive qualities to your love—for example, your constantly being worried about and preoccupied with the relationship? If so, what would be left if you took the obsession away? Is the obsession a substitute for love?

10. Is your commitment to the relationship one that, if you had the opportunity to decide now, you would still make, or is it based on the way the relationship once was but is no longer?

11. Is your relationship still interesting, alive, and changing, or is it stagnant?

12. Do you love the person for him or herself, or for what you want him or her to be?

13. What is your attachment style in your relationship, and what is your partner's? Do they mesh? (For example, if you are both avoidant, you are likely to run into trouble.)

14. What is your style of loving in your relationship, and what is your partner's? Do they match?

15. How much do you care about what happens to

your partner, and how much does your partner care about what happens to you?

There are no right or wrong answers to these questions, but your pattern of responses can teach you a lot about yourself, your partner, and what holds you together—or is tearing you apart.

If there has been a problem in theories of love, it has been that some that have focused on part of the phenomenon have often been seen as theories of the phenomenon as a whole. A goal for the future ought to be the integration of existing theories into a unified and more comprehensive theory, with subsequent research aimed at testing it.[82] Thus, I believe we are heading in a direction where it will be possible to understand liking and loving as labels for a variety of interrelated phenomena, rather than as single phenomena whose complexities defy scientific analysis.

Attraction: What Makes It? What Breaks It?

LOVE would seem to be a part of attraction: you can be attracted to someone you do not love; but if you love someone, you are likely to have been drawn, to begin with, by some appealing quality in him or her (though it need not be physical appearance). What, then, is it that attracts two people to each other in the first place? What makes them more or less likely to become involved in a loving relationship? These questions are addressed by the area of research called interpersonal attraction.[1]

There is considerably more empirical research on interpersonal attraction than on love. Indeed, interpersonal attraction has long been considered a field within psychology, and the study of love just a small drop in this large pond. The study of attraction has generated more research and also probably has been considered more "acceptable," both within psychology and outside it, than the study of love. There are several reasons for this preference. First, researchers have been able to identify concrete environmental factors that generate attraction. The best examples, each of which will be considered in turn in this chapter, are physical attractiveness, arousal, proximity of two people to each other, reciprocity (in the sense that the attraction to someone else is mutual), similarity of one person to the other, and barriers that make it difficult to act on one's attraction to another. Studies of attraction have tended to be studies of how these fairly concrete variables affect attraction. Love has no clearly definable set of concrete variables like these to study.

Second, people have preferred to study interpersonal attraction over love because interpersonal attraction is more easily measurable. People have been happy to accept as measures of attraction little quizzes asking a small number of less than profound questions: How much do you like being with so-and-so? Or, how much would you like to do something (such as be in an experiment) with such-and-such? No one would claim that a handful of such questions measures all there is to being attracted to someone, but investigators seem content to deal with just a portion of attraction. With love, perhaps the expectations are higher. Somehow, the investigator is expected to measure the whole thing.

Third, there seem to be at least somewhat objective standards for attraction. No one finds it particularly odd to say that, by the standards of a given society, some people are perceived as more attractive than others, but it is invidious to say that some people are more lovable than others. Society has no clear, objective standard for "lovability"; and indeed, even the idea of such a standard seems unpleasant, which brings us to the last reason why people have generally preferred to study attraction over love.

Fourth and finally, the study of love is much more threatening to people than is the study of attraction. Most people have come to terms with being attractive in some degree. They may believe they are more attractive than others believe them to be, but they have some sense of how others perceive them (which, of course, may be wrong), and they probably have come to terms with their perception. But few people know and probably want to know how lovable or even loved they are, and love research threatens to tell them. One may be afraid to find out the results and then, when one does find them out, be not quite sure what to do about them if they do not meet one's expectations. Yet I would argue that it is better to recognize, and try to ameliorate, any discrepancy between such expectations, rather than to live in an ignorance that reality may eventually explode.

For all these reasons, then, interpersonal attraction has been a more popular subject for study than has love. In this chapter, I shall discuss some of the main findings in this literature, discussing the primary variables that affect the attraction of one person to another: physical attractiveness, arousal, proximity, reciprocity, similarity, and barriers.

Physical Attractiveness

One of the most famous studies in the interpersonal attraction literature—and one of the most depressing—was done by Elaine Hatfield (formerly Walster) and her colleagues.[2] The study was conducted to test the so-called *matching hypothesis*, according to which people look for partners whose level of interpersonal attractiveness, broadly defined, matches their own. The context of the study was a "computer dance," at which 376 college men were paired with 376 college women. They were each informed that the basis of the pairing was their profile of scores on a personality test administered at an earlier session when they signed up for the dance. The setting, therefore, was seen by these men and women as similar to that provided by standard computer-dating services.

In fact, the individuals were randomly assigned to each other, the sole restriction being that men were paired with women. The researchers collected information about each person so as to try to determine what aspects of the pairs would lead to greater or lesser success on the initial date at the computer dance. The idea was that people who were better matches would enjoy their date more; and the question addressed was: What constitutes a better match? Unbeknownst to the individuals, each had been rated on physical attractiveness at the initial session in which the personality test had been given. After the date, each person was asked to complete a brief questionnaire assessing the date.

The investigators found that only one factor influenced how much a person liked his or her date, how much a person wanted to see the date again, and how often the men actually asked the women for future dates. That single factor was the physical attractiveness of the date: the more physically attractive the date, the higher the ratings. Not even matching effects were found, whereby people liked dates whose attractiveness matched their own. Rather, almost everyone preferred the more physically attractive dates.

Why was physical attraction so important? After all, few people would admit to counting physical attractiveness so much in their choice of people to date or in how much they enjoy dates. I believe that there are two reasons. First, since most personal attributes take some time to judge while physical attractiveness is registered immediately, it is one of the few attributes that can be assessed with any accuracy after a first date. Second, since contact on a first date tends to be superficial, the superficial aspects of a person are likely to be salient. The implication is fairly clear: If you really want to get to know someone, don't let the first date count too much. Or if you do want to go beyond physical attraction, don't count on mixers! You probably will find out very little and are likely to overweigh physical attractiveness.

One possibility, of course, is that the sole importance of physical attractiveness and the failure of the matching hypothesis were due to the fact that partners were assigned. In the normal course of life, people choose their dates and risk rejection when they ask someone out. The risk of rejection may cause people to play it safe and look for partners who match themselves, rather than those who are highly attractive physically. Because the dates in this study were assigned, neither partner had to risk rejection by the other.

Ellen Berscheid and her colleagues tested the possibility that risk of rejection accounted for the results.[3] In another experiment, individuals again were led to believe that they were signing up for a computer date. Half the people signed up under conditions similar to those of the previous experiment, in which they were led to believe that they would go to the dance with their assigned partners. The other half were led to believe that their prospective dates would have the chance to turn them down after a short meeting. While there were no differences in effects of physical attractiveness between the two groups, the researchers did find that more physically attractive individuals wanted more physically attractive dates—a result consistent with the matching hypothesis. In their next experiment, Berscheid and her colleagues asked individuals to choose a date from six photographs of members of the opposite sex who varied in physical attractiveness (according to independent raters). These researchers found that the possibility of rejection again did not affect the preferred level of attractiveness of the date; but, consistent with the matching hypothesis, more attractive individuals chose more attractive photos for their dates.

Work by Bernard Murstein also provides support for the matching hypothesis.[4] In one study, Murstein had judges rate the physical attractiveness of photos of ninety-nine couples who were either engaged or going steady, as well as the attractiveness of a set of couples consisting of randomly matched men and women. Couples who were actually involved with each other were rated, on the average, to be more similar in physical attractiveness than couples who were not involved with each other. Murstein has also found that middle-aged, middle-class couples tend to be matched on physical attractiveness.

My own view is that the researchers have not fully considered all of the variables that may lead to matching in physical attractiveness. One such variable, I believe, is a person's perception of what he or she deserves. Even though one might ideally like someone more physically attractive than oneself, one may not feel deserving of such a person. Just as some people feel uncomfortable when they receive a reward they do not believe they deserve, some may be uncomfortable with a date who is much more attractive than they are. Or they may be able to handle a date without too much difficulty but believe that the relationship would not work in the long term. This situation may be explained by equity theory (see pages 119–21). A person who believes that his or her partner is much more attractive than he or she is may also believe that it would just take too much effort, over the long term, to restore equity and even, indeed, that equity cannot be achieved.

Two apparently opposing stereotypes seem to exist side by side in our culture. One is that what is beautiful is good, and vice versa.[5] Perhaps its most famous expression is Keats's "beauty is truth, truth beauty." The opposing view is that you should not judge a book by its cover, or beauty is only skin deep. According to this view, superficial beauty often is a cover for shallowness and lack of emotional depth, whereas superficial plainness may hide a gem in the rough. Indeed, people who are not physically attractive may well need to develop their internal resources so as to compensate in some way for their lack of physical attractiveness. Several studies have been done to examine these alternative views.

One study, by Kenneth Dion, Ellen Berscheid, and Elaine Walster, required college men and women to rate photographs of three people of varying physical attractiveness on a large number of characteristics.[6] Half of the individuals rated same-sex photos; the other half, opposite-sex photos. The results were clear: the more physically attractive people in the photos were judged to have better personalities, greater marital happiness, more occupational success, more social and professional happiness, and more happiness in life than the less attractive people. There was no evidence of jealousy, although the investigators tested for it by trying to see whether raters might belittle very attractive photos of members of the same sex as making the raters look bad by comparison.

It is important to appreciate exactly what is being studied here: namely, people's perceptions of others' personalities, happiness, success, and so on. Perceptions do not always correspond to actualities. Clearly, there are very attractive people who are unhappy, as the suicides of famous actors and actresses occasionally show. The blissful lives we imagine very attractive people to have exist only in the eyes of the beholders.

Harold Sigall and David Landy found that when a male is associated with an attractive female, he makes a much more favorable overall impression on people and is better liked than when he is associated with an unattractive female.[7] This better impression is made on both males and females. This result suggests a beautiful woman may have a sort of radiating effect on the man associated with her. It has often been asserted that some men choose beautiful women in order to enhance their own attractiveness—as, for example, the marriage of Aristotle Onassis to Jacqueline Kennedy.

A more disturbing finding is also that of Sigall and Landy, who had individuals rate the quality of an essay when a photo of the writer was attached to it.[8] The photos attached to the essays varied in attractiveness, but the same essay was used in each case. A given subject saw each essay paired with only one photo. More attractive looking persons received better ratings on their essays, independent of the actual quality of the essay. Thus, it appears that physical attractiveness can bias the way in which a person's work is judged. This finding has important implications for college and graduate school applications, which until recently often recommended or required the attachment of a photo to the application, and also for job applications that require a photograph.

It is sometimes said that Richard M. Nixon lost his televised debates with John F. Kennedy as much for physical appearance as for anything else. Kennedy looked relaxed and "up"; Nixon, tense and "down." Part of the latter's problem was that his heavy beard left him with a pronounced "five o'clock shadow." In recent years, of course, as politics has increasingly become a media event, ever greater attention is paid to physical appearance.

The effects of physical attractiveness may differ for men and women. Daniel Bar-Tal and Leonard Saxe found that female spouses tend to be evaluated for physical attractiveness independently of their husband's physical attractiveness, whereas evaluations of the husband are affected by the wife's attractiveness.[9] When an unattractive man was married to a beautiful woman, it was assumed by the subjects that he must have some exceptional compensating qualities—for example, high income or high occupational status.

These assumptions are, again, borne out by the precepts of equity theory. Couples may use a variety of resources to try to achieve equity: money, brains, or background may all substitute for other resources or for each other.

It appears that, in evaluating potential mates, men place more value on women's physical attractiveness than women do on men's.[10] However, not all men appear to count physical attractiveness equally. In a recent study, Mark Snyder, Ellen Berscheid, and Peter Glick contrasted the importance of women's physical attractiveness to men who were either high or low in an attribute called *self-monitoring*.[11] High self-monitors are people who tend to tailor their behavior to the situation, in the sense that they act one way with one person and a different way with another person so as to maximize their fit with each. Low self-monitors are more consistent in behavioral interaction: they tend to act more or less the same way no matter whom they are with. Their attitude is, "This is who I am, and you can take it or leave it."

Snyder and his colleagues found that men who are high self-monitors value looks more than do men who are low self-monitors.[12] Even more important was the finding that when men were given a choice between dating a woman described as physically attractive but not terribly nice versus one who was physically not very attractive but really quite nice, high self-monitors preferred the more physically attractive date whereas low self-monitors preferred the less physically attractive date who was described as being the nicer person. This result suggests that high self-monitoring men may be more concerned with the radiating effect of a beautiful woman than are the low self-monitors.

One of the most interesting studies examining the effects of physical attractiveness monitored a ten-minute phone conversation between a man and a woman. Mark Snyder, Elizabeth Tanke, and Ellen Berscheid conducted this study in which men and women who were previously unacquainted were given the opportunity, allegedly, to get to know each other.[13] The men were each shown a photo of the woman to whom they were talking. Half the time the photo was of a beautiful woman and half the time, of a very unattractive woman. Unbeknownst to the men, the photos were not of the woman to whom each was talking. The conversations between the men and the women were recorded, and judges who were blind to the photographs that each of the men saw rated either the men's or women's conversation on several dimensions.

The judges listening to the males' part of the conversation judged the men who thought they were talking to the attractive women as more social, sexually warm, permissive, interesting, and attractive than the men who thought they were talking to the unattractive females. Similarly, the judges listening only to the females' part of the conversation judged the women who were thought to be attractive by their male partners as more sociable, poised, sexually warm, and outgoing. In other words, when the men thought that they were talking to a very attractive woman, both they and the woman seemed more attractive in the phone conversation than when the men thought that they were talking to an unattractive woman. In essence, being thought beautiful made the women react in a more attractive way and made the men act more attractively. In this case, belief becomes reality.

The results of these various studies on physical attractiveness could be depressing if relationships ended with initial encounters. On the one hand, the studies seem to confirm what some of us fear—that physical attractiveness matters a great deal early in relationships. But as time goes on, other variables become more feasible to evaluate and more important to relationships. Moreover, even early in relationships, physical attractiveness is not equally important to everyone.

It would be worth studying how perceptions of a person's physical attractiveness change as people get to know each other better. What has been looked at is how perceptions of physical attractiveness affect the way we feel about people, but at least as important is how the way we feel about people affects our perception of their physical attractiveness. I have found, as have many others I know, that my perception of a person's physical attractiveness often increases if I like a person, and decreases if I do not. Over time, liking may affect perception of physical attractiveness as much as perceptions of physical attractiveness affect liking.

Arousal

There is an old trick that some men who pursue women have adopted almost intuitively: in order to arouse a woman's interest in them, they take the woman to some event that is emotionally stimulating, such as a wrestling or boxing match. For many women, of course, a good ballet or play may have a better effect. The intuition is that emotional arousal somehow acts as an aphrodisiac. In fact, there is now evidence that arousal does act in just this way.

Perhaps the most famous experiment demonstrating the link between arousal and attraction was conducted by Donald Dutton and Arthur Aron.[14] The experiment was conducted in an unusual setting—a scenic spot frequented by tourists, which had two bridges in different places. One bridge extended over a deep gorge and swayed from side to side while people walked across it. For most people, walking across this bridge was terrifying. The other bridge was stable and not high off the ground. Walking across it did not arouse anxiety. Male subjects were assigned to walk across one bridge or the other, and as they walked across the bridge, they were met by an assistant of the experimenter, who was either male or female. The assistant asked each person to answer a few questions and to write a brief story in response to a picture. The picture was from the Thematic Apperception Test, a test for measuring personality needs. After the individuals wrote the story, the research assistant gave them his or her phone number and remarked that they should feel free to call the assistant at home if they would like further information about the experiment. The experimenters were particularly interested in scoring the stories for sexual imagery. They found that the highest level of sexual imagery in the stories was obtained by those men who walked across the anxiety-evoking suspension bridge and were met by a female assistant. Moreover, men in this condition were more likely to call the research assistant at home.

The Dutton and Aron research supports the stereotype in myriad books, plays, and movies that people who endure stress together are likely to be attracted to each other. Indeed, many "office affairs" are likely to start with two people being brought together by their sharing of a common stress and their resolving their problems together. Thus, it is important for couples in relationships to continue to confront mutual challenges together, and not to leave them for the office or the home for only one of the two partners to confront. By all means, set reachable goals, but if and when you reach them, set new ones. Relationships that stand still are really moving backward.

A second experiment by Dutton and Aron showed the effect of arousal in an anxiety-provoking setting.[15] Male subjects came to participate in an experiment. Some of the subjects were told that they were about to receive a series of strong and painful electric shocks; others, that they would receive only weak and nonpainful electric shocks. While they were waiting, the male subjects were introduced to a young woman who was alleged to be another subject in the experiment, but who was in fact "planted" by the experimenters. While the subjects were waiting to receive the shocks, they were asked to fill out a questionnaire evaluating the young woman. Subjects expecting to receive the strong and painful shocks evaluated the woman more favorably than did subjects who expected to receive the weak and painless shocks. None of the subjects ever really received the shocks, which were mentioned merely as a device either to arouse or not to arouse the experimental subjects.

This experiment, like the earlier one, shows the importance of arousal in generating attraction. One is more likely to be attracted to another if one is aroused, even if the arousal does not come from that person. On the one hand, this work shows that arousal matters. Whether you are meeting someone for the first time or taking a night on the town after raising three children, generating excitement helps keep a relationship going. At the same time, it is important to emphasize that the studies on arousal, like those on physical attractiveness, deal with the earliest stage of a relationship—initial attraction. With time, people who do not arouse you at first may come to arouse you, although the reverse can also be true. Planning surprises, having fun, and doing new and exciting things are always important in relationships.

Proximity

Of the potentially millions of partners with whom one might become involved in a romantic relationship, one meets only an infinitesimal fraction. Many of us choose a future mate on the basis of having met and truly gotten to know less than a dozen contenders, and it is the rare person who meets, and gets to know well, more than two dozen. The most important factor determining whom you meet is also the simplest—namely, proximity. You are most likely to meet those people to whom, for one reason or another, you are physically near.

Two classic studies examined the effects of proximity on interpersonal attraction. The first was conducted by Leon Festinger and his colleagues in the early 1950s.[16] Festinger and his colleagues investigated patterns of friendship among military veterans and their wives who lived in two student housing projects at the Massachusetts Institute of Technology. The two housing projects had different architectural designs, so that it was possible to investigate the effects of proximity in two fairly different settings. The most basic finding was that people who lived closer to each other were more likely to become friends than were people who lived farther apart. People who lived in centrally located apartments were more likely to form more friendships than were people who lived in apartments toward the end of a floor. Predictably, the friends of the people living near the middle of the hallway tended to be people on that floor. People living in apartments near stairways were much more likely to make friends with people living on the floor above, because they were in a position to interact with these people when they were going up the staircase. The underlying lesson here is that, in choosing a place to live, you are also choosing a set of people with whom to live.

A second major study was conducted by Theodore Newcomb, under circumstances rare in social psychology.[17] Most psychologists have to decide whether they want the experimental control of a laboratory setting or the greater real-world validity of a field setting. Newcomb was able to have both when he was given the opportunity to create a dormitory situation for students at the University of Michigan. For each of two years, seventeen male college students lived in his dormitory without rent in exchange for participating in his experiment on the formation of friendships.

The results were generally consistent with those of Festinger and his colleagues. During the first year of the experiment, Newcomb found no evidence that physical proximity influenced interpersonal attraction. But during the second year—with an entirely different set of people living in the dormitory—proximity did affect attraction, with roommates liking each other more than did those who did not room together. What might have been the cause of the discrepancy between the results during the two years? During the first year, roommates had been assigned at random; during the second year, room assignments were based on a matching of the individuals' values and attitudes as expressed prior to their moving into the dormitory. Half of the students were assigned to live with others whose initial attitudes agreed with theirs; the other half were assigned to live with those whose initial attitudes were quite different. Regardless of assignments, though, the general effect still held: roommates were more likely to be friends than were non-roommates. It was never really clear why Newcomb obtained the significant effects of proximity during the second but not the first year.

Another study of the effects of proximity was conducted by Mady Segal, who mailed questionnaires to fifty-two students in the Maryland State Police Training Academy.[18] The students were asked to name their three closest friends in the force after their six-week training. In the academy, students were not randomly assigned to seating and placement in classes. However, the basis of assignment was alphabetical order of last names, which hardly seems like a basis for forming friendships. Nevertheless, Segal found that alphabetical ordering had a strong effect on friendship. Of sixty-five friendships, almost half were formed between trainees whose last names began with the same or adjacent letters.

The effects of proximity can be mixed. On the one hand, proximity may generate attraction, as shown in the studies described so far. Indeed, in respect to the mere exposure effect (see pages 90–92), according to which mere repeated exposure of a person to a stimulus is a sufficient condition for that person to come to like that stimulus more, Zajonc has found that the effect will work not only for people but for things.[19] Thus, exposure to Chinese characters, photographs, and similar objects increases liking for them. An experiment by Susan Saegert, Walter Swap, and Robert Zajonc showed that even liking for unpleasant-tasting substances increases upon repeated exposure to them.[20]

On the other hand, there is the view that familiarity breeds contempt, that getting to know a person too well can lead to the downfall of a friendship. There is evidence for the "familiarity breeds contempt" effect as well. In a study, Ebbe Ebbesen, Glenn Kjos, and Vladimir Konecni found that, in a middle-class condominium complex in California, proximity was associated both with greater liking and with greater disliking.[21] Moreover, the effect of proximity was greater on disliking than on liking: whereas 62 percent of people's friendships were with other residents in the same area, 70 percent of people's dislikings were also in the same area.

While it is not possible to determine precisely when familiarity breeds fondness, and when contempt, I can speculate a bit. The more you know a person, the more opportunity that person has to reward or punish you; and you, them. One determinant, then, of whether familiarity will lead to positive or negative feelings is whether you are giving your partner primarily reward or punishment: that is, whether you are reinforcing him or her; or, rather, whether the other *feels* reinforced. One punishment is likely to have a more substantial effect than one reward; what you believe to be a reward may not be for the other person, and what you take to be neutral may be perceived by the other as a punishment.

A second factor that may determine the effect of familiarity is the extent to which one associates the familiarity with arousal and excitement. Familiarity can provide opportunities for doing rewarding things together (and the rewards rub off on people, making them seem more attractive) or be an excuse for letting boredom become the order of the day. People have different levels of excitement that they find to be optimal, and what is too little for one person can be too much for another.

The third factor that I believe makes a difference is a person's expectations. If you expect to be bored, then you are likely to act in ways that will make you bored: you generate a self-fulfilling prophecy. But if you see getting to know a person better as a window of practically limitless opportunity for new kinds of shared experience and excitement, then that is likely to be just what you get.

Reciprocity

We tend to like those who like us, an idea that motivated a study by Carl Backman and Paul Secord.[22] Moreover, what counts for our liking is not necessarily how much the other actually likes us, but rather how much we *think* the other likes us.

In the Backman-Secord experiment, people who were previously unacquainted with each other were formed into small discussion groups. Prior to their formation, each person was informed individually that, on the basis of personality-test information (which was phony), the experimenters were able to tell that certain members of the group, but not others, would be very attracted to that person. An informal group session was then actually held at a first meeting. After this meeting, the experimenter told the members of the group that they might eventually be paired off, and so asked them to rank each of the three other members of his or her group in terms of preference as a potential discussion partner. The whole group continued to meet for a total of six sessions, and a similar ranking procedure for preferred-discussion partners was obtained after the third and the sixth as well as after the first session. The investigators found that, at the end of the first session, subjects preferred as potential discussion partners those other group members whom the subjects had been told would like them on the basis of the phony personality-test data. Thus, the belief that another will like you can lead to your liking that other. By the third session, however, the effect of the phony data had disappeared, as subjects were now in a position to discover whom they genuinely liked and who liked them.

In a related experiment, Richard Stapleton, Peter Nacci, and James Tedeschi showed that when subjects were evaluated by another person, their evaluation of that other was strongly influenced by the way in which they had been evaluated by him or her.[23] We all have felt, to some extent, the repercussions of our own evaluations of others and, indeed, may hesitate to criticize powerful people in our lives lest we be criticized in turn.

Reciprocity appears to be important in the area of self-disclosure. Generally, people are more likely to like others who are willing to show themselves as they really are.[24] When we bare ourselves to another, we usually expect that person to do the same. If someone does not, we feel uncomfortable and less attracted to him or her.

The findings on reciprocity have a straightforward implication for relationships, one that has been recognized since the earliest human society: that is, that one tends to get back what one gives. People who exploit others are usually recognized as such sooner or later, and then others react to them in kind. In the long run, exploitation is probably not in your own self-interest in a relationship, even if you take a selfish point of view, because when you are eventually found out, you will likely get back what you gave. Of course, the Golden Rule may work on the average, but it does not necessarily work in individual cases. Some people are "black holes": they take, take, and take more and still give nothing in return. Others are able to give but reluctant to take. Psychology affirms what religion, philosophy, and literature have told us for a long time: what we give is what we get.

Similarity

The saying that "birds of a feather flock together" seems to be supported by the empirical literature on interpersonal attraction. On the whole, more similar individuals are more likely to be attracted to each other.

Similarity can take many forms, several of which have been related to increased interpersonal attraction. Perhaps the most basic set of variables is demographic; research shows that similarity in demographic variables such as age, religion, education, physical health, ethnic background, economic background, self-esteem, and the like are associated with increased interpersonal attraction.[25] There is at least some suggestion that individuals who are attracted to each other have similar personalities, and studies have suggested that having similar personalities is associated with marital satisfaction.[26] Attracted couples are also more likely to be similar in attitudes than are unattracted ones.[27] As I noted earlier, couples in ongoing relationships are also more likely to be similar in physical attractiveness than are couples matched in age but not in physical attractiveness.

Perhaps the most well-known and vocal proponent of the similarity-breeds-attraction view is Donn Byrne. As noted in chapter 4, Byrne has written extensively on his attempts to predict personal attraction on the basis of similarity. Many of Byrne's studies have entailed a single experimental procedure. His subjects, generally college students, start off by answering questionnaire items intended to measure their personality attributes and attitudes. Subjects are then shown the questionnaire of another individual whom they have not met. Unbeknownst to them, the unknown subject is a phony, and his or her responses have been manipulated so as to be either similar or dissimilar to those of the genuine subject. The genuine subject is left to form a general impression of the other person and to rate him or her on what Byrne calls the Interpersonal Judgment Scale. The Interpersonal Judgment Scale contains several items, two of which are critical: one regards personal feelings toward the unknown other, and the other regards the subject's willingness to work with the other in an experiment. Ratings on these two items, added together, are considered to be a measure of attraction toward the phony other. Byrne has found that scores on the Interpersonal Judgment Scale are linearly related to the amount of similarity between the subject's and the phony other's patterns of responses. In particular, similarity in attitude is an excellent predictor of attraction as measured by Byrne's scale. His measure of interpersonal attraction is general and global, and it is not clear that the strength of the relation that he obtained would pertain to a more complex and variegated measure of attraction.

How general is the relation of similarity to attraction? We know that there must be a few basic differences, not the least of which is gender! Ted Huston and George Levinger suggested four reasons that similarity may be so important.[28] First, people may find similarity to be rewarding to them. The very fact of similarity may directly lead to increased attraction to the person. Second, similarity may increase self-esteem: hearing someone express similar attitudes or values may enhance your view of yourself, as through similarity you may receive support for the positions you take in life. Third, similarity may portend a bright future: people may have greater confidence in the future of a relationship with someone who is more rather than less similar to them. Finally, it may be that it is not just similarity in demographics or attitudes or whatever that directly influences interpersonal attraction, but also the similarity in emotional responses thereby generated. In other words, people who are similar in a variety of ways may respond to various situations in an emotionally congruent manner and therefore be more likely to be attracted to each other.

Barriers

One of the longest-running and most successful of off-Broadway plays is the *Fantasticks*. The play is about a boy and a girl whose fathers are sworn enemies and have, as a result, erected a high wall separating their properties. The boy and girl come to know each other, fall in love, and go to great lengths to see each other in secret trysts. The fathers, upon discovering the relationship between their children, discourage them but eventually come to the conclusion that they will not be able to prevent the relationship. Hence, they tear down the wall. But as soon as they tear down the wall, problems emerge. What once had been a close and harmonious relationship becomes more distant and discordant. Eventually, the boy goes off to see the world; and the girl, left behind, also gets to see what else is around. After many trials and tribulations, the boy and the girl are reunited. But now the fathers, having learned a lesson, rebuild the wall in order to create an obstacle separating the two. The lesson they have learned is that love seems to flourish only in the face of obstacles. The theme of the *Fantasticks* is actually supported by psychological research. Richard Driscoll, Keith Davis, and Milton Lipetz found that parental interference in a relationship tends to bring the partners in it closer together; and that—as the parents in the *Fantasticks* found out—if parents want to discourage a relationship, the worst thing they can do is actively to interfere with it.[29]

Couples sometimes glue themselves together by creating outside enemies who are out to get them. The enemies may be friends, parents-in-law, stepchildren, or, for

that matter, the IRS. Sometimes, of course, one's perception of these external enemies is not paranoid but realistic: sometimes people or agencies are out to get a couple.
But it is useful to have an external enemy—so long as it is
relatively impotent. Enemy-seeking has its drawbacks:
couples who get in the habit may eventually find the
enemy in one another.

The principle underlying the story of the *Fantasticks* is
sometimes called the "hard-to-get effect" (see pages
86–88). As I have said, when Elaine Walster and her
colleagues investigated this effect, they found that it is
itself hard to get: that is, it is not that people who are hard
to get are more attractive, but that we tend to prefer
people who are harder for others but easier for ourselves
to get.[30] R. A. Wright and R. J. Contrada questioned the
results of Walster and her colleagues on several grounds,
and found that we tend to be attracted to people who are
at least somewhat selective in whom they date.[31] However, we are more attracted to people who are moderately
selective than to people who are extremely selective. The
extremely selective people are often seen as conceited
and as having too high an opinion of themselves.

In conclusion, unless at least some of the factors
in interpersonal attraction—physical attractiveness,
arousal, proximity, reciprocity, similarity, and barriers—
are operating for a couple, it is unlikely that they will
reach the point of falling in love.

What Matters When?

IF you were solicited for a major financial investment that was likely to pay off just over 50 percent of the time, or asked to play Russian roulette with the same probability of not being killed, chances are that you would neither make the investment nor play the game. Yet people routinely enter into marriages with roughly the same probability of success. Few people start out expecting to become victims of divorce, any more than smokers expect to become victims of lung cancer or Californians of earthquake. Yet, if the divorce rate remains constant, close to half of the men and women currently entering into marriages can expect eventually to divorce.

Perhaps many intimate relationships, including marriages, terminate because people make poor decisions about a potential partner: they misevaluate the evidence or do not seek the most useful evidence in the first place. Another explanation, the focus of this chapter, is not that people pick the wrong partners, but that they select partners on the basis of what matters early in an intimate relationship rather than what might matter over the long run. And, of course, intimate relationships and the people in them change over time in ways that are not fully predictable to begin with. Now psychological research has made it possible at least to discern the characteristics of a relationship, as well as of the partners in it, that will vary in importance over time. Thus, one may have a better chance, at the beginning of a relationship, of predicting its success in the long as well as the short term. In this chapter, I discuss studies of changes in what matters when in relationships, and in the next chapter, I will discuss theories of what underlies the changes.

Studies of Relationship Change

Two major studies of what changes over time in relationships have been conducted by Zick Rubin and his associates. The first study, part of Rubin's dissertation, involved a follow-up of 182 couples six months after an initial questionnaire session.[1] Fully 87 percent of the original 364 respondents replied. Couples were in close agreement in reporting changes, if any, in the intensity of their relationship. Five of six couples were still together; 60 percent of couples reported that their relationships had become more intense, 19 percent reported no change in intensity, and 21 percent reported a decrease in intensity. Most of the couples in the last category had broken up. The relationships most likely to have broken up were those that had lasted either for the shortest or for the longest time. Apparently, the shortest-termers in the original study were still unstable, and the longest-termers were susceptible to being in relationships that were coming close to having run their course. Scores on Rubin's Loving Scale predicted favorable progress in the relationships to only a slight degree.[2] But the correlations of love-scale scores and progress in relationships were higher for those individuals who had indicated, in the initial study, that they lived in accordance with more romantic ideals, as captured by such statements as "A person should marry whomever he loves regardless of social position" and "As long as they at least love one another, two people should have no difficulty getting along together in marriage." For couples in which both partners were romantic, the correlations between initial love-scale scores and progress six months later were moderate, somewhat higher for men than for women. Correlations for the Rubin Liking Scale were in the same direction, but weaker.

This study helps explain why some seemingly loveless relationships can go on and on, whereas others terminate rapidly. Most of us know couples who stay together in what seem to be dead relationships (at least emotionally), and other couples who break up as soon as one member of the couple stops feeling "in love." The critical issue is the perception of each member of the couple regarding how important love, and especially romantic love, is for the survival of a relationship. For example, in the storgic (best-friend) love of John Lee's theory of love styles (chapter 4), lovers are not likely to become distressed if their relationship cools off: indeed, it may never have been anything but cool. Erotic lovers, on the other hand, may be very distressed. An additional intervening variable is what the members of a couple expect not just for relationships in general but for a given relationship in particular. Some people, for example, adore erotic relationships but do not expect a marriage to survive as this kind of relationship over the long term.

The biggest problem, and a frequent one, is when each member of a couple has a different perception either of the importance of love in a relationship or of what love means in their relationship. Cathy and George provide a case in point. After being married for over a decade, they appeared to have everything; a nice house, two successful careers, four wonderful children, lots of discretionary money to spend, status in the community, and practically anything else a couple could want. The problem was that Cathy was unhappy, but George was not. Cathy felt she had everything and yet nothing. However great her life looked, it was empty except for her love of her four children and their love of her. What love she may have once had for George had given way to what she referred to as "patience." She tolerated him, but found herself emotionally disengaged. She felt that there had to be more to life, and love, than this. At the time I knew her, she was considering giving up on the marriage, and the nice house and the money and the picture-perfect environment she lived in, to seek a man whom she could feel really crazy about. George felt that Cathy would be crazy to give up what they had because they had it all. And George was right—for George. His notion of love was much more placid than Cathy's. Passionate feelings were not important to him in a marriage, and he was comfortable with modest amounts of intimacy. He and Cathy had a commitment to each other, and that commitment had brought them all they wanted, and more. But the lack of passion and intimacy in the relationship was increasingly frustrating to Cathy, and she didn't know what to do about it. During my last conversation with her, she was still deciding, as she had been for the past five years, and might well be for another five or more.

Unfortunately, there is no one right answer to Cathy's problem, because it involves so many factors. She will have to take into account not only her feelings for George, or the lack thereof, but also the emotional needs of the children, financial security, effects on living arrangements, and so on. It is not surprising that she, like many others in her position, finds herself in a state of prolonged indecision.

The initial Rubin study examined relationships over the course of only six months. Charles Hill, Zick Rubin, and Anne Peplau conducted a longer longitudinal study —"Breakups before Marriage: The End of 103 Affairs," which has become something of a classic[3]—over a period of two years. In this study, Hill and his colleagues examined factors that predict termination of intimate relationships among college students prior to marriage and found that unequal involvement in a relationship, as well as discrepancies in age, educational aspirations, intelligence, and physical attractiveness, were predictive of breakups. The timing of breakups was closely related to the school calendar: they tended to occur at the natural beginnings and ends of school terms. The decision to terminate a relationship was seldom mutual, and women were more likely than men both to perceive problems in a relationship and to make the decision to terminate it.

This study affirms the importance of similarity and reciprocity in relationships. It also illustrates how dissimilarities that may not be problematical over the short term can become so over the long term. Consider, for example, unequal involvement. Early on, a person may be flattered (and even floored) by the high level of involvement another exhibits toward him or her. And if the person has felt relatively unloved for a long time, the interest of the other may be especially welcome. The person may feel less toward the other but be so grateful for the love received that he or she is content to be the more loved partner.

Stacey was in just this position. At twenty-five, she had been in few relationships, none of which had lasted long, and was starting to panic. She had recently heard of a study that supposedly showed that her chances of marrying were already becoming remote, and she really wanted to have children as well as a good relationship. When Charles, whom she had recently met, declared his love for her, she was almost ecstatic, despite the fact that she did not feel much for him. She stayed with him for over a year and then left the relationship. She had hoped to "learn to love" Charles, but never did. Moreover, she had become frustrated being in a relationship that was grossly asymmetrical. She now felt suffocated by Charles's love, probably because she was unable to reciprocate it.

An age difference can also be an unpredictable factor in a loving relationship. The most common difference, of course, is for the man to be older than the woman. When the difference is large, problems may result over the long term. Lydia was delighted with Joe on first meeting: she was twenty-three, and he was forty-nine. Lydia, who had had a troubled relationship with her father, was looking for the father figure she never had. Joe was it. Within a year after meeting, Joe and Lydia were married. By the age of thirty, Lydia no longer needed or wanted a father figure. She had worked through her early troubled relationship with her father, largely with Joe's help. Joe, at fifty-six, was viewing his life as winding down, while Lydia was looking now to start winding her life up. The couple encountered serious difficulties, which eventually they worked through. Joe and Lydia saw a counselor and realized that part of their problem was not in their objective age difference but in Joe's perception of himself at fifty-six as ready to wind down. His psychological rather than biological age was the problem. As Joe began to realize that he need not be an old man at fifty-six, he was able to rally to save a marriage that meant a lot to him.

Differences in education and educational aspirations can also affect the well-being of a marriage. Don married a woman while she was an undergraduate and he a medical student about to get his degree. Sally dropped out of school but told Don she later wanted to go back, finish, and have a career. Don didn't take what she said seriously, because a lot of women seemed to be talking that way at the time—maybe, he thought, to save face. Most of them, he believed, ultimately settled down, had children, and provided the kind of tranquil, stable family life he wanted while he pursued his career as a doctor. Don later discovered that Sally was totally serious in her educational aspirations—so serious that she wanted to finish school before having children. She did—minus Don, who was last heard of looking for another wife to be the docile homebody he wanted.

As for intelligence, almost everyone seems to be looking for an intelligent partner these days; and in academia, I encounter many people who seem to equate intelligence with godliness, or almost. A match in intelligence makes sense in that someone who is very intelligent may become bored with someone who is distinctly lacking in intelligence. But intelligence takes many forms, not all of them measurable by academic honors or other clear signs. One can be seriously misled by equating a potential partner's success or failure in school with his or her intellectual prowess and compatibility.

What Matters When?

Both of the Rubin studies involved relatively short-term longitudinal designs. A study by Richard Cimbalo, Virginia Faling, and Patricia Mousaw involved a cross-sectional analysis of thirty-two couples married fifteen years or less.[4] The investigators found that over time the importance of sex increased whereas the importance of security decreased. Love scores also decreased over time.

Five Basic Questions

In this section, I address five basic questions about changes in intimate relationships over time:

1. What attributes of a relationship do males and females view as *important* for the success of an intimate relationship at different points in it?
2. What attributes of a relationship *characterize* the relationship at different points?
3. To what extent do ratings of *importance* of various attributes *predict success* of a relationship at different points in it?
4. To what extent do ratings of *characteristicness* of various attributes *predict success* of a relationship at different points in it?
5. What differences are there between the sexes in what is important to and what is characteristic of relationships?

To address these questions, Sandra Wright and I did a preliminary and then a major study: the first to gather clusters of feelings about and activities in intimate relationships; and the second, with a new set of subjects, to examine these questions in terms of the clusters.

CLUSTERING ATTRIBUTES

In the preliminary study, 32 subjects, half men and half women, were recruited via advertisements in a local newspaper; none were Yale students. The subjects were asked to rate the relatedness of each possible pair of 32 statements on a scale of 1 to 9, where 1 indicated that the statements were "not at all related" and 9 indicated that they were "very closely related"; between these were intermediate degrees of relatedness. The complete set of statements, which also formed the basis for the main study, is shown in table 6.1. The 496 pairs of statements (all possible combinations of the 32 statements taken two at a time) were presented in four different orders to control for biases that might result if everyone answered the questions in the same order.

We analyzed the data through *cluster analysis*, which identifies groupings of attributes: that is, the attributes people see as being connected. We identified ten major clusters, which were in descending order of importance: communication/support, understanding/appreciation, tolerance/acceptance, flexibility/modifiability, values/ abilities, family/religion, finances/chores, physical attraction/romance, liking/friendship, and fidelity (see table 6.2). For the most part, these clusters are cohesive and sensible, and indicate a fairly wide range of bases for what works and what does not in a close relationship, ranging from feelings about one another to actions to situational variables that affect how well the relationship is going. These clusters formed a useful basis for some of the data analyses in the main experiment.

The ordering as well as the contents of the clusters

198

What Matters When?

TABLE 6.1

The Sternberg-Wright Close Relationships Questionnaire

---

1. Your ability to communicate well with your partner
2. Your own physical attractiveness
3. Your understanding of your partner's wants and needs
4. Your having good times with your partner
5. Your finding time to spend with your partner
6. Your sharing interests with your partner
7. Your sharing values with your partner
8. Your ability to make love
9. Your ability to meet your partner's financial expectations
10. How interesting you are to your partner
11. Your handling of your children (if you have them)
12. Your handling of your parents
13. Your handling of your partner's parents
14. Your ability to listen attentively to your partner
15. Your ability to empathize with your partner
16. The freedom you are willing to give your partner
17. Your exclusive fidelity to your partner
18. Your willingness to change in response to your partner
19. Your willingness to do household tasks
20. Your appreciation of your partner
21. Your willingness to tolerate your partner's flaws
22. Your ability to get along with your partner's friends and associates
23. Your respect for your partner
24. Your match to your partner's intellectual level
25. Your match to your partner's religious beliefs
26. Your knowledge of what your partner is like
27. Your expressions of affection toward your partner
28. Your pride in your partner's accomplishments
29. Your supportiveness of your partner
30. Your acceptance of your partner for the person he or she is
31. Your romantic love for your partner
32. Your liking of your partner

Note: On the full questionnaire, the number of statements is doubled; in other words, each statement appears in two forms, the first with respect to your relation to your partner (as shown), the second with respect to your partner's perceived relation to you. For example, the second form of statement 1 would be, ''Your partner's ability to communicate with you,'' and the second form of statement 2 would be, ''Your partner's physical attractiveness.''

indicate how important people feel each of these clusters is to a loving relationship. In placing the highest value on communication and support, people show they want

TABLE 6.2

Clusters Formed from the Sternberg-Wright Close Relationships Scale

	Cluster Name	Scale Items
1	Communication/Support	1 ability to communicate 14 ability to listen attentively 15 ability to empathize 29 supportiveness
2	Understanding/Appreciation	3 understanding wants and needs 20 appreciation 23 respect 26 knowledge
3	Tolerance/Acceptance	21 tolerance of flaws 30 acceptance of partner as a person
4	Flexibility/Modifiability	16 willingness to give freedom 18 willingness to change
5	Values/Abilities	7 sharing values 22 getting along with partner's friends 24 match to partner's intellectual level 28 pride in partner's accomplishments
6	Family/Religion	11 handling of children 12 handling of your parents 13 handling of partner's parents 25 match in religious beliefs
7	Finances/Chores	9 meeting financial expectations 19 willingness to do household tasks
8	Physical Attraction/ Romance	2 physical attractiveness 8 ability to make love 27 expressing affection 31 romantic love
9	Liking/Friendship	4 having good times together 5 finding time to be together 6 sharing interests 10 interestingness to other 32 liking of other
10	Fidelity	17 exclusive fidelity to other

Note: Clusters are listed in order of strength.

someone who can not only communicate effectively how he or she feels, but also listen attentively. Listening is perhaps the most underemphasized of intellectual skills. We are taught to read, and our reading comprehension is endlessly assessed. We are also taught to write and to speak effectively. But for the most part, we are never given direct instruction in listening. Some people do not know how to listen. Others do not want to, being so preoccupied with their own thoughts and problems that they tune another person out in next to no time. If you want to make a major improvement in your relationship in a minimum of time, try listening carefully to what your partner says, and—equally important—show your empathy by putting yourself in his or her place. Again, the Golden Rule! If you want your partner to understand your position, try to understand his or hers. And then support your partner. This does not mean endorsing every stand he or she may take, but showing that person that you care for him or her whatever that stand may be.

The second cluster is understanding and appreciation of the other. Everyone wants to be understood and appreciated, and more people feel underappreciated than overappreciated. Early on in a relationship, one is well able to find a person's strong points but often seems to miss his or her weak points. On the other hand, after knowing someone for a while, one seems to become expert at finding weak points at the expense of strong points. Relationships would be happier if people were more balanced in their approach and tried to be honest with themselves about both their strengths and weaknesses and those of a partner.

The elements in the third cluster—tolerance and acceptance—are, in the long run, indispensable for a relationship to work. The flaws you can overlook or even findapappealing in the short run may wear thin in the long run. Tony and Luanne, for example, seem always to be in debt. Although he blames her, and she, him, both are responsible. Tony has a weakness for stereo equipment and indulges frequently, while Luanne has a weakness for expensive jewelry. Although she gets very excited about each new piece, she is soon ready to move on to the next. Their nearly ruinous financial situation would spell the end of many relationships. They stay together, however, perhaps because each accepts the other's weakness in exchange for acceptance of his or her own.

If your partner cannot accept or at least tolerate you the way you are, you still have at least one option open within the realm of what works. You can change to become more like what your partner wants by exercising the flexibility and modifiability of the fourth cluster. This can be a hazardous venture. If you effect a change in yourself, you have to be sure that it is compatible with your basic personality and character. Otherwise, you may come to resent the change and thereby undermine your relationship. Ultimately, it is unlikely such a change will last: people seldom sustain changes that leave them feeling untrue to themselves.

Some partners may be so sure that what they want for the other is the "right thing" that they strongly encourage the other to seek professional help. To take an extreme case, Kurt was thinking of leaving Trudy, and she thought he was crazy. She begged him to see a therapist, which he did, and he thus gained the strength to leave her.

Being in a relationship is a fine balance between giving up and gaining freedom. When you enter into a committed relationship, you normally give up some freedoms in exchange for gaining others. But if you are to keep things working, the limits you try to set on your partner should be reasonable. If they are not, you may be sowing the seeds of the relationship's destruction. Margo, for example, was extremely demanding of Hal's time. Not only did she want as much of it as possible, but she wanted him to account for almost every minute of it. When Hal would do things she didn't like, she would remonstrate forcefully. Eventually, Hal started lying to keep the peace, and then decided to leave altogether. He got sick both of accounting for every minute of his time, and of lying.

The fifth cluster generally deals with matches in both values and abilities, which I have already discussed. The item in this cluster worthy of special mention, though, is pride in a partner's accomplishments. One is likely to compliment one's partner fairly frequently on his or her accomplishments early in a relationship, but less so as the years pass. People like to be complimented on the things they take pride in, and last year's compliments, or last month's, or last week's, need to be reinforced today.

The sixth cluster pertains to family and religious matters—how you handle children, parents, and religion, which is often integral to family life. The seventh cluster pertains to finance and chores; and the eighth, to physical attraction and romance. The ninth cluster is liking and friendship; and the tenth, the weakest, consists of a single item dealing with exclusive fidelity to the other. Although this cluster came out last, its weakness may be simply a function of the fact that only one item measured exclusive fidelity, and this attribute does not tend to relate strongly to other ones.

There is no magic prescription for exclusive sexual fidelity. While I know many couples with so-called open relationships, a majority expect exclusive fidelity. Different things may work for different people, but my impression is that "open" relationships work a lot less well in practice than in principle, or at least according to some people's principles. I know few people who can adjust over the long term to a partner's having sexual relations with others. In more cases then not, sexual jealousy eats the relationship alive, and it does not seem to help that the members of the couple are "allowed" to see others.

HOW IMPORTANT AND CHARACTERISTIC ARE THE CLUSTERS?

In our main study, we sought to address directly the five questions posed earlier in this chapter. The participants in the main study were forty men and forty women from the New Haven area ranging in age from seventeen to sixty-nine, with an average of thirty-one years. They were divided into three groups, depending on the duration of their current intimate relationship: short-term (twenty-six participants, with relationships ranging from .1 year to 2 years), medium-term (thirty participants, with relationships ranging from 2 to 5 years), and long-term (twenty-four participants, with relationships ranging from 5 to 36 years). Average durations in the three groups were .8 year, 3.2 years, and 12.5 years, respectively. Although we divided the participants into three groups in order approximately to equalize the number of participants in each group, our long-term group varied substantially in duration of relationship and may have shown substantial differences. Ultimately, another study with more participants will be needed to determine these differences.

Materials included:

1. A demographic questionnaire, asking about family background, age, number of past relationships, and related items.

2. A scale querying about changes in the relationship since it began.
3. A relationship satisfaction questionnaire, asking questions regarding satisfaction, happiness, intimacy, closeness, rewardingness, and importance of the relationship.
4. The Sternberg-Wright Close Relationships Scale, to be filled out with respect to how important each statement was in contributing to satisfaction in the relationship.
5. The Sternberg-Wright scale, to be filled out with respect to how characteristic each of the items of the scale was with respect to the relationship.
6. The Rubin Loving Scale.
7. The Rubin Liking Scale.
8. An abbreviated form of the Close Relationships Scale of Levinger, Rands, and Talaber.[5]

All of the various scales inquiring about a subject's close relationship were phrased in a way that allowed ratings on a scale of 1 (low) to 9 (high), with the exact scale labels varying as appropriate to each scale. Subjects were asked to fill out the last six scales (3–8) with respect, first, to the current state of the relationship and, second, to the state of the relationship when the subject first fell in love with the partner.

Sandra Wright and I constructed our Close Relationships Scale on the basis of past theory and research as well as our own experiences and those of people we knew. We wanted to sample broadly within the realm of relationships so as to include a wide variety of thoughts and feelings that seemed important to us and others for the maintenance of relationships. We claim only to have sampled the realm of relationships, however; we have not included everything that might possibly be relevant in such a scale.

Ratings differed in time rated (present versus past), type of rating (importance versus characteristicness), person rated (self versus partner), and item cluster (ten clusters in all).

Clusters with particularly high ratings—that is, those attributes people see as most important to close relationships—were communication/support (1), understanding/appreciation (2), tolerance/acceptance (3), liking/friendship (9), and fidelity (10). Clusters with particularly low ratings were family/religion (6) and finances/chores (7).

The clusters that were rated high were not necessarily those that came out strongest in the earlier cluster analysis, because "strength" has a different meaning in each study. In the preliminary study, a cluster was strong if lots of people recognized the items within it as fitting together. Here, a cluster came out as strong if lots of people recognized it as *important* to relationships.

These cluster values make intuitive as well as theoretical sense in terms of the triangular theory of love.[6] According to this theory, the four clusters with the highest values (communication/support, understanding/appreciation, tolerance/acceptance, liking/friendship) all belong to the intimacy component of love and are the only clusters in the full cluster analysis pertaining to intimacy. The last cluster, also with a high value, is the one and only cluster pertaining to an action reflecting commitment (fidelity). Clusters with the lowest values (family/religion, finances/chores) reflect pragmatic considerations in a close relationship that are not viewed, in the context of the triangular theory, as directly related to love. After the top clusters, which pertain to intimacy and commitment, comes the one cluster pertaining to the passion component—physical attraction/romance—and then comes flexibility/modifiability, which does not directly pertain to any component. In short, the clusters with the higher perceived importance ratings for close loving relationships are pertinent to the triangular theory of love, whereas the clusters with the lower perceived importance ratings are not pertinent.

This pattern of results suggests that the components of love, as specified by the triangular theory, are just those aspects of relationships that people see as particularly important to the survival of a relationship—a nice validation of the triangular theory, especially since the Sternberg-Wright scale was not constructed explicitly to test it. But the results also show that important as love is, it is not all that matters to a relationship. Many of the day-to-day things that matter, such as agreement on how to handle children or finances, have little or nothing to do with love.

In some of the clusters, importance ratings tend to be higher than characteristicness ratings; whereas in other clusters, the reverse tends to be true. Clusters in which the importance ratings are uniformly higher (that is, for all durations of relationship, and for both self and other) are communication/support (1), understanding/appreciation (2), tolerance/acceptance (3), and liking/friendship (9). These are, again, exactly those clusters pertaining to the intimacy component of love, indicating that the subjects perceived intimacy as more important to, rather than characteristic of, their close loving relationship. Clusters in which the characteristicness ratings are uniformly higher than the importance ratings are values/ abilities (5), family/religion (6), and finances/chores (7); all but one of these are irrelevant to the triangular theory of love and, from an intuitive standpoint as well, seem to be those clusters least directly relevant to love per se. In other words, people perceive as more characteristic than important in a relationship those aspects of it that are not particularly relevant to love, at least according to the precepts of the triangular theory.

We found that the ratings for oneself (how one feels about the other) were uniformly higher than the ratings for the other (how the other feels about oneself) for the clusters of understanding/appreciation (2), tolerance/acceptance (3), and flexibility/modifiability (4). Ratings of the other were never uniformly higher than ratings of the self, although, over all, fidelity was rated higher for the partner than for oneself. Thus, people tended to see themselves as the more involved partner, and also as rating attributes measured by the questionnaire as more highly important than would the other partner, for some but not for all attributes. In particular, they saw themselves as understanding and appreciating the other more, as tolerating and accepting the other more, and as being the more flexible person.

This set of findings suggests a central difficulty in making relationships work. If both partners see themselves as being more understanding, appreciative, tolerant, and accepting, it is going to be hard to achieve feelings of equity in a relationship: each partner feels as if he or she is contributing more than half to what makes the relationship work. You must thus try better to understand each other's point of view, and why each of you tends to feel that you are contributing more than half. If you cannot do this, and each partner feels undervalued, the relationship may start to erode. Role playing helps: next time you discuss a serious matter, reverse roles, and do your best to think like your partner. You may come to understand better why he or she feels like the greater contributor, and your partner may start to understand why you feel that way. If, like most couples, you have never before role played, it may be a good idea to start role playing with a less serious matter and to work your way up.

The difference between ratings of the self versus other differed from one cluster to another by different amounts for the ratings of the present versus the ratings of the beginning of the relationship. In other words, the difference between your perceptions of yourself and of your partner varies over time. For example, the first cluster (communication/support) showed a larger difference in characteristicness between self and other ratings for the present than for the present. The second cluster (understanding/appreciation) also showed larger differences in the present than in the past. Also, the difference between ratings for the present and for the beginning of a relationship was larger for some clusters than for others. For example, finances/chores was rated much higher in the present than in the past, whereas physical attraction/romance was rated higher for the beginning of the relationship than for the present.

The discrepancy between ratings of self-to-other and other-to-self was greater for the ratings of the present than for the ratings of the past. In other words, there is greater perceived asymmetry between the feelings of oneself and one's partner in the present than in the past. These ratings were generally in the direction of present ratings for oneself being higher than those for the partner. People seem to feel more and more over time as if they are losing their partner. Thus, any increasing asymmetry in ratings is in the direction of higher ratings for one's feelings toward the other than for the other's feelings toward oneself. Moreover, the difference between present and past ratings of self versus other was greater in the middle term than in the short or the long term, especially for importance ratings. We also observed a sex difference. Men's ratings for the past showed somewhat greater discrepancies between self-to-other and other-to-self than did women's ratings. In other words, men perceive more of a discrepancy between past, but not present, feelings, between themselves and their partner.

In respect to the effect of time of rating, two clusters with distinctly higher importance ratings for the present in the relationship than for its beginning were family/religion and finances/chores. In other words, these pragmatic issues have taken on greater importance as the couple has had to adjust to the realities of being together and getting on in the everyday world. None of the clusters had distinctly higher ratings for the past than for the present.

These results suggest, then, that one of the reasons relationships may "go bad" is that the things that matter earlier are different from the things that matter later, but we tend to choose partners on the basis of the things that matter earlier rather than later in a relationship. Couples would be wise to discuss early in a relationship pragmatic issues such as having and bringing up a family, religious differences, and handling of finances and chores. These discussions should take place as soon as a couple feel there is a good chance that they may wish to stay together on a long-term or permanent basis. It is probably no coincidence that couples entering into second marriages often have a more pragmatic orientation than do couples entering into first marriages: the couples with the experience of a marriage (or more than one) behind them better realize how important pragmatic issues can become.

The difference between the importance and characteristicness ratings was greater for current ratings than for ratings at the beginning of the relationship for the clusters of communication/support (1) and understanding/appreciation (2), two of the intimacy clusters. In other words, the discrepancy between the importance of each of the two attributes of intimacy and their characteristicness is perceived to be greater now than at the beginning of the rated close relationships. Participants perceive their relationships as currently more deficient in intimacy than when they first fell in love, as would be predicted by the triangular theory: that is, as couples start to operate more smoothly, with less disruption, their perception of intimacy will decrease.

Women tended to give lower characteristicness ratings, but not lower importance ratings, than did men. In other words, women tended to view their relationships as being in poorer shape than did men, as shown by their assigning lower characteristicness ratings to positive attributes of relationships than did men. But these lower characteristicness ratings did not merely reflect a bias in the use of the scale: the women did not perceive the attributes listed in the questionnaire as any less important than did the men. This result is consistent with the general finding in the literature that women are, at least on the average, more attuned to what is going on in a relationship than are men.

THE IMPORTANCE OF VARIOUS ATTRIBUTES OVER TIME

Comparisons were made for individual items regarding changes over the course of a relationship. Four attributes of relationships were found to increase in importance over the three durations: sharing values, willingness to change in response to each other, willingness to tolerate each other's flaws, and match in religious beliefs. The second and third items are of particular interest, I believe, because they show the importance of flexibility in a relationship. To make things work, either you need to change in a way that better suits your partner, or your partner has to come to accept an aspect of your behavior as "the way you are" and as something not likely to change.

Three attributes of relationships decreased in importance over the three segments of time: interestingness to each other, handling of each other's parents, and listening attentively to each other. One can see why handling of parents would become, on the average, less important. Parents often try to have a say in whether a given relationship turns serious. But once it has, in fact, done so, the parental impact decreases. The decreasing importance of interestingness suggests that couples tend over time to find outside interests. But this decrease, coupled with the decrease in the perceived importance of listening attentively, does not bode well. If couples perceive maintaining the other's interest and listening as less important over time, they may stop working on two of the things that could matter most in the long term. In my view, then, people are mistaken in assigning decreasing importance to these elements over time, and pay for their mistake in terms of relationships that do, in fact, become less intimate. If you want to maintain intimacy, then listen attentively and try to remain interesting to each other.

Five attributes were found to increase in importance in relationships from short to medium duration, and afterward to decrease in importance: physical attractiveness, ability to make love, ability to empathize, knowledge of what each other is like, and expression of affection toward each other. Just one attribute was found to decrease in importance and then to increase: match in intellectual level.

Why should aspects connected to passion—physical attractiveness, ability to make love, affection—first increase in importance and then decrease? Early on, when a couple is very much in love, sheer physical technique and how attractive a person is may be overwhelmed in importance by the thrill of just being in love. As the heat of the love begins to decrease, as it usually does, and a relationship starts to cool, the thrill of being in love may no longer be sufficient to compensate for, say, lack of technique in bed. The "honeymoon" period having ended, couples may experience disillusionment as they see each other through glasses whose rosiness is fading. But these passion-related elements decrease in importance over the very long term, probably in part because of changing expectations about what each person, and a relationship, can reasonably offer an older adult.

There were some interesting sex differences. First, males and females agreed that female physical attractiveness is more important than male physical attractiveness. Second, males believed that shared interests are more important than did females. Third, males believed that the ability to make love is more important than did females. Fourth, males and females agreed that male financial ability is more important than female financial ability. Fifth, females believed that handling of parents is more important than did males; however, both males and females agreed that handling of the female's parents is more important than handling of the male's parents. Sixth, females believed that exclusive fidelity is more important than did males; but males believed that exclusive fidelity is more important for women than for men, whereas women believed that it is equally important for both partners. Seventh, males rated more highly the importance of their willingness to do chores than females rated the importance of male willingness to do chores. Eighth, females believed that ability to get along with the other's friends is more important than did males. Finally, males believed that match in religious beliefs is more important than did females.

These patterns of sex differences show that old sexual stereotypes do not die easily. Even in the late 1980s, when these data were collected, the beliefs of men and women are surprisingly sex-stereotypical: women's looks count more than men's, for example, and it is men who should be judged for their ability to generate income. Perhaps the most troubling result, from some points of view, is the double standard of men, but not women, with respect to sexual fidelity. The results clearly showed that men believe that sexual fidelity *is* important—for women.

THE CHARACTERISTICNESS OF VARIOUS ATTRIBUTES OVER TIME

There is a striking variety in the patterns of increase and decrease in various attributes of relationships over time. Only one attribute increased in characteristicness over the three durations: match in religious beliefs. Eight attributes decreased in characteristicness over the three durations: ability to communicate with each other, physical attractiveness, having good times, sharing interests, ability to make love, ability to listen, respect for each other, and romantic love for each other.

It would be easy to find these results depressing. Many

important aspects of a relationship are viewed as on a continual downswing. Not much is seen as on the upswing: <u>people seem to become less and less happy in their relationships as time passes</u>. Actually, the results are even more discouraging than they look, since these data are for relationships in which people have, in fact, stayed together. The data would almost certainly have been worse had we included ratings of relationships in which couples had broken up.

Two attributes were found first to increase in characteristicness and then to decrease: knowledge of what each other is like and liking of each other. Finally, five attributes were found <u>first to decrease and then to increase</u>: giving freedom to each other, exclusive fidelity, tolerance of each other's flaws, ability to get along with each other's friends, and acceptance of each other as each is.

<u>Several results stand out</u>. First, one feels initially that one is getting to know the other person better, and then that one is losing what one has gained. This result shows the importance of change in a relationship. When one meets someone, one often expects him or her to be more or less the same person for an indefinite period of time. As time goes on, one gets to know the person better, expecting the information gleaned to be valid on a permanent basis. But much of it is not, because people do change. And when a person starts to change, one may well feel one is knowing him or her less and less—especially if, as the earlier results showed, one starts to devalue the importance of good listening and of remaining interesting to the other.

In statistics, *statistical regression* describes the effect whereby a person who does particularly well at something one time is likely, on the average, not to do as well the next time around; conversely, someone who does unusually poorly on one round is likely to do better the next time around. Statistical regression explains why the baseball player rated as the most valuable rookie during his first year on a team usually does not equal that record of performance in the second year. It also explains why the least valuable player will usually do better in his second year—if he is still allowed to play.

I believe that something of a statistical-regression effect operates in relationships, and that it provides one explanation of why many aspects of relationships seem to get worse over time. When two people meet and decide to form a relationship, the chances are that each is at a point in life when he or she is particularly well suited to the other. Otherwise, they would not stay together. But since people change, then statistical regression alone would predict that over time the two are likely to become less suited to each other. In effect, there is almost nowhere to go except down.

There is not much that can be done about the effect of statistical regression. It has nothing to do with psychology per se but applies as well to nonhumans, and to inanimate objects as to animate ones. We can, though, try to keep growing together rather than apart, and this means paying attention to each other, listening, and doing what we can to remain an integral part of each other's life.

A second result of interest in these data is that relationships seem to go through at least one hard point, or crisis, and most probably go through more than one. Whether it is called the "seven-year itch" (which may come after fewer or more than seven years) or something else, there appears to be a decline in exclusive fidelity, tolerance, and acceptance of each other after some years, but these things improve later on. This result does not, by any means, guarantee improvement if you and your partner stay together. It is based only on people who have stayed together, and might have been different if we had asked people to rate relationships in which there had been a breakup.

Again, there were interesting sex differences, which overwhelmingly indicated that males perceived the relationship as better than did females. First, males rated communication as better than did females. Males rated their communication skills as higher than the females', whereas females rated their communication skills as higher than the males'. Second, males and females agreed that women are better at finding time to spend with men than the latter are at finding time to spend with women. Third, males rated love making in the relationship as better than did females. Fourth, males rated the financial situation as better than did females. Fifth, males rated handling of parents as better than did females. Sixth, males rated listening as better in the relationship than did females. Seventh, females rated exclusive fidelity as higher in the relationship than did males (indicating that there may be some lack of knowledge on the part of the females). Eighth, males rated tolerance of flaws as higher than did females. Ninth, males rated romantic love as higher than did females. Finally, males rated liking as higher than did females.

Of the many possible reasons men may be more positive about their relationships than are women, any or all may be correct. One possibility is that women are more astute, and that men are denying the problems in their relationships. A second possibility is that the women are more critical and expect more of a relationship. But I believe that both the men and the women are right. The relationship actually works differentially well for the two of them, with better outcomes, on the average, for men than for women. Mortality statistics actually bear out this argument: single men die earlier and are more susceptible to sickness and accidents than are married men; but the reverse is true for women. Thus, even in concrete, health-related terms, men stand more to gain from long-term relationships than do women, even though it seems that they are often the more reluctant sex to enter into them.

PREDICTION OF SUCCESS FROM IMPORTANCE RATINGS

The statistical technique of *multiple regression* was used to predict rated satisfaction with the relationship from each of the importance variables. In multiple regression, one attempts to predict scores on one variable from scores on a group of others. For example, if I wanted to predict a person's income from other variables, I might want to use such variables as the person's age, social class, level of occupation, number of years in the occupation, and so on. In these analyses, we did not ask people what they thought became more or less important over time, but used statistical analysis to determine what actually became more or less important in predicting relationship satisfaction.

Two attributes showed an increasing pattern of correlation with success: finding time to be with each other and willingness to change in response to each other. In other words, higher scores on these attributes became more predictive over time of satisfaction with the relationship. People who were satisfied with their relationships found more time to be with each other and were willing to change for each other. I believe that the "finding time" variable may actually be a proxy for other things. In particular, you are more likely to find time to be with someone if you positively enjoy being with them, and you are less likely to find the time if you find every minute of his or her company aversive. Thus, it may not be the time itself that matters so much as what taking that time represents.

Only one attribute showed a decreasing pattern of correlation with success: exclusive fidelity. In other words, exclusive fidelity mattered more to the success of a relationship earlier during it than later. Again, there were some sex differences, all in favor of better prediction for males. Interestingness of partner, willingness to change in response to partner, willingness to do chores, knowledge of other, and taking pride in each other's accomplishments were all better predictors of satisfaction for males than for females. To put things another way, we were better able to predict men's happiness in their relationships than women's happiness, based on the importance ratings in our Close Relationships Questionnaire.

PREDICTION OF SUCCESS FROM CHARACTERISTICNESS RATINGS

In these analyses, we used the characteristicness ratings rather than the importance ratings to predict success in relationships. Five attributes showed an increasing pattern of correlation with success: understanding each other's wants and needs, sharing values with each other, ability to listen to each other, knowledge of what each other is like, and supportiveness of each other. Two attributes showed a decreasing pattern of correlation with success: exclusive fidelity and pride in each other's accomplishments. Again, there were some sex differences, but all but one were in favor of better prediction for females. Physical attraction was more important for males than for females. But understanding each other's needs, sharing values, ability to listen to each other, appreciation of each other, and match in religious beliefs were all more important for women. Satisfaction in a relationship for males seems to be based more on what they perceive as important in a relationship, whereas satisfaction for females seems to be based more on what the relationship is actually like.

I believe that the most important result to come out of this set of analyses is the difference in what predicts happiness in a relationship for men versus women. Men count more than women what is important to them in a relationship. Women count more than men the way things actually are. In other words, men weight more the abstraction of the way things *should be*, whereas women weight more the concrete situation as it actually *exists*.

In summary, what matters to a relationship seems to change substantially over time, both with respect to what is important to it and with respect to what actually characterizes it. We might better predict long-term satisfaction with relationships if we gave more attention to the variables that will matter in the long run, and perhaps a bit less attention to those that matter in the short run.

CORRELATING THE STERNBERG-WRIGHT SCALE WITH OTHER MEASURES

If the Sternberg-Wright Close Relationships Scale achieves its aim of measuring important aspects of close interpersonal relationships, it should show significant and substantial correlations with other measures of germane aspects of close relationships. The Sternberg-Wright measure does correlate moderately with the Rubin Loving and Liking Scales, the Levinger, Rands, and Talaber Close

What Matters When?

Relationships Scale, and our own satisfaction scale.[7] Most of the clusters showed significant correlations with the Rubin and Levinger scales. Of greatest interest probably were the correlations with satisfaction. Clusters with characteristicness ratings showing particularly high correlations with the satisfaction measure were communication/support, understanding/appreciation, tolerance/acceptance, values/abilities, and liking/friendship. Those clusters best predicting satisfaction included all of the intimacy clusters obtained from the cluster analysis and only one other cluster not directly associated with intimacy (values/abilities), although it is perhaps indirectly associated. In other words, it appears that the best predictors of satisfaction were those aspects of the relationship pertaining to the intimacy component of the triangular theory of love. The passion cluster (physical attraction/romance) showed a lower correlation for current self to other; and exclusive fidelity, often taken as a sign of commitment, showed the lowest correlation. Correlations for importance ratings were lower, on the average, than were correlations for characteristicness ratings.

Characteristicness ratings for the present better predict present satisfaction than they do past satisfaction, whereas importance ratings for the present better predict past satisfaction than they do present. In other words, if you want to know how happy people are in a relationship right now, ask them what does and does not characterize their relationship. If you want to know how happy they were in the past, ask about what they view as important. Perhaps importance of an attribute, and especially agreed-upon importance of an attribute, was important to predicting satisfaction early on in relationships; but over time, importance and agreement about importance stopped being enough. The question became whether a couple could continue over time to implement what was important in their relationship, or whether even the things the couple believed to be important to the sustenance of the relationship fell by the wayside in face of the pragmatic realities of life.

Summary and Conclusions

In general, higher ratings of importance were assigned to elements specified as central to the intimacy and commitment components of my triangular theory of love. Intermediate importance was assigned to elements of its passion component. And the least importance was assigned to elements irrelevant to the theory. Although the study was not designed to test the triangular theory, the results suggest that the triangular theory taps central aspects of close loving relationships; and that, over the long term, maintaining intimacy—communication, sharing, support, and the like—is more important than maintaining passion.

The most simplistic accounts of love, such as the one-factor types of model discussed by Sternberg and Grajek (see pages 5–6), treat love as a simple, unidimensional entity that does not vary across space or time.[8] More complex theories recognize that love has multiple elements, and that these elements may be possessed in different degrees at different times and in different places. Several theories, such as those of Berscheid and of Sternberg—part of which is based upon Berscheid—make fairly specific claims both about what is important in a relationship and about what changes over time.[9] The results of this study were quite consistent with the predictions of these theories.

As I mentioned earlier, clusters assigned the greatest weights for importance to a close relationship were those of the intimacy and commitment components of Sternberg's triangular theory, with a cluster emanating from the passion component following in importance immediately thereafter. The theory also predicts that there will be a decline over time (beyond the earliest stages of an intimate loving relationship) in manifest intimacy and in experienced passion displayed in an intimate relationship. In fact, all of the items showing decreases in characteristicness ratings over time fell into the intimacy and passion components of the triangular theory. Intimacy included the ability to communicate with each other, to have good times together, to share interests, and to respect each other. Passion included physical attractiveness, the ability to make love, and romantic love for each other. Thus, the time patterns shown in this study are in accordance with the predictions of the triangular theory, predictions not tested in another study that was designed as a direct test of the triangular theory.[10]

The results of the present study are also consistent with Levinger's model of relationship development, although this model is somewhat less specific than the others in terms of predicting exactly what behavior will change over the course of a relationship.[11] According to Levinger, the development of relationships can be likened to the progressively greater intersection of two circles. The closer two people become, the more their "circles intersect." A relationship falls apart if or when the circles start to diverge again, and the couple find that they have less and less in common.

Characteristicness ratings provided good statistical prediction of satisfaction in intimate relationships, whereas importance ratings provided weaker, although still often statistically significant, prediction. Importance seems to bear more upon past than present satisfaction, suggesting that over time couples may lose some of their ideals about how relationships should be.

This study showed some of the attributes of an intimate relationship that change over time, as well as those that do not change. At the same time, we recognize the limitations of the cross-sectional design, such as the one we employed. People who have been in relationships longer are, on the average, older, and hence there may be some confounding of length of relationship with cohort: older couples may simply value and experience different things, regardless of how long their relationship has been. Moreover, other variables may be confounded with length of relationship, such as stability of other life circumstances and ability to commit oneself to a relationship over the long term. As always, cross-sectional data of the kind collected in our study need to be supplemented by longitudinal data, collected over time, in order for reasonably firm conclusions to be drawn. Nevertheless, we believe that our data provide at least hypotheses for a longitudinal study. Of course, longitudinal studies have their own problems, such as the almost inevitable differential dropout rates (people still in relationships over the long term are not going to be a representative sample of those who were in relationships in their earlier phases) and possible cohort effects (that is, when people were born) within the sample studied. Thus, neither cross-sectional nor longitudinal designs are perfect in themselves but, ideally, are used in combination.

Beginnings, Middles, and Endings: The Course of a Relationship

Having presented some of the data we have collected on what changes in relationships over time, I shall now turn to theories of how relationships are formed, how they progress, and how they end.

Beginnings: How Relationships Are Formed

Several theories have been developed about how people select particular partners: similarity, complementarity, sequential filtering, stimulus-value-role, and dyadic formation.

SIMILARITY

Until recently, the received view was, as expressed in the writings of Donn Byrne, that people select mates who are similar to themselves (see pages 185–87). Thus, according to the similarity view, we tend to select as mates people who reward us, and probably the single most rewarding aspect of a potential mate is similarity to oneself. It is obvious that people look for others similar to themselves in at least some fundamental ways, but theorists who talk merely about similarity often do not make clear the ways in which we want a partner to be similar or different. One group of theorists particularly concerned with this issue has investigated complementarity.

COMPLEMENTARITY

Some theorists have suggested that we look for people as mates primarily not because they are *similar* to us, but rather because they are *complementary* to us: that is, they excel in or do something we do not excel in or do. Thus, if you don't like doing dishes or cleaning house, you might want a mate who would do these things. If you don't like handling finances, it would make good sense to find someone who does. If you talk a lot, then you might want to find somebody who listens.

The best-known theory of complementarity is that of Robert Winch, which is based on a specific brand of personality theory—namely, Henry Murray's theory of needs.[1] The idea is that each of us has a set of needs. For example, some people are high in the need for nurturance, to be pampered or taken care of, and thus naturally want a partner who is nurturing. A person high in the need for domination would look for someone who is submissive. Thus, according to this theory, you look for someone who is complementary to you in that he or she will fulfill your particular needs.

I believe that Winch's theory is on the right track, although it has been difficult to collect data that confirm it. Most tests of the theory assume some broad set of needs and then check on whether people are complementary with respect to it. But these investigators have tended not to take into account the fact that particular needs do not have the same importance to everybody. The need for domination (or submission) might be really important to one person but of no importance to another. In order adequately to test this theory, we need to know not only what the needs are but also how important each one is to a given person.

SEQUENTIAL FILTERING THEORY

It would seem reasonable to combine the similarity and complementarity points of view—as Alan Kerckhoff and Keith Davis did in their sequential filtering theory. According to this theory, one first looks for people who are similar to oneself in the basics, such as social class, religion, race, upbringing, and so on. If one continues in a relationship, and begins to view the partner as a potential mate, one seeks similarity also in personal values. Finally, complementarity begins to play a role in the course of the relationship over a somewhat longer time. According to Kerckhoff and Davis, one is likely to value and stay in a relationship if a potential mate also fills one's needs.

In their famous 1962 study of 130 dating couples of college age, 94 of whom were retested seven months after an initial session, Kerckhoff and Davis proposed that degree of consensus of values and degree of complementarity of needs would be critical both for the maintenance of a relationship and for its progression toward a permanent union.[2] The idea, based upon the Kerckhoff and Davis model, is that value consensus should appear as an important issue earlier, and need complementarity as an important issue later. Basically, Kerckhoff and Davis's data supported the importance of value consensus in the short term but not in the long, and the importance of need complementarity in the long term but not the short. Thus, according to these researchers, the similarity and complementarity views are not contradictory but rather both apply at different points in the development of a relationship that might lead to marriage.

Although the Kerckhoff-Davis model is attractive, its support is mixed. When, for example, George Levinger, David Senn, and Bruce Jorgensen attempted to repeat and expand the Kerckhoff-Davis findings, neither value consensus nor need complementarity proved to be important to the progress of a relationship.[3] Because the sample of Levinger and his colleagues was more than three times as large as Kerckhoff and Davis's, the former's results inevitably call the latter's model into question. Levinger and his colleagues did find a particularly good predictor of relationship progress from one testing session to a second one: the best measure of progress was the couple's prediction of what their progress would be over time. Thus, what a couple thought would happen to them was a better predictor of what would actually happen to them than were either value consensus or need complementarity.

I believe that this simple result is important. In the attempt to understand love or any other phenomenon, it is easy to overlook the obvious. We can formulate fairly complicated predictive models of what works and what does not, but sometimes the simplest predictors are the best. In this case, if you want to know what is going to happen to people in a relationship, ask them. David Buss of the University of Michigan has done just that, asking people to specify acts that exemplify love (such as agreeing to marry someone).[4] There is a good chance that these prophecies will come true, if only because prophecies are often self-fulfilling. If you believe that a relationship won't work, it probably won't. If you believe it will work, there is no guarantee that it will, but you are at least likely to give it an honest, dedicated try.

STIMULUS-VALUE-ROLE THEORY

Bernard Murstein has proposed the stimulus-value-role theory of mate selection and relationship development, which is a bit more refined than the Kerckhoff-Davis model, while sharing some common elements.[5] According to Murstein, in order for two people to be attracted to one another, they need initially to respond to each other on a basic, simple level—physical appearance, financial position, religious or ethnic background, style of dress, first impression of personality, and the like. Basically, one gets together with people whose assets and liabilities, or strengths and weaknesses, seem to provide a likely match to oneself.

When people do get together, then values start to become more important. A relationship is likely to continue on the road to permanent union if, at a deeper level, one finds that one shares personal, family, and generalized values with the other person. Important here are such values as views about having and raising children, the importance of religion in life, earning and spending money, time spent on work versus time spent on play, and so on. Even if one is initially attracted to someone, the relationship is unlikely to forge ahead unless, in the second stage, the partners can achieve some degree of value consensus. If they cannot, they are likely to view the relationship as superficial, and to seek other, more compatible partners.

In the third and last stage, which continues the filtering process whereby one weeds out people not compatible with oneself, role issues become important. Can one find, in the day-to-day functioning of the relationship, complementary roles such that one feels comfortable interacting with the other person? Here arise such issues as allocation of labor: who takes care of the house, the finances, the social life of the couple, and so on. One can have values similar to those of another person but find that one's role expectations for oneself and the other do not coincide. In other words, there may be some roles that both partners want and other roles that neither wants. Unless they can work out division of labor and allocation of responsibility, the relationship is unlikely to continue or, if it does, to succeed. To support this theory, Murstein has collected a substantial amount of data, which show that relationships fail for different reasons at different times along the lines predicted by the theory.

THEORY OF DYADIC FORMATION

Robert Lewis has proposed a theory of processes that he believes are essential for the formation of a close relationship.[6] He argues that early processes need to be successfully completed before moving on to later ones. The six processes on his list are perceiving similarities, achieving pair rapport, attaining openness in communication through mutual self-disclosure, achieving comfortable roles for each person, achieving roles that are comfortable for the other as well as for oneself, and attaining so-called *dyadic crystallization*, whereby commitment to each other and identity as a couple are established.

In sum, theories of relationship formation have tended to build on each other—from the theories of similarity and complementarity to Kerckhoff and Davis's attempt to combine the two. Murstein's and Lewis's elaborations seem to give a fairly good account of at least some of the important things involved in mate selection.

Relationship Development

Whereas the theories I have considered so far have concentrated on mate selection and the steps that seem to lead toward a permanent union, other theories look at relationship development over the longer term, often viewing relationships from beginning to end. One of the best-known theories of relationship development was proposed by George Levinger and J. D. Snoek, who attempted to think of it in terms of a single dimension of how couples relate.[7]

STAGE THEORY

Stage 0, according to Levinger and Snoek, is a stage of no contact. It is the relationship—or, to be more accurate, the non-relationship—each of us has with all but a handful of the people in the world. Basically, one goes through life unaware of most people; one knows that they exist, but one's life is essentially unaffected by them.

Stage 1 of the Levinger-Snoek theory is awareness. At this stage, one becomes aware of the other as a potential partner in a relationship. For example, a friend may call up and mention that so-and-so is available, and suggest calling. Or one may hear that a certain person's relationship has just broken up, so that this person might be eligible. There is, as yet, no contact.

At stage 2, the potential partners meet. They may have a first conversation over the phone or a first face-to-face encounter, but the contact is superficial and is characterized by their independence as individuals. This stage would correspond to the "stimulus" stage in Murstein's stimulus-value-role theory.

Stage 3 of relationship development, mutuality, is divided into three substages: minor intersection, moderate intersection, and major intersection. The levels of intersection simply refer to the amount of interdependence that the couple achieves.

In later work, elaborating on his notion of mutuality, Levinger has noted that it actually has three aspects.[8] The first aspect is what he calls *involvement*. The second aspect, *commitment*, refers to the strength of the boundaries between the two people. Thus, two people can be quite close to one another, yet be relatively uncommitted. In such uncommitted relationships, the strength of boundaries would be strong, even though the couple seem to be close. In more committed relationships, the boundaries become weaker, and there is more of a fusion between the two lives. The third aspect of mutuality is *symmetry* between the two individuals, which calls attention to the fact that the two people in a relationship may not be equally close to one another: one may have more investment in the relationship than does the other.

The general course of relationship development is for the couple to become progressively closer. Levinger has recognized, of course, that over the life course, relationships do not always continue to become closer and, in his later work, has noted stages of relationship maintenance and decay.[9]

SOCIAL-PENETRATION THEORY

One of the more elaborate theories of relationship development is the social-penetration theory of Irwin Altman and Dalmas Taylor.[10] *Social penetration* refers both to external behavior and to internal feelings that precede, accompany, and follow behavior. Basically, according to Altman and Taylor, our interactions with others have two aspects: breadth and depth. *Breadth* refers to the range of topics we discuss and to the interactions we have. *Depth* refers to the level at which we discuss and interact on each of these topics. Relationships vary in terms of the breadth and depth of social penetration. For example, with someone who is merely an acquaintance, one's interactions will be on a limited number of topics at a superficial depth. In a casual friendship, one may interact on more topics but still not get to their core. In a deeper friendship or the beginning of an intimate relationship, the range of topics continues to expand at the same time that we begin to discuss them deeply. Finally, relationships that become truly intimate increase further in both breadth and depth. In other words, the partners begin to share all of themselves, interacting on all topics, those not only in the present but also in areas of concern from their past and for their future. They discuss these topics in greater detail and with great feeling. The extent of breadth and depth indicates the degree of social penetration.

Not all relationships proceed breadth-first. Occasionally, one may have an intense interaction with another, but only in a limited range of topics. The "stranger on the train" phenomenon, whereby one spills out some aspect of one's life story to a person one has met casually and expects never to see again, is an example of a relationship in which considerable depth may be achieved for only a few topics. Or one may have a friendship with a particular person in which one bares one's soul, but probably in only a specific area of concern that happens to be at the forefront of one's mind at the moment and needs to be vented.

Decay and Dissolution

The evidence generally suggests that marital happiness tends to decline over time. Investigators such as Richard Cimbalo, Virginia Faling, and Patricia Mousaw have found a relatively steady decline in marital satisfaction: marriages seem to drive along a road that eventually goes downhill.[11] P. C. Pineo has suggested that the decline in marital satisfaction is due to two primary factors: fading of the romance that characterizes premarital courtship, and almost inevitable decrease in compatibility.[12] Presumably, when people marry, they often feel that they are "best fits" to each other. If this is indeed true, or close to true, then almost any changes that occur are likely to be for the worse. In an interesting twist on this "best fit" notion, William Graziano and Lynn Musser picked up on the idea of Theodore Reik and others that people often get involved in relationships because of their own self-doubts, particularly doubts about their personal worth.[13] Once in a successful relationship, one's self-image improves because of the reinforcement provided by the partner. But then the relationship may decline because the need that motivated the relationship has been fulfilled.

For example, Carl, who was very insecure, looked long and hard for a woman who could bolster his fragile ego, and finally found such a one in Marybeth. She was exceptional: most women tired of constantly bolstering a man who was so pathetically insecure, but Marybeth seemed to have boundless energy in this regard. She was truly John Lee's "agapic" style of lover (see page 152): she gave, and gave, and gave. Finally, she gave so much that Carl actually began to feel better about himself. But by now, he had come to associate his relationship with Marybeth with his feelings of insecurity, and no longer wanted to deal with those feelings or even acknowledge that they had ever existed. So he went out and found himself a new love. He also found out, when she left him, that his feelings of insecurity had never really ended. He returned to Marybeth, who took him back, and they are today in the only groove that seems to work for them, with Marybeth continually feeding Carl's weak ego.

Not everyone believes that the course of happiness in marriage always leads downhill. Some investigators, such as Boyd Rollins and his colleagues, believe that marital satisfaction is at a high during the early years, goes down during the middle years, and goes up again during the later years.[14] One reason for this U-shaped pattern is probably the effect of raising children. It is well documented that the coming of children into a marriage creates new strains and is associated with a decrease in marital happiness. As the children grow up and eventually move away, there is evidence that marriages again improve.[15]

Children are not the only source of increasing discontent in close relationships. Another is what might be referred to as *role strain*—the conflict over who is supposed to do what in a relationship.[16] While at one time role expectations for men and women were relatively clear, today they are not. With all the pressures on couples to earn income, have children, maintain a nice house, entertain themselves, and have a meaningful relationship, many couples find that the magnitude of the tasks confronting them exceeds their ability to get them done. And their ability to get their tasks done may be further hindered by confusion over what tasks are whose responsibility. Over time, the strain of such role confusion can become a major source of discontent.

People are constantly making attributions—as in respect to role responsibility—about themselves and each other—attributions that are likely to become particularly crucial in times of conflict. Bruce Orvis, Harold Kelley, and Deborah Butler have suggested that attributional processes are especially important in relationships that have entered a period of conflict.[17] *Attributional processes* are the interpretations you give about yourself, others, and situations.

These investigators' first proposition is that attributional processes are active primarily during times of conflict. It is during such times that one is most concerned about motives, both of a partner and of oneself. In contrast, when things are going well, one is less concerned about who did what and why. Several researchers have found that one is more likely to explore the motives of another individual when one feels the need to control his or her behavior[18]—a reasonable attitude, because conflict with another indicates that one has lost control over that person's behavior, and a first step toward regaining at least some control is figuring out why he or she is behaving that way. When one has at least some understanding of the other's actions, one is more likely to feel able to regain control of that person.

For example, Ann's husband, Bill, worked late, but she never questioned it while her relationship with him was going well. But then things started going less well, and she started to ask questions and make attributions about behavior that in the past she had always taken for granted. And she started with Bill's working late at the office. Whereas earlier she hadn't given it a second—or at least a third—thought, now she found herself wondering what he was doing and with whom. She didn't know for a fact that he was doing anything with anyone, but once she got started thinking that way, she found it difficult to shut it off. As it happens, Bill was working late because he was working late, and when the couple resolved their difficulties, the doubts that were, for Ann, symptomatic of their difficulties went away.

Orvis and his colleagues also proposed that each of us believes that we understand the reasons for our own behavior and that these reasons justify that behavior. According to these researchers, our attributional processes change during conflict. They are not objective or impartial but, rather, are largely egocentric and self-serving. We believe that we know why we act the way we do, and that our motives are good.

Third, and perhaps most interesting, Orvis and his colleagues suggest that attributional conflicts regarding motives are often unresolvable. Initially, most conflicts will concern who did what, but eventually such conflicts will turn to the further issue of why. Thus, the two partners, each believing that he or she is motivated by good reasons and intentions, may reach an impasse in which each protests his or her own innocence and points out the other's guilt. Once arguments concentrate on innocence and guilt, the partners become increasingly self-serving rather than trying to resolve the conflict. For example, Jimmy and Lea, like many couples, seem almost never to resolve any of their arguments. They start off arguing over matters of substance but quickly come to matters of guilt and innocence. For example, if they argue over money, an argument over what should be purchased degenerates into an argument over who is a spendthrift. Once the argument has taken this turn, there is no longer any hope of resolution, because matters of guilt and innocence are not ones they are in a position to resolve; and the issues they are in a position to resolve never really get discussed.

Harold Kelley has pointed out that, once conflict arises, the partners to it become especially susceptible to the *fundamental attribution error*—the tendency to see the causes of their own behavior as *situational* (controlled by events in the environment) but the causes of the behavior of others as *dispositional* (controlled by what they are like as people).[19] In other words, when one does things that might seem unpleasant to others or even to oneself, one is likely to cite the situation as the cause of one's actions: one has been pressured into it by others, or there seemed to be no other choice, or the situation dictated a quick decision. In contrast, one tends to view other people as motivated by their own dispositions. Thus, if someone does something you don't like, you tend to interpret it as confirming your suspicions about who he or she really is.

Clearly, these conflicts about motives are destructive, because one tends to see oneself as good and the other as not so good. Indeed, much research now confirms Kelley's view that the results of attributional conflicts tend to be negative and destructive.[20] If one does indeed conclude that one is stuck with somebody who isn't a very good person, one may consider terminating the relationship or finding another one. Research by William Doherty suggests that women are somewhat more susceptible to a negative attributional style than are men: in other words, women are more likely to be critical, of themselves as well as of others. Perhaps this is one reason for the finding described in chapter 6 that women tend to be less happy with their relationships than are men.[21]

F. Fincham and K. O'Leary investigated the attributional processes of happy and unhappy couples.[22] The subjects were asked to imagine that their spouses had behaved in a certain way, to rate the possible causes for the behavior, and to indicate what they would feel and do in response to the behavior. Half of the imagined situations involved favorable actions; and the other half, unfavorable actions by the spouse. The investigators found that couples in happy marriages generally saw favorable actions by the spouse as likely to occur, as resulting from the spouse's wishes as well as their own, and as drawing out favorable reactions from themselves. Unfavorable actions, in contrast, were viewed as relatively rare and involuntary. Thus, the unfavorable actions received a situational rather than a dispositional attribution, even though they pertained to the other partner. Unhappy couples showed opposite results: unfavorable behavior was seen as common, extensive, deliberate, and provoking. Moreover, favorable behavior was generally discounted. Supporting these results, Neil Jacobson and his colleagues have found that happy couples tend to emphasize the role of dispositional causes for favorable behavior, and the role of situational factors for unfavorable behavior. Unhappy couples tend to do the reverse.

What all this means is that it may not be people's actions but how we perceive those actions that affects, and is affected by, the quality of a relationship. The very same actions may be perceived in radically different ways, depending on whether a person is happy or unhappy with the state of his or her relationship. Thus it was with Ann, who did not make a negative attribution about her husband's working late until she became unhappy with the relationship.

Arthur and Grace are another case in point. For a long time they had a reasonably happy, if somewhat dull, relationship. Then Arthur met someone else and entered into an affair with her. But he could neither accept responsibility for the affair nor admit that, to the extent his relationship with Grace was unexciting, it was at least half his fault. Arthur became extremely critical of Grace, lambasting her for behavior that she had shown all along but that he had never before criticized or even felt particularly critical of. He was using the new negative attributions to excuse his infidelity.

In sum, if happy in a relationship, we tend to magnify the importance of the positive and to minimize the importance of the negative, whereas if unhappy in a relationship, we do the opposite. Moreover, if unhappy, we also tend to emphasize situational factors for the positive and dispositional factors for the negative.[23] For example, when you are unhappy with someone, you may attribute that person's being nice to the weather, but see bad behavior as intrinsic to him or her. Or when someone you don't trust is nice to you, you may interpret the niceness as ingratiation—as an attempt to get something.

Jacobson and his colleagues, in studying happy and unhappy couples, found that unhappy couples are more responsive than happy couples to negative events, such as disagreements. Among the happy couples, the number of negative events occurring during a day has only a weak relationship to overall daily satisfaction; whereas for un-happy couples, the number of negative events is highly related to daily satisfaction.[24] But unhappy couples also appeared to be more responsive to positive events, such as news of a bonus or of a child's success in school—a find-ing that suggests that unhappy couples are more reactive over all. In other words, each member responds more strongly to things. This finding suggests that the partners in an unhappy relationship who make a deliberate effort to behave positively toward each other are likely to notice and respond in kind. As the positive actions increase, the unhappy couple may become more happy. This outcome will not occur, however, unless the couple can learn not to attribute positive actions to particular situations. In other words, if one makes excuses for a positive action rather than just enjoying it, it will not have a positive effect. For example, each member of the couple might say that the other member is behaving in a more positive way because of an agreement to improve the relationship rather than because he or she is genuinely a good person. Getting out of this morass is no easy feat.

There is yet another step one can take toward improv-ing one's relationships, based on the research of Margaret Madden and Ronnie Janoff-Bulman.[25] One can assume more responsibility for what happens in a relationship. If you credit yourself for the good things that happen but blame the other person for the bad things, there is no hope for improvement. But if you can make a concerted and good-faith effort to see the other person's point of view, and put yourself in his or her shoes, you may see how you also are responsible for the problems in the relationship. Instead of assigning all or almost all of the blame to the other person, you should take on some of it yourself and try to understand how the other person's actions may, in part, be reactions to your actions. Madden and Janoff-Bulman found that having a sense of control in marital interaction is crucial for happiness: each member of the couple needs to feel some sense of responsibility for what has happened, and some sense of control for what can happen in the future. Indeed, if you feel that your actions are totally determined by the situation, you have little control over yourself, and if you feel that the other person's actions are totally due to the way he or she is, you have no control over him or her. Thus, you need to acknowledge your role as a source of your own behavior and the role of the situational origins of the other's behavior, thereby overcoming the fundamental attribution error.

This is not to say that we should always follow a path looking for improvement. Some relationships genuinely do not and cannot work, or simply were not meant to be. With a partner who is physically or mentally abusive and unable to change, the search for good reasons for his or her behavior may not lead to a more favorable outcome. Perhaps the hardest part of a relationship is knowing when to try to salvage things and when not to. Sometimes people need the help of an objective third party, such as a therapist, in order to sort things out.

A recent experience I had when visiting Japan illustrates the misunderstanding that can occur in close interpersonal relationships. A Japanese graduate student, who seemed well conversant with English, agreed to be my guide for a day-long tour of Tokyo. Several times, she referred to me as an "Aryan," and I found myself becoming angry. In the first place, the Second World War had ended some time ago, and I was disturbed that the nonsense label of *Aryan* persisted in the mind of the Japanese. Second, I was upset because I have few, if any, characteristics that would identify me as an Aryan: I am not blond, or blue-eyed, or of the right background. Finally, at the risk of insulting my hostess, I remarked on her inappropriate use of the label. I explained to her that I was not an Aryan, and that, moreover, there is really no such thing. She looked at me, perplexed, and said that she didn't understand. Before long, we both realized that the word she was saying—or at least meaning to say—was *alien*. The Japanese have great difficulty in hearing or pronouncing the *L* sound in English, often confusing it with the *R*. Later in the conversation, when I mentioned the Berlin Wall, she wondered whether a new war had broken out.

The point is that my guide was making distinctions that were different from mine. Although I thought she heard mine, she was really hearing her own—just as she thought that I was hearing her distinctions, whereas really I was hearing my own. In a relationship, we may each divide up the world differently, but we accept our own parsing and assume that others do as well. In fact, my Japanese guide and I were each hearing both what we said and what the other said from our separate points of view—each of which seemed valid, given the distinctions we had learned.

In interpersonal interactions, people often do the same thing: they do not hear each other. One or the other partner may say the same thing time after time, and be amazed, if not insulted, that he or she does not seem to be understood correctly. The listener is hearing from his or her own vantage point and set of categories. As a result, the conflict never gets settled.

I found this incident helpful in understanding an interpersonal conflict I was having myself at the time. I had been having disagreements with someone close to me;

despite repeated discussions, we seemed unable to resolve them. Moreover, we kept re-enacting the same scripts as we sought to resolve our conflicts. I realized that neither of us was genuinely hearing what the other was saying. Rather, we were hearing it in terms of our own ways of seeing things, ways that did not apply to the other.

In interpersonal interactions, people tend to fall into *scripts*: that is, scenarios that have a fairly predictable beginning, middle, and end. Not only do we have scripts of our own making, but we classify the remarks of others according to the set of scripts we happen to have. If the other individual has different scripts, we are likely to misinterpret what he or she is saying.

Often, in interactions, people repeat the same scripts over and over, just as though they were acting the same part again and again in a drama. One may think that one's script meshes with another's, when in fact it does not. It is as if a couple were dancing and failed to notice that each partner was doing a different step because each was moving to different music. In trying to resolve interpersonal conflicts, it is essential not only to hear what the other is saying but to understand it in the context of the other person's life. Whether you accept another's way of seeing things, in order to communicate fruitfully with a person you need at least to try to understand that way.

Sometimes one is simply unable to understand either the other individual's behavior or the scripts that generate it. For one reason or another, the other person's scripts are just too different from one's own. When such lack of understanding occurs, the optimal solution is probably not to fall back on one's own script. Sometimes, one has to make the leap of faith, trusting that the other person has good intentions. Obviously, one cannot have faith in everyone. But actions and motives that are not understood at one point in life can often be understood later. If you really want reconciliation and to keep the relationship, it is wise to give yourself a fair stretch of time to understand the other person, and avoid letting conflict escalate into successively higher levels.

People create scripts in order to make sense of what is going on not only during a relationship but after one ends. Often neither party to a relationship quite understands what went wrong. It is as though the relationship, in its final days, took on a life of its own—perhaps a life that seemed almost incomprehensible to either partner. Breakups are usually distressing, and in order to deal satisfactorily with that distress, one may create hypothetical scripts about what went wrong. One may attribute the breakup to the other person's disloyalty, inconsideration, or greed; or, in part, to one's own lack of effort in trying to make things work. But more often than not, the script points to the other person as bearing a major share of the responsibility for the breakup. People may need such self-serving scripts to get over a relationship and move on.

There is a well-known effect in psychology called the *Zeigarnik effect,* by which people tend to recall incomplete events better than completed ones. If one wants to get over a relationship and put it out of mind, one needs to give it some completion, and a script accounting for what went wrong may fulfill this need. Often the creation of such scripts is a difficult task, because they almost never do full justice to what happened; and at some level, one knows that the script one has created is an oversimplification. The script may nevertheless help one to move on.

Scripts of this kind almost always are inaccurate to some degree, and their benefit may ultimately be offset by their inaccuracies. For one thing, they prevent you from relating in a meaningful way to the partner in the former relationship. You may continue to have to work with the partner, either in your job or in bringing up the children. Better understanding of the partner and of his or her relation to yourself helps you to work with your former partner.

Second, breaking up can help you better to understand yourself and the way you relate to others. The more inaccurate your script, the less understanding of yourself and others you achieve; indeed, you may learn little from the breakup and proceed to repeat the same mistakes in future relationships. If you hope to learn from your past and to apply what you have learned to new relationships, then you need at least a fairly accurate understanding of what went wrong and of how to avoid it in future relationships.

Finally, to the extent that your script is inaccurate and you know it, you may continue to get a Zeigarnik effect from your knowledge that the story is not really completed. You would do better to try to improve the accuracy of the script so as to conclude the story of the past relationship. If you cannot do so, the relationship may live on in your head, always looking for a resolution that you know you have not yet found.

GETTING OVER A RELATIONSHIP

People are often surprised by how difficult—or how easy—it is to get over a relationship.[26] Whether it is easy or hard to get over the other person can depend on a variety of factors, one of which is the difference between your emotional involvement with the other person and the amount of benefit you actually got from the relationship. Berscheid has pointed out that people who are highly emotionally involved in a relationship, but actually receive little from it in terms of objective gains and benefits, may find it easier to get over the relationship than they expect. Similarly, people who are not deeply involved emotionally, but benefit a great deal from the relationship, may find it harder than they expect to get over it.[27] Thus, the actual difficulty of getting over a relationship does not necessarily bear out anticipated difficulty.

In helping yourself get over a relationship with another, probably the most important thing is to build your self-esteem and sense of independence. Often when a relationship ends, you cannot imagine living without the other person. Life seems as if it cannot go on. But it will. Or you may feel that you could live without the other person if you could only find another to take his or her place. People often spend long periods of time looking for another person to help them get out of a particular relationship. In effect, they want to leave one person for another in order to ease the transition. In fact, having another person for whom you leave may make things easier in the short run, but is not likely to do so in the long run. For one thing, the new relationship is more likely than not ultimately to fail: since it has been built on a particular set of circumstances, when the situation changes, so will the relationship. Moreover, residual feelings of guilt in one or the other person may render it difficult to continue the relationship. Finally, there is always the possibility that the person who has left the first individual for the other may leave the other for someone else, or vice versa.

For example, Paul and Margie started an office affair that grew into a full-blown romance. Paul was married; Margie was not and never had been. After much soul searching, Paul left his marriage for her. But as soon as he left, a relationship that had been almost conflict free became incredibly conflict ridden. It turned out that, unbeknownst to her, part of Margie's attraction to and comfort with Paul emanated from his being married. So long as he was married, Margie felt "safe." But once Paul left his marriage, he started making demands that she found herself unable to meet. She had thought she was ready for a commitment, just so long as a commitment was impossible. But when it became possible, Margie felt pressured, and ultimately terminated the relationship.

In the long run, it is probably best to leave not for another but for yourself. The decision is not that you would rather be with another than with the first person, but that you would rather be alone than with the first person. The decisions to leave one person and to join another should, if at all possible, be independent, both to take the pressure off the new relationship and to ensure that leaving the first partner was the right decision. Later you can find comfort in knowing that you left because it was right for you rather than because you thought the grass was greener elsewhere, especially if you find that the grass is not actually greener. In ending a close relationship, people generally need to rebuild their sense of self-esteem and independence, and although friends can be helpful, ultimately it is one's own responsibility. You can be truly successful in your relationship with another only if you have a good relationship with yourself, and often when a relationship with a significant other ends, your relationship with yourself is in need of building and possibly repair. It therefore pays to develop a liking of yourself and to take charge of your own life; once you have rebuilt and created a new and independent life, then look for another from a position of strength. If this all sounds obvious, so it is, but it is nevertheless true, and more difficult to do than to talk about.

This strategy pays off in many ways—not only for the individual, but in helping one attract a better potential partner. People tend not to be attracted to others who are perceived as overly needy or lacking in self-esteem. People want to be wanted for themselves, not to help someone get over another relationship, in which case they may be cast aside later.

FORMING A NEW RELATIONSHIP

A mistake that people often make in seeking a new relationship is to look too fast and then try to move the new relationship too quickly. Rapid expression of love and affection often turns other people off, because they feel that they cannot possibly be loved for who they are, but rather only for the image the other has created in his or her mind. Allow yourself the time genuinely to get to know the other so that you, as well as the other, will know that if you express great love or affection, it is because of who the other is rather than because of an image you have built up in your mind.

And while you are looking for this new relationship, do your best to see the other as he or she is rather than as you wish him or her to be. In this period, you may be somewhat desperate and wish to project certain characteristics onto a person that he or she may not have. If you allow yourself enough time, you are less likely to fall into the trap of involving yourself in a rerun of your past relationship, whereby the new person differs from your past partner only in surface characteristics. You are also less likely to look for another person whose main attraction is in being the complete opposite of your former partner. Rather, look for independence in your new selection, choosing someone who is right for you, given your needs and wants. Give yourself time to find out who you really are and only then look to become serious with another. Remember also that if you are unhappy with yourself, you cannot expect another to be happy with you.

Disengagement of Intimate Relationships

Many relationships ultimately cease to work, and it is helpful to know not only *why* they have ceased—for example, loss of intimacy, passion, or commitment—but also *how*. A recent book by Diane Vaughan, a sociologist, addresses the question of what happens when relationships stop working.[28]

IT STARTS WITH A SECRET: THE THEORY OF DIANE VAUGHAN

According to Vaughan, disengagement, or what she calls *uncoupling*, begins with a secret. One of the partners in the relationship begins to feel uncomfortable in it. This discomfort may begin early, even before the wedding, or after many years. But the critical thing is that the disengagement begins unilaterally and quietly: the dissatisfied partner generally says nothing. He or she may not even consciously realize that something is wrong, or just what is wrong; or be certain of the implications of the feelings: will they lead to a separation or are they just temporary and of passing importance? Since the dissatisfied partner
not want to say anything before being absolutely

sure of what is wrong, he or she creates a private world in which to mull over those feelings.

In creating this private world, the dissatisfied partner, generally unintentionally, initiates a breach of communication. The partner, while not necessarily viewing himself or herself as lying, nevertheless withholds information that would be important to the other partner. Secrecy permits one to think about things, to develop plans, and generally to figure out what to do. But the other partner, being uninformed of the dissatisfaction, is powerless to do anything about the situation. Eventually the dissatisfied partner—the initiator—begins to try to convey his or her dissatisfaction to the partner—but finds it difficult, because he or she may still not have quite figured out the problem. Unable to communicate fully and accurately the source of the dissatisfaction, the initiator will generally not directly confront the partner in a way that allows the latter to address the basic issues, but rather displays dissatisfaction in subtle ways, many of which may not even be understood by the partner as indicating global dissatisfaction.

Vaughan points out that the initiator's first attempts to communicate unhappiness are, in part, an attempt to save the relationship. By indicating dissatisfaction, the initiator is trying to change the partner or the relationship so as to create a situation acceptable to the partner. The efforts of the initiator seldom result in quick success. This lack of success is hardly surprising, since the partner does not yet realize the nature and extent of the dissatisfaction. Indeed, some of the initiator's remarks may camouflage rather than reveal the sources of dissatisfaction. So the initiator remains unhappy, and the partner is likely not to be in a position to do anything about it.

The initiator, unhappy with the relationship, turns to

alternative sources of satisfaction—outside activities, new friends, or an affair. As the initiator begins to form a new life, the partner may wonder what is going on and why. The partner may attribute the changes to second childhood or a further sowing of oats, while the relationship itself is the true source of dissatisfaction. Eventually the initiator will create a separate social life which may take increasing amounts of time and energy. The partner may be shut out of this new life and not even know the full extent of what is happening in it.

Often the initiator will enter into a new meaningful relationship, sexual or not, as a means for venting dissatisfaction and frustration and for finding an alternative. The new relationship, which may even be partially based on fantasy, may satisfy the need of the initiator to form new ties. This situation further increases the need for secrecy, so that the gulf between the initiator and the partner is likely to expand.

Vaughan points out that what happens in disengagement is in many respects the exact opposite of what happens when one is drawn to someone else initially. In falling in love with someone, one tends to concentrate on his or her favorable traits. One notices how one is similar to and compatible with this new partner, and attempts to view any differences as complementary. As a relationship grows, there occurs the "fallen angel" phenomenon: no other can live up to the degree of perfection one may have hoped for. But if the relationship starts to disengage, the focus of the initiator shifts to the unfavorable qualities of the partner, who is then redefined in terms of his or her objectionable traits. The initiator concentrates on the points of difference with the partner, seeing them now as disturbing and unattractive. The initiator is likely to recast the history of the relationship, seeing negative aspects in what before had been positively construed events. The relationship is suddenly seen in a new and unfavorable light. The initiator becomes prey to the fact that there is no objective historical account of the past, and shapes the past to fit the needs of the present.

The initiator's increasing dissatisfaction becomes more apparent both to others and to the initiator. Whereas earlier the initiator may have expressed discontent with the hope of saving the relationship, now his or her intent is to convince the partner that the relationship is troubled or perhaps even cannot be salvaged. The initiator expresses dissatisfaction not only to the partner but to others as well. The initiator informs close friends and colleagues that all is not as it should be in his or her personal relationship with the partner. There may be jokes about the partner, angry exclamations, or subtle digs. But the message is conveyed in one way or another. The initiator is likely to avoid those with a vested interest in continuing the relationship, because they make the initiator uncomfortable. Instead, the initiator is likely to select as friends at this time only those who will provide support for his or her intended moves.

By this time, it is extremely common that the initiator has found what Vaughan refers to as a *transitional person:* that is, someone who helps the initiator through the transition that is beginning to play a greater part in the initiator's life. The transitional person, who may be a lover or a friend, is someone who helps the initiator ease himself or herself out of the old relationship. Sometimes there may be more than one transitional person, each such person taking on a different role. For example, a psychotherapist and a lover would play different roles, each helping the initiator to leave an old life and find a new one.

As the initiator more and more expresses increasing discontent, the social perception of the couple may change. They are likely to be viewed as in distress. Sometimes the partner may be the last to know just how amiss things have become. Initiators are likely to look for information about the transition they are experiencing, either through books, magazines, plays, movies, or whatever. Noticing how others have dealt with similar transitions, they try to apply this information to their own lives. The initiator pushes toward a new life and is gradually pulled away from the old one. The initiator may become increasingly detached from the old relationship and spend ever less time engaging in it. As initiator and partner grow further apart, the role of separate friends is likely to become greater. Whereas, before, the emphasis in the relationship may have been upon mutual friends and acquaintances, now each individual looks for his or her own support group.

Symbolic behavior may become especially important at this time, such as the initiator's removal of the wedding ring (to which he or she has suddenly become "allergic") or the undermining of actions that had been done together but are now suddenly done apart, such as going on trips. By now, the initiator is well out of the relationship, whereas the partner may still be firmly entrenched within it. For the partner, the relationship is still central to his or her life and identity, and he or she may now seriously wonder about what is going on.

It often seems incredible that two people can live together and one go so far afield without the other's noticing. Partners often describe themselves as unaware or only vaguely aware of things having gone wrong. At the same time, the initiator is likely to report that he or she has made repeated efforts to apprise the partner of the seriousness of the situation. Clearly, a major breakdown in communication has taken place, because the two partners see the situation as so very different.

What has happened, according to Vaughan, is that they have colluded in a cover-up. The initiator is indirect and subtle in order to protect one or both partners. The partner takes what is said more or less at face value, not looking to find any deeper meaning. If the initiator makes one complaint after another, these complaints are taken as stated rather than as symptomatic of a deeper problem in the relationship. While recognizing that something is wrong, the partner may view it as a normal part of ongoing relationships. The partner may keep things private, as the commonplace view in our society is that marital problems should be a private matter. At the same time, the initiator, viewing the relationship as deeply troubled, is likely communicating his or her dissatisfaction publicly. The partner may believe that any problem is not in the relationship but in the initiator, and suggest that the initiator seek professional or other help. Ironically, in so doing, the initiator finds a new ally in the march toward disengagement. Since it is the nature of therapy that the patient stress his or her point of view, the chances are good that the situation will be defined in terms satisfactory to the initiator rather than to the partner.

Eventually, the collusion breaks down, and the cover-up fails. Now confrontations are likely to become direct. The initiator who is far enough along, and certain that he or she wants out, is likely to become bolder, having less to risk by direct expression of his or her feelings. For the initiator, the question now may be not whether to leave, but how. At this point, the initiator may start making concrete preparations for a new life, such as a secret bank account or the hiding of assets from the partner. The initiator may talk to a lawyer and start devising a plan for how to get out. He or she may even have a date in mind at which time the decision to split is to be communicated to the partner. As the date begins to loom, the initiator continues preparing for a new life. Often the date does not quite materialize when it is supposed to. Something else may come up—such as a crisis in the extended family or problems on the job or of health—and temporarily delay the planned date of separation.

By now, the partner is likely to view the relationship as troubled, whereas the initiator is likely to view it as over. The confrontation emerges, but the initiator is unwilling to take responsibility for it. Rather, he or she tries to find some way of shifting at least some of the burden of the conflict to the partner. Sometimes the initiator tries to goad the partner further into making a "fatal mistake," which is likely to be a manifestation of some behavior that the initiator can describe as totally unacceptable. This mistake may also be a failure to initiate a behavior that the initiator would view as necessary. For example, if the partner reacts with a highly emotional outburst, the initiator may say that this proves what he or she has feared all along—that the partner is wholly irrational. The initiator is likely to decrease interaction with the partner and may even start violating formerly tacit rules of the relationship. The partner, eventually realizing that something is seriously wrong, may take on the role of a detective, trying to figure out just what is going on. He or she may look for evidence in the initiator's actions, personal possessions, or through communications from others.

Once an overt confrontation has been reached, both partners are ready and willing to acknowledge that the relationship is deeply troubled, and are likely to enter into negotiations to salvage it. But the two members are not negotiating on equal footing, because the initiator feels that he or she has already tried. Attempts at communication and to improve the relationship have been made, and nothing seems to work. For the initiator, then, the relationship may already be over or past the point of no return. Thus, although the partner makes a belated but hopeful attempt to render change, the initiator may merely appear to try while intending to ease his or her way out of the relationship. The partner is likely to devote increased priority and energy to the relationship and to make a concerted effort to persuade the initiator to stay. This effort may save the relationship, but usually it fails because by this time the initiator is well on the way toward a radically different life. The initiator has become, in some sense, a different person, and may feel as if the partner does not know him or her any more. Any changes are likely to be superficial and not touching the root of the real problem in the relationship. Moreover, both partners are likely to sense that this is a period of trying, and that what is happening is not really the relationship but something else—an attempt to find the relationship. Although the partner seeks stability in returning to what was, the relationship seems to keep reverting to its degenerated state.

At this point, the power balance in the relationship is fundamentally unequal. The initiator, as the less involved person, has far greater power than the partner, because it is the former who has the power to continue the relationship or to leave it. Ultimately, the initiator may suggest a temporary separation, which makes the state of the relationship a matter of public note. The separation is likely to lead the couple even farther apart: whereas the partner may see the separation as the last hope for reconciliation, the initiator is likely to see it as the first physical step toward the ultimate termination of the relationship.

It is sometimes asked, who finds the separation easier—the man or the woman? Often it is said that the man finds it easier, if only for economic reasons. But, according to Vaughan, much more important than the sex of the individual is the role in the separation: the initiator is far better prepared for the separation and is likely to be the one who finds it easier. The initiator has been gradually easing into the separated role; whereas for the partner, the separation may be sudden, with little preparation or forethought. This is not to say that the separation may not be hard for the initiator. Moreover, the partner may, in some instances, try to make life harder for the initiator out of spite or revenge. The partner may hope to prove to the initiator that life on his or her own is substantially worse than life as a couple. But the partner's attempts to make life difficult for the initiator are likely to boomerang, making the initiator only more determined to stay outside the relationship. The total amount of mourning and grief suffered by each member of the former couple may be equal, but for the initiator it has been spread out over a longer time. The other partner, who must mourn in a relatively shorter time, may be at wit's end. Each must find new friends and try to maintain some of the old friendships from the marriage. A competition may ensue whereby each of the partners tries to sway friends of the now-separated couple toward his or her point of view. Usually it is difficult for people to be friends with both partners, and they may be forced to make a choice. Some may withdraw entirely, unwilling to choose between the two members of the couple who have now been torn apart.

What started off as a temporary separation is likely to become permanent, because much of what happens during the separation involves increasing independence of the partners from each other. Moreover, one partner may so antagonize the other that whatever little hope there may once have been is now lost. Now the second partner must go through the same redefinition of the relationship that the initiator underwent earlier. The partner, like the initiator of the past, must begin to see the chinks in the armor and define the now-dying relationship as one that perhaps was not so good after all. The partner may not wish to redefine the relationship negatively; but, according to Vaughan, such a redefinition is important for the partner's well-being because of the need to put the relationship behind one. The redefinition may be hard, especially if the partner has latent feelings of failure. In order successfully to undergo the transition, the partner must realize that both members of the former couple are partially responsible.

What happens now may seem strange in many respects to both partners, because they have now become outside observers of each other's life. Much of what they hear about the other they may hear from third persons, whether friends or children. They must now both come to view the relationship as beyond saving, although many partners do not take this view until the initiator has formed a new public relationship with somebody else.

Reconciliation can occur, and occasionally does, but Vaughan points out that it is difficult. To achieve a genuine reconciliation, both of the partners must redefine the other person and their relationship in a positive way. Moreover, they have to change the public definition of themselves—now that of a separated couple. The reconciliation cannot be a return to what was, but rather must be a transition to yet something else. If it is a return, it is much more likely to fail than to succeed. It will work only if a new relationship is formed that is stronger, more durable, and more realistic than the one the partners had before.

This process of disengagement, as characterized by Vaughan, does not describe all breakups equally well. Many breakups do, however, show similar patterns; and as a sociologist, Vaughan has documented them with striking success.

CREATING A SCRIPT OF DISENGAGEMENT: THE THEORY OF ROBERT WEISS

Another classic work on disengagement is Robert Weiss's book on marital separation.[29] He opens by considering why the rate of marital separation has risen over the years. Of several reasons, the first is socioeconomic: both men and women are better off economically than they once were, and modern society places great emphasis on individual rights, so both partners are better able to be socially and economically independent. Second, whereas divorce was once considered scandalous, it no longer is; thus, people, deterred in the past by the social stigma of divorce, are more likely to pursue this course now. Third, he notes that organized religion has become more permissive, with even some Roman Catholic priests increasingly accepting the notion of secular divorce. According to Weiss, we Americans, perhaps more than anyone else in the world, value what we see as our rise to the unimpeded pursuit of happiness; and if this route requires a divorce, so be it.

Weiss believes that during the separation, each partner forms an account or a history of the marital failure, which is essentially a script describing the relationship and its downfall. The account may include a few or many of the major events that signified what went wrong. It is not only a chronology but an assignment of blame: through the account, the partners partition the blame between themselves, also including the effect of outside persons and circumstances on the separation. Thus, they account for both dispositions and situations in their account.

The accounts of husband and wife are likely to differ, and an outside listener hearing the two might not even realize that they are accounts of the same marriage. Each partner has selected and reinterpreted events in such a way as to render them favorable to the self and palatable in providing an understanding of what now seems to have gone wrong. In many of these accounts, Weiss found that men or women mourned not the marriage but rather the years they devoted to it. Another common theme was that each spouse wanted different things from life. Some accounts stressed chronic failings of the other spouse; and others noted things that, although irritating, would scarcely seem as important to an outside observer as they did to the separated couple. Some couples had lost their ability to talk to each other, and others engaged in infidelity. Although infidelity may contribute to the demise of a marriage, it is itself often a symptom of things that have already gone wrong. A common aspect of the failing marriage is the existence of interchanges that have the effect of invalidating each partner's view of himself or herself. Even though they may not mean to, members of the couple may look for their own self-validation at the expense of the other. Rejection may come in many forms, and the members of the couple may have great difficulty in maintaining their self-esteem.

An especially important insight of Weiss's lies in his

discussion of the erosion of love and the persistence of attachment. He observes that even though a couple's love for each other may well be dissipated, their sense of attachment to each other may remain. Even if they have argued a lot, they miss the arguing. The members of the couple may experience the same kind of separation anxiety that each as a child once experienced when temporarily separated from the mother.

From Weiss's point of view, it is important to distinguish between love and attachment. According to him, love usually involves some degree of idealization, trust, identification, and complementarity. Attachment, which usually accompanies love, is a bonding to another that gives rise to feelings of being at home and at ease with the other. Although love and attachment are separate things, it is easy to confuse the two, and some couples inevitably do.

The loss of attachment can give rise to a wide variety of emotions, including ones as diverse as stress and euphoria. Separation distress is the focusing of attention on the lost person, together with intense discomfort because of the loss. It results not just from being alone but from being without the other person specifically. In separation distress, one may experience apprehension, anxiety, or fear. Some people experience euphoria rather than distress—as though a black cloud has lifted from their lives, or as though they were walking on air. Although this reaction of euphoria seems distinct from distress, Weiss points out that the two may be related: euphoria may result from the realization that the attachment figure, previously thought to be necessary to your life, really is not, and that you can manage on your own. But such euphoria is just another way of managing the same thing—namely, the loss of the individual to whom you are attached.

Weiss notes several factors that affect separation distress. One is forewarning. Separations that occur after a seemingly good marriage are much more difficult for that partner than separations that occur after a seemingly inharmonious marriage. To the partner who has viewed the marriage as satisfactory, the separation may appear to have come from nowhere.

A second factor that affects distress is the length of the marriage. Weiss believes that there is a cutoff period of two years, before which the separation distress is considerably less than afterward. Couples in their first two years have not fully integrated their marriage into the fabric of their lives; but after that time, according to Weiss, the length of the marriage seems to make little difference in the amount of distress the members of the couple feel.

A third factor is who is the leaver and who is the left, with the difference between the two apparently involving more the character of the distress than its intensity. According to Weiss, however, the definition of which spouse has decided to separate is largely arbitrary, the marriage having become nearly intolerable for both. For Weiss, only rarely does one spouse decide on the separation while the other opposes it. In contrast, Vaughan argues that, on the average, the person who is left feels the greater distress. My own experience in the reading of the literature is more in accord with Vaughan's view than with Weiss's. Leaving is tough, but being left is tougher. For one thing, the person who leaves is more likely to be prepared for the split than is the person who is left, who may, in fact, be caught totally off guard. For another thing, it is the leaver who makes the decision, and the person who is left will often not accede willingly to it. And finally, the leaver is the one exerting the power in the relationship; as a result, the partner may feel not only alone but powerless and perhaps unworthy.

A fourth factor affecting stress is the presence of someone new, who can help deflect some of the sorrow and pain of the separation. While obviously this person cannot take away all of the distress, he or she can help the uncoupled partner to channel energy into building something new and turn it away from reminiscing about something old. Finally, Weiss notes that the quality of the postmarital relationship affects the degree of distress. How the husband and wife treat each other after the separation will be a major determinant of how they adjust. Obviously, better treatment will lead to better adjustment.

Weiss argues that a major consequence of the separation is a disruption of identity. People become unsure of just who they are. To some extent, your social identity, and perhaps your psychological identity as well, is in a state of transition. You may find yourself susceptible to self-deprecation and guilt, whether you are the leaver or the left. You may have problems in planning for the future because you are uncertain of what it holds. You may find yourself obsessively reviewing the marriage, trying to figure out what went wrong. Ironically, this crisis of identity comes at a time when many decisions have to be made; yet the ability of the person to make them is impaired. Even ability to work is impaired, and Weiss has found that people in the middle of a separation often do their best at work whose intellectual challenge is engaging but not maximal. One of the most difficult aspects of the separation is that what was once a well-defined relationship becomes ill defined. Whereas before there may have been certain rules, many of them tacit, now it is not clear what the rules are, and the couple must redefine their relationship. In some cases, they may have little to do with each other. But more often, their lives are sufficiently entangled so that they need to engage in fairly regular communication, especially if there are children, and they need to make a great effort to figure out what form their relationship will now take. There are likely to be sources of conflicts of interest regarding property division, support, custody of children, visitation rights, and so on—all of which make hammering out a new relationship exceedingly difficult. In many cases, the relationship will become worse than it was before.

Some partners are so averse to separation that they consider reconciliation. It is not known what proportion of separated couples eventually reconcile; but it is known that the further along the couple is toward divorce, the less likely a reconciliation is to take place. If the separation was impulsive, reconciliation may take place quickly. But if it was deliberate, and there is actually a filing for a divorce, the chances are only about 1 in 8 that a reconciliation will eventually take place. It appears that the chance of a reconciliation working out are only about 50-50; and as I noted earlier, a redefinition of the relationship is needed in order for the reconciliation to succeed. One danger of reconciliation is that if it does not work, one or both of the members of the couple may have exhausted their resources in terms of being able to initiate or cope with a second separation.

Ultimately, if the separation continues, both members of the now-defunct couple need to start over. For both members of the couple, there will be a transition period unlike anything that has come before and probably anything that will happen again: it marks the ending of one period of life and the beginning of the next. Weiss suggests that a new partner can be more effective than any system for relieving loneliness. But unless one takes the time honestly and realistically to assess what went wrong and what one's contribution was, the same problems may arise in the new relationship that plagued the old. If the separated partners can grow from the experience and correct their weaknesses, the disengagement may ultimately be a cause of bounty in life rather than of despair.

The Triangle of Love

As WE ALL KNOW, love can be seen as dark and dreary as well as bright and wonderful. This dichotomy has held among researchers of love as well as among the men or the women in love. The early clinical theories of Freud and Reik, for example, emphasized a somewhat pessimistic side of love. For Freud, love was largely the sublimation of sexual desire—a way of channeling sexual drives into an activity that would be more socially acceptable on more occasions and that would leave room for work. Reik saw love as what people turn to when they are down and out. While the neo-Freudian theorists, such as Maslow, saw love in a more positive light, they tended to think, I believe, in terms of "bad love" (thus, Reik, and Maslow's deficiency-love) and "good love" (Maslow's being-love, which sounds so good that one wonders whether anyone ever really achieves it). In modern times, the reinforcement theorists abandoned values altogether, leaving us with the impoverished notion that one is attracted to others as a function of the way one is reinforced by them. This kind of theory seems no more complete than were the clinical theories. The cognitive theory (according to which love is arousal labeled as love) seems very incomplete. Now—in seeing love as consisting of a triangular relationship among intimacy, passion, and decision/commitment shifting in importance and value over time—I believe we have a theory that accounts more completely and correctly than any other for the many aspects of this fundamental relationship between men and women.

Not only is the triangular theory more nearly comprehensive; it refutes many of the notions about love that people have long held to be "obvious." For example:

1.   Two of the best predictors of how happy you are in a relationship are how you feel about your partner and how your partner feels about you.

2.   One way to predict how you and your partner will fare in a marriage is to see how things go if you live together first.

3.   The way to handle a partner with low self-esteem is to bolster the partner's ego.

4.   Today religion is much less important to a successful match than it used to be, as evidenced by the increasing numbers of people intermarrying across religious faiths.

5.   One way to find out how loving a person is, is to look at how loving his or her family is.

6.   Passion and sex are most important at the beginning of a relationship.

7.   "Chemistry" is the unpredictable wild card in a relationship.

8.   The key to better communication is for you and your partner to get to know each other better.

Every one of these statements is "obvious." And every

one is wrong. But they do not *seem* wrong; indeed, they seem eminently plausible and have to many people for a long time. Yet let us consider each of these statements in light both of the scientific study of love and especially of the triangular theory I have outlined in the previous chapters.

1.   The first statement would seem to be the most obvious; and yet Barnes and I have found it to be in error. How you feel about your partner is *not* a particularly good predictor of happiness in a relationship unless you take into account your ideal for that relationship. You may love someone, but your ideal for what you expect may be so high that you are never satisfied. Moreover, how your partner feels about you is not what is crucial to your happiness: what really matters is how you think your partner feels about you. And we know from the Sternberg-Barnes study that the relationship between how someone feels about you, and how you think that person feels about you, is not particularly strong. Most importantly, perhaps, neither how you feel about your partner nor how your partner feels about you is a major predictor of happiness. The best predictor is the difference between how you perceive your partner to feel about you and how you would like your partner to feel about you.

2.   Although living together before marriage seems as if it should be a good trial for marriage, the divorce rate in the United States for people who live together before marriage is no lower than that for those who do not live together. In Sweden, it is worse. Why should this be?

First, recall Jack Brehm's theory of reactance, according to which one tends to react against threats to one's freedom of choice. And marriage is a distinct threat to one's freedom of choice, because it constitutes a choice already made. When a couple lives together outside the bonds of marriage, either partner is free to leave at any time, however hard such leavetaking may be and fraught with awkwardness, pain, and sorrow. But neither one of a married couple can just walk away: there are laws requiring some legal settlement—a divorce—before the relationship can be fully terminated. Thus, marriage, in constraining one's freedom, is more likely to engender reactance than does living together.

Second, couples who live together before marriage are likely to be more reluctant than average to make a binding commitment, and more likely than average to experience reactance upon a threat to their freedom of choice. They are likely thus to see marriage as not only changing their relationship significantly but as curtailing their freedom significantly as well.

3. Almost every one of us prefers people who agree with us to people who do not, who constantly criticize our beliefs or our very selves. The person with low self-esteem is no exception. Thus, a man who believes himself to be no good is likely to feel rewarded upon hearing someone agree with that opinion—whether he is aware of that feeling or not—and ultimately is more likely to be attracted to a woman who treats him in the rotten way he expects than to a woman who treats him nicely, as he doesn't expect.

Passing on compliments, however well meant, to someone with low self-esteem will only be interpreted by that person as a sign of your lack of perspicacity. The best approach to the man (or woman) of low self-esteem is to find ways of raising his consciousness of being successful in particular tasks, so that he cannot help but compliment himself. You can then reinforce that self-perception.

4. Religion still matters: either because couples who think they do not care start to care when they have chil-

dren; or because many values are tied up with religious upbringing, even if one no longer perceives oneself as religious. Sternberg and Wright found nothing increased more in importance than religion in relationships over time. So if you and a potential partner differ in religion, you should discuss the issue and make a real attempt to discover whether in this area you will be able to succeed over the long as well as the short term.

5.   How loving a family a person comes from is a poor predictor of how much that person will love you. Susan Grajek and I found only trivial prediction from family closeness to love in a close relationship with an adult partner.

6.   Passion and sex increase rather than decrease in importance over the first few years of a relationship, and decrease in importance somewhat over the very long term, according to my study with Sandra Wright of what matters when in relationships. As habituation sets into a passionate relationship, the couple's ability to sustain some spark of passion and an interesting sex life becomes more and not less important.

7.   The physical attraction between two people, often called "chemistry," is not wholly unpredictable. We tend to feel passion for people who fulfill certain needs we have, such as for dominance, submission, affiliation, or praise. Some of these needs we may be unaware of, and some may be essentially maladaptive. For example, you will probably not come out ahead in many competitive situations if you always need to feel dominated, and you may also lose your competitive edge if you feel you always must dominate. So accept whatever chemistry you feel toward someone, but make sure that beyond it the relationship can still work.

8.   Research, as I have discussed earlier, shows that as

you get to know a partner really well it may become harder to communicate if one or both of you have learned that telling the truth is ultimately more costly than telling a lie. A couple can do themselves in if they count on fiction over fact.

Thus, the scientific study of love has exploded many of the old wives' tales that people have unfortunately all too often tried to live by in making their relationships work. Another result, and one with ramifications far beyond the scientist's office, is a very practical one.

Putting the Theory into Practice

As I have indicated throughout this book, the findings of my own research on love, as well as that of other psychologists, can provide a wealth of practical advice in respect both to what makes a loving relationship succeed and to common problems in any loving relationship.

TEN RULES FOR A SUCCESSFUL RELATIONSHIP

At the risk of repeating myself, let me spell out ten rules that men and women who seek a satisfying loving relationship will find helpful:

1. *Successful partners do not take their relationship for granted.* Nowhere are the seeds of the destruction of a relationship more likely to sprout than when its members take each other for granted. When a couple are dating, they usually make an extra effort to impress each other by paying attention to the way they look, act, and set priorities. The motivation for this behavior seems to be, in part, advertising rather than a completely honest show of feel-

ings—as becomes evident when the partners, secured through marriage, move on to other things: acquiring wealth, advancing careers, raising children, gaining social position, or whatever. Some people may no longer take the time to make their relationship work, or have personal pride in it. During dating, the members of a couple are much more aware of the threat of losing each other and so make an extra effort to keep the relationship stimulating. A dating relationship can be compared to an agreement written in paper and pencil. Once married, a couple feels that the agreement is etched in stone. But stone is not indestructible and will, under certain conditions, crumble.

Sometimes the tendency for married couples to focus on everything but the relationship is not intentional. The rewards and punishments of work are often tangible. Success means promotions and more money, whereas failure means less money and possibly even the loss of a job. The rewards and punishments of relationships, however, are not as obvious. It is easy to take a relationship for granted, because you seem to "have it." There are no tangible rewards corresponding to promotions or increases in salary, and often no immediate punishments if you put the relationship "on hold." Whereas children will obviously suffer if left unattended, the spouse or the lover, being an adult, will not show immediate signs of neglect. But relationships, like flower gardens, need to be nurtured. If they do not grow, they will wither away sooner or later, and die. Unfortunately, the price of taking a relationship for granted often does not show up for some time. The partner may seem to accept the situation, and then one day ask for a divorce. You do not want to be taken for granted; neither does your partner. The relationship needs constantly to be renewed and nurtured.

2. *Successful partners make their relationship the first priority.* During the courting phase, people often give their relationship first priority, because there is something concrete they want—the love and possibly the marital commitment of the other person. As time goes on, the press of careers, family, and other things tempt us to put our relationships on the back burner—where they are likely to burn out. The relationship may share first priority with other things, but once it falls behind them, it is jeopardized.

3. *Successful partners actively seek to meet each other's needs.* A gift is less of a gift when it is demanded or actively solicited than when given of a person's own free will. The very act of giving a gift in response to someone else's request or demand reduces the meaning of the word *gift*. The situation becomes one of requested or even forced compliance. If we view gifts in a general way, as all of those things that we can do to advance the life of another, then we can understand why active meeting of needs, initiated by one of the partners, is much more effective than passive or requested meeting of needs. Active, self-initiated meeting of needs shows that you understand and care for the other and, moreover, wish to do something about your feelings. Don't wait for the request to be made. Do it, whatever it is, before you are asked, and the value of what you do will be much greater.

4. *Successful partners know when, and when not, to change in response to the other.* Our research shows that successful partners are flexible: they are willing to change in response to each other's needs. The triangular theory of love predicts that relationships will frequently be in a state of flux with respect to the balance of intimacy, passion, and commitment. Only by being flexible are the partners in a relationship able to meet the challenge to

grow that each change in the nature of the relationship requires. Successful partners can give in as the situation demands, but also know when not to give in. They know what they can and cannot be, and will not strive to comply with requests that they simply cannot fulfill while remaining true to themselves.

5. *Successful partners value themselves.* As I noted earlier, Abraham Maslow distinguished between deficiency-love and being-love: in deficiency-love, you seek out another in order to remedy some lack in yourself; in being-love, you seek another in order to enhance an already adequate self.[1] In fact, most loves are probably not pure cases of either deficiency-love or being-love, but are a blend, varying over time. One who seeks in another person the sense of worth one cannot find in oneself is likely to be disappointed. You cannot find salvation in a relationship. The projections one often places on another of traits one lacks but wishes one had may tell less about the other person than about what one wants the other person to be. Thus, I come to the next characteristic of a relationship that works.

6. *Successful partners love each other, not their idealizations of each other.* It is much easier to fall in love with an ideal than with a real person, as discussed in chapter 1. Ideals are unflawed; they do not make "unreasonable" demands; they have all the characteristics one wants from true love; they do not talk back; indeed, they are just what we want them to be. The problem with ideals is that they exist only in one's head. One may be in love, but with a fantasized ideal rather than with a real person. Love based on idealization can go on for some time. You tend to see only what you want to see and to ignore or make excuses for the rest. But sooner or later the bubble will burst. You eventually get to know the person and are

disappointed because he or she does not match up to the hypothetical ideal. In successful relationships, the partners love each other for who they are, not for who they want each other to be.

7. *Successful partners tolerate what they cannot change.* Some things we can change about another; other things we cannot. The important thing is to have the wisdom to recognize which is which. But although you may not always be correct about what is changeable, you need to learn to tolerate the things about the other person that you may not like that you cannot change—or else give up on the relationship. If your partner is moody, and always has been, it is likely that he or she will continue to be moody. And it is unlikely that you can change this basic quality. If your partner tends to be messy around the house, chances are that he or she will stay that way or resent it if forced to change. If you cannot live with it, you should not have entered into the relationship in the first place. The point is simply that there are many major things that can be wrong with people; if the only things you have to tolerate are minor, be thankful.

8. *Successful partners are open with each other.* No one is perfect, but few will admit their faults. Sometimes it seems so much easier to lie, or to withhold the truth, than to admit to errors and shortcomings. The problem is that omissions, distortions, and outright lies tend to be cancerous. Once they start, they tend to spread and, ultimately, to infiltrate and possibly to destroy the relationship. Once you see you can get away with a little lie, maybe the next time you will try a slightly bigger one. Once you withhold your feelings and see that what could have been a tooth-and-nail fight has been replaced by the placidity of ignorance, it is easy to say nothing the next time as well. Ultimately, each partner says less and less, or whatever

one does say is empty and of little importance. Although the relationship may continue, it has lost much of its meaning and depth. All that is left is a shell, but by now the partners may not even be aware of how little remains inside.

9. *Successful partners make good times together and grow through the bad ones.* They purposely create joint activities that will be enjoyable both in their own right and in the companionship each partner can supply. Rather than wait for good times to happen, they create them. At the same time, they recognize that there will be bad times, but use these as an opportunity for growth. Even if you are truly honest with each other, you will not prevent some bad times—but you will pave the road for mutual growth and come out stronger.

10. *Successful partners do unto each other as they would have the other do unto them.* We all learn the Golden Rule in childhood, and many of us even continue to believe in it, but in a way often separated from our day-to-day lives. We often want to give less than we get, or to be treated in ways we are not prepared to offer the other. If you truly want your relationship to work, see things from the other's point of view in order to develop the empathy and understanding that underly every successful close relationship.

PROBLEMS IN LOVING RELATIONSHIPS

In studying the triangle of love, we have found twelve common problems in loving relationships:

1. *"I'm bored with my relationship."* Boredom often sets in when manifest intimacy starts to decrease or when passion habituates. If you are bored, then your relationship is not giving you sufficient positive reinforcement or

novelty to sustain you. Everyone needs rewards and novelty, but people differ in the amounts they need. Since doing pleasant things with someone often radiates onto the person, sit down and make a list of things you could do with your partner, and then start doing them. If you need more novelty, then make sure that some of the things on your list are not only fun but different. Also, think of a list of things that your partner could do that would be rewarding for you; and talk to your partner about his or her doing them, in exchange for your doing the same for your partner. Most of all, take responsibility for making your relationship more interesting. Don't wait for it to happen: make it happen.

2. *"We fight a lot."* When you fight a lot, you sacrifice the possibilities for growth of intimacy. Make a pact with your partner: next time you start a fight, either of you can say "Stop!" and at that point you both agree to stop immediately. Fighting can be a habit; and to break the habit, you have to make the same effort you would to break any other bad habit. All couples fight occasionally, but regular fighting can become a script for the two of you, one that can be called out by even the slightest and sometimes silliest disagreement. When one of you says "Stop," agree to use the opportunity to figure out what is behind the fight. Agree to discuss the sources of the disagreement and to work out a compromise. Fighting tends to acquire a certain kind of "functional autonomy"—a life of its own, independent of any genuine disagreements. Thus, fighting may actually decrease your chance of achieving a compromise, because you may find yourself concentrating on the fight and techniques of effective (or damaging) fighting rather than on the source of disagreement. You need not use the "stop" rule every time you fight. Agree with your partner to use it the next time,

and maybe just for every other fight thereafter. You can thereby compare the effectiveness of your resolution of conflicts when you do and don't fight. If you prefer fighting, or find it necessary for resolving your conflicts, consider seeing a counselor with your partner. You may need outside help if, given the choice, you find that fighting is your preferred script.

3. *"My partner doesn't understand me."* Unless you have reached the heights of intimacy, you're probably right. Moreover, you probably don't fully understand yourself either. One of the biggest problems in any relationship is the expectation, or hope, that one's partner has extrasensory perception. But there are no documented cases of ESP. And even if it should exist, don't expect your partner to be the undocumented case. Agree with your partner to sit down one day or evening when you have at least a couple of hours of uninterrupted time and can have a soul-to-soul talk. Agree that each of you will take one aspect of yourself that you are convinced your partner misunderstands, and use the time to explain this aspect of yourself thoroughly (for example, why you drink too much or never drink; why you are impatient with people; why you believe in "spare the rod and spoil the child"). Say what it is, how you became that way (to the best of your knowledge), how the aspect of yourself manifests itself in your behavior, and how you expect to be treated in view of this aspect of yourself. No interruptions are allowed, although your partner should feel free to make a list of questions or comments for later. After you have finished, your partner should have as much time as he or she needs to ask questions or make comments, and then he or she should agree to do the same thing you have done. You just need one more element in your pact. What each of you says should be respected by

the other person, and not be used against or thrown up to him or her.

If you feel you are not achieving mutual understanding, supplement the next session in the following way: reverse roles. Do the exact same thing you did in the last session, but speak from your partner's view, and have your partner speak from your point of view. By thus reversing each other's roles, you may better understand your partner's position. Have as many such sessions as necessary until you and your partner feel you have achieved a better understanding of each other. If you have not reached a better understanding, again, you should consider counseling.

4. *"My partner and I don't communicate well."* I have argued in this book that intimacy is the core component of love, and difficult or impossible to achieve without good communication. If you don't communicate well with your partner, the first step you need to take is to figure out why. One possibility is that one or both of you has just gotten into the habit of not saying much, or at least not much of substance. Another possibility is that you are simply afraid to tell your partner what's on your mind for fear of being beaten down, verbally if not physically. You thus find it safer to be silent. A third possibility is that you feel your partner doesn't listen; or that, if he or she listens, it doesn't matter since there seems to be no understanding of what you say anyway.

Whatever the course, find a time when you and your partner can be together for at least a couple of hours. If you have to, take the phone off the hook and leave your children with a babysitter. Agree that during this time, each of you will raise one issue that is of concern to the two of you jointly or to only one of you. But it has to be something you care about. Now use half the time to discuss your issue, and half the time to discuss your partner's. Next time, reverse the order. But each time, each of you has to agree to give your partner's as well as your own issue your full and undivided attention. And agree to do your best to help your partner resolve whatever his or her issue may be.

5. *"I find myself attracted to others"; or, "My partner seems to be attracted to others."* You are not alone. Almost every other couple is in the same position, especially as passion starts to habituate, or when your commitment to your relationship is lagging. There are two important questions to ask: Why the attraction to others? and What are you (or your partner) doing about it? It is normal and common to be attracted to others. But if it is becoming a problem for either you or your partner due to the frequency or intensity with which it occurs, then you may want to take action. One solution is for you or your partner to make yourself more attractive—by losing weight, doing exercise, dressing better, or, in general, paying more attention to your appearance.

Another possible problem is that one or the other of you is not particularly adept at love making and could use guidance. If this is the problem, I recommend Alexandra Penney's books on lovemaking.[2] If these are not enough, professional sex counseling may be in order.

A third possible problem is that your partner may have some characteristic or habit that turns you off, or vice versa. Ask. Sometimes these habits are easy to change; but, again, you cannot expect your partner to change, nor can your partner expect you to change, unless you discuss the issue first. Say what is on your mind, or ask your partner to say what is on his or hers.

A last possibility is that one or the other of you may just be very susceptible to members of the opposite sex. Accept it as part of the way you are (or your partner is), unless the attractions are turning out to be more than just that. Then you need either to help yourselves or to seek outside help.

6. *"I just can't commit myself to this relationship."* People differ in the extent to which they can commit to another, and probably no one reaches the maximum possible in this component. Inability to commit oneself to a relationship is a problem only if it disturbs either of the partners. If one or the other of you believe that a greater commitment is in order, then you indeed have a problem, especially because the fact that generally the less committed person wields the greater power in the relationship creates an imbalance in both commitment and power.

There are several solutions to the problem of unequal commitment. The first is nothing. The partners can agree to accept things the way they are. In effect, the more committed person agrees to accept less than he or she would like. Both partners should realize that there is danger from both sides. The less committed person may indeed stay that way, or leave the relationship for another, especially for one he or she believes has greater potential for commitment. But the more committed person may also leave, out of frustration or disgust or for another relationship that promises to be more rewarding.

A second possibility is for the less committed person to agree to a greater commitment. At the risk of saying something unpopular, I do not recommend this option unless the less committed individual is truly ready to become more committed. Without such readiness, this person is likely to become ever more resentful and even to feel as though he or she has been railroaded into the agreement.

A third possibility is for the couple to agree to terminate the relationship, or at least to restructure it so that each partner feels totally free and is able to seek out someone else in a more committed relationship. Sometimes this is the best option, especially if one partner feels that he or she is wasting "the best years of life" waiting for the relationship to go somewhere it is not going. Some people, however, cannot commit themselves fully to anything or anyone, and you may be with one of those people. If you decide that you are, you should truly allow each partner enough space to find someone else, rather than just saying that, in principle, either person could leave; whereas in practice, neither person has the space or freedom to seek out another relationship.

7. *"We have nothing in common any more."* Intimacy often decreases as people grow and find that they are growing apart rather than together. The first thing you want to do is to find out whether this is, in fact, really the case. If it is, you may genuinely be in trouble and have to consider counseling or possibly restructuring or terminating the relationship. But usually it is not true. Rather, what has happened is that the parts of you that are in common have been submerged. If this is the case, as it probably is, there are three possible options.

First, try to restore to your relationship those parts of you that are common but have gone below the surface. If there are things you used to do together but have stopped doing, start doing them again. If you used to like going to the theater, but let it drop out of your life, put it back again. Start dredging up the common interests you have let lapse.

Maybe you don't like doing together any more, or can't do any more, the things you used to like doing together. Since you moved to Iowa from California, surfing or scuba diving is not as practical as it used to be. In this case, your second option is to make a concentrated effort to find new interests that you share. The new things may be new for both of you and open up unknown dimensions of the relationship.

The third option is probably the most painful. It may be that you have discovered that you still do have things in common, but that these are those aspects of yourself you like least. Indeed, your partner may evoke in you memories of a person you once were but no longer want to be. You know those parts of you are still there, but they are precisely those parts of yourself that you do not want to bring to the surface. In such cases, the partner is often a punishing stimulus because of his or her ability to evoke memories that are unpleasant or even painful. Your option is either radically to change the relationship or to leave it. There is little sense in leaving the way it is a relationship that makes you feel bad about yourself or the other person.

8. *"My partner makes too many demands on me."* One's reaction to the perception of too many demands is often to withhold intimacy; and, of course, reactance theory says that we start chafing at the bit when our freedom is taken away from us. Indeed, we often want things largely because we cannot have them. When I was younger, I read a poem by Stephen Crane about a man who sees a ball of gold in the sky. The man really wanted that ball of gold. He decides to go for it, and spends much time and effort building an edifice high enough so that he can go up and get it. When he goes there, he grabs the ball, only to find to his very great distress that the ball is made of lead. Bitterly disappointed and with great anguish, he makes his way back to the ground, leaving the worthless

ball in the sky. When he returns to the ground, he takes one last look up into the sky, and there it is—a ball of gold.

Relationships can be the same way. We often want precisely what we cannot have or is not allowed us. If your partner makes too many demands on you, you may find yourself a living example of reactance theory, wanting to do precisely the opposite of what he or she wants. It therefore makes sense for you and your partner to sit down when you have plenty of unfettered time to decide what are and are not reasonable demands, and ask your partner to do the same. You may not be able to relieve yourself of all the demands that make you uncomfortable, but you may be able to reduce them, and to do the same for your partner.

9. *"I don't like spending time with my partner."* A frequent source of disagreement between members of a couple is the feeling of one of them that they don't spend enough time together. If the feeling is mutual, then all it takes is a resolve to make time. The problem is more serious if one of the couple does not like spending time with the other. If this is the case, you first need to admit it to yourself. It may be a hard admission to make, because couples are not supposed to feel that way about each other. Once you admit it, you need to figure out why you do not like to be with your partner. If it is for one of the reasons discussed in the other eleven problems, then you might try the recommendations associated with that problem. But there is another reason that I think is more common than we like to admit: it is, quite simply, that we would enjoy doing something else more or feel that something else is a better use of our time. If this is the case, remember that relationships are no exception to the rule

that we often lose what we don't use. See if you can find any enjoyment with your partner that he or she is not now supplying. If you cannot, seek outside help to determine whether what you do have is worth something. It may well be, but it may be that you need outside counseling to figure out why (or why not). But intimacy is not a function only of amount of time, but of what you do with the time you have.

10. *"My partner's values are distasteful or aversive to me."* Sometimes you discover, perhaps fairly late in a relationship, that you and your partner have serious differences in values. For example, you may have thought you had the same ideas about religion, or raising children, or making money, and then discover that you do not. Or your values or those of your partner may change, leaving you with a difference you never had before. Because intimacy depends partly on shared values, you may find the quality of your relationship declining.

Value conflicts can be difficult to handle or even to face up to. Since values tend to be basic to a person and his or her definition of self, they are not easy to change. You probably cannot change your partner's values; and unless they are clearly pernicious (for example, it is good to murder people, or hard drug use is acceptable in moderation), you probably should not even try to effect a change. You are better off agreeing to disagree, and possibly working out compromises of action that partly reflect the values of both of you, even if they don't fully reflect what either of you believes. For example, if you disagree about how to discipline children, work out a compromise that each of you can live with. (But don't be inconsistent in discipline, because there are few things more confusing to children than inconsistent discipline.) Or if you disagree about how to spend money, have a pot of money that is for each of you singly, as well as a collective pot, and agree that either partner can use the single pot in whatever way he or she sees fit (short of illegality, of course). Don't even try to make every purchase a consensus purchase, because one or both of you is going to end up frustrated. Chances are neither of you will be very happy. In general, I think that value conflicts are best handled by a combination of compromise with a policy of spheres of disagreement: you allow your partner to do things in his or her way within certain domains, and he or she allows the same for you.

11. *"We have different ideas of what love is."* From what I can observe, no two people have exactly the same idea of what love is. And as we have seen, people can have different triangles of what they believe love should be. The question that matters is not whether two people have different ideas of what love is, but rather what practical difference those ideas make. I think that this problem is much more common than people recognize, because they tend not to confront what love means either to themselves or to their partner. But I think the confrontation is worthwhile, because you may find that your partner is expressing love to you in ways you do not recognize as love. Conversely, you may be expressing love to your partner in ways he or she does not recognize as such. So I would encourage you to undertake a joint venture with your partner. Each of you should spend your spare time for one week thinking what love for your partner means to you, how you express it in action, and how it is not expressed in action but is there anyway in terms of feelings you have for your partner. Keep notes on all that comes to mind. Then, at the end of the week,

each of you exchange your notes with the other. You may not only learn a lot, but see expressions of love that you have missed for years as well. After reading each other's notes, discuss how each of you could make the other experience the love you feel.

12. *"My partner does not support me."* Often we enter into a relationship to get the support we feel that we could not get in any other way. We are therefore profoundly disappointed when we find that the support we counted on is on the wane. By the time we notice the problem, it may be because we feel we are getting hardly any support at all. And support is a crucial part of intimacy. How to get it back? The first step has been taken when you recognize that you no longer have it. Decide what you want; then ask for it. Again, don't count on telepathy. And be willing to give support in return for getting it. I have been in various relationships where I felt I was giving support, but the other person didn't recognize it. In such instances, I would view myself as supporting someone, and then, out of the blue—at least so it seemed to me—the person would express feelings that I was not being supportive. But then, when I would ask what I could do to show my support, the response I got was so general or distant that I would have no idea what the person really wanted. So if there is something you want, be concrete and down-to-earth about it. Do not be so vague or abstract as to leave the person with no particular actions to perform. To get what you want, you have to be clear in asking for it. And ask for what the other person has in him or her to give, and no more. Relationships are not improved by asking for what someone does not have to offer. They are improved by taking the best of what each has to give.

Unanswered Questions

My work and that of other scientists has only begun to solve the riddles of love. In this book, I have concentrated on what we know about love. Let me end by suggesting three areas where there is a great deal we do not know about love, and where research seems to me particularly urgent.

The first concerns parental love for children, and children's love for their parents. Parents and children—young children, especially—exhibit an unconditionality in their relationships rare in relationships between spouses (or unmarried lovers, for that matter). Children and parents can go through the most trying times together, and yet their love comes out unscathed. A better understanding of the mechanisms underlying love between parents and children might allow us to apply what we have learned to relationships between adults, and thereby make these relationships better—and more forgiving.

The second issue is what attracts people to each other in the first place and maintains or dissolves the attraction over time. Although there has been extensive research on this issue (much of it described in this book), I believe it has barely scratched the surface. A better understanding of the bases for initial and maintained attraction would help us construct interventions that might help people find others with whom they are compatible and screen out those with whom they are not compatible, and also help them maintain the love that often gets lost over the years.

The third issue, and the one I myself am pursuing at the moment (and to which I devoted this chapter), is the formation of strategies that make relationships work. We are often afraid that if we overanalyze our relationships, we will lose them. But I think that we more often lose relationships because we do not understand them. Consider, for example, a common occurrence in relationships: recurrent arguments over the same topic. We have all been in relationships where there is some issue that we are just unable to resolve, and no sooner do we think we have it licked than it rears its head once again, often in some new form. A couple may find themselves arguing again and again over money, or time spent together, or the support one member of the couple gives to the other. Often these arguments continue because the members of the couple are defining the issue differently. In the case of time, for example, one member of the couple defines time spent away from the spouse as showing lack of caring, whereas the other defines it as a display of caring, in that the time is perhaps being spent on earning money that facilitates, or may even be necessary for the survival of, the relationship. If we mutually work toward strategies that would please both members of the couple, we might improve our relationships considerably. While we need to take a more thoughtful approach to relationships, there is, of course, more to relationships than thought.

As a scientist, I feel no qualms about saying that I believe in the magic of love, but I also believe that my research has helped me better understand those experiences. And it has enabled me to step back at times and to attempt to apply some of what I know both to my own relationships and to those of others. While it has not saved me from making mistakes, it has helped me learn a bit more from those mistakes than I otherwise might. If

The Triangle of Love

anything, my work in science has helped me appreciate even more the magic of love, and how little I know about it. The more I have learned about the triangle of love, the more I have come to realize the many dimensions of love that neither science nor any other discipline has yet grasped.

NOTES

Chapter 1. In Quest of Love

1. C. Spearman, *The Abilities of Man* (New York: Macmillan, 1927); G. H. Thomson, *The Factorial Analysis of Human Ability.* (London: University of London Press, 1939); L. L. Thurstone, *Primary Mental Abilities* (Chicago: University of Chicago Press, 1938).

2. C. Spearman, " 'General Intelligence' Objectively Determined and Measured," *American Journal of Psychology* 15(1904): 201–93.

3. R. J. Sternberg and S. Grajek, "The Nature of Love," *Journal of Personality and Social Psychology* 47(1984): 312–29.

4. Z. Rubin, Liking and Loving Scales (1973); G. Levinger, Interpersonal Scales (1980).

5. J. W. Thibaut and H. H. Kelley, *The Social Psychology of Groups* (New York: John Wiley, 1959).

6. Ibid., pp. 81–82.

7. R. J. Sternberg and M. Barnes, "Real and Ideal Others in Romantic Relationships: Is Four a Crowd?" *Journal of Personality and Social Psychology* 49(1985): 1586–1608.

Chapter 2. The Ingredients of Love

1. Obviously, the relationships were not completely one-sided, but rather differed from one another in emphasis on the various components.

2. For more detail on the various components, see R. J. Sternberg, "A Triangular Theory of Love," *Psychological Review* 93 (1986): 119–35.

3. H. H. Kelley, "Analyzing Close Relationships," in H. H. Kelley et al., eds., *Close Relationships*, pp. 20–67 (New York: W. H. Freeman, 1983).

4. L. B. Rubin, *Just Friends* (New York: Harper & Row, 1985).

5. S. M. Jourard, *Self-Disclosure: An Experimental Analysis of the Transparent Self* (New York: John Wiley, 1971).

6. V. J. Derlega, M. Wilson, and A. L. Chaikin, "Friendship and Disclosure Reciprocity," *Journal of Personality and Social Psychology* 34(1976): 578–82.

7. T. L. Morton, "Intimacy and Reciprocity of Exchange: A Comparison of Spouses and Strangers," *Journal of Personality and Social Psychology* 36(1978): 72–81.

8. P. C. Cozby, "Self-Disclosure, Reciprocity, and Liking," *Sociometry* 35(1972): 151–60.

9. E. Hatfield, and G. W. Walster, *A New Look at Love* (Reading, Mass.: Addison-Wesley, 1981), p. 9. Elaine Hatfield has also published under the name Elaine Walster.

10. H. H. Kelley, "Love and Commitment," in H. H. Kelley et al., eds., *Close Relationships*, pp. 265–314 (New York: W. H. Freeman, 1983).

11. D. Tennov, *Love and Limerence* (New York: Stein & Day, 1979).

12. Hatfield and Walster, *A New Look at Love*.

13. S. Duck, *Friends for Life* (New York: St. Martin's, 1983).

14. E. Berscheid and E. H. Walster, *Interpersonal Attraction*, 2nd ed. (Reading, Mass.: Addison-Wesley, 1978).

15. E. Berscheid, "Emotion," in H. H. Kelley et al., eds., *Close Relationships*, pp. 110–68 (New York: W. H. Freeman, 1983); G. Mandler, "The Generation of Emotion: A Psychological Theory," in R. Plutchik and H. Kellerman, eds., *Emotion: Theory, Research and Experience*, vol. I: *Theories of Emotion*, pp. 219–43 (New York: Academic Press, 1980).

16. R. Schank and R. Abelson, *Scripts, Plans, Goals, and Understanding* (Hillsdale, N.J: Lawrence Erlbaum, 1977).

17. K. R. Livingston, "Love as a Process of Reducing Uncertainty," in K. S. Pope, ed., *On Love and Loving*, pp. 133–51 (San Francisco: Jossey-Bass, 1980).

18. Berscheid, "Emotion."

19. R. L. Solomon, "The Opponent-Process Theory of Acquired Motivation: The Costs of Pleasure and the Benefits of Pain," *American Psychologist* 35(1980): 691–712.

20. S. Peele and A. Brodsky, *Love and Addiction* (New York: New American Library, 1976).

21. J. W. Thibaut and H. H. Kelley, *The Social Psychology of Groups* (New York: John Wiley, 1959).

Notes

22. R. J. Sternberg and M. Barnes, "Real and Ideal Others in Romantic Relationships: Is Four a Crowd?" *Journal of Personality and Social Psychology* 49(1985): 1586–1608.

23. D. J. Bem, "Self-Perception Theory," *Advances in Experimental Social Psychology* 6(1972): 1–62.

Chapter 3. Looking at Love: Applying the Triangular Theory

1. E. Walster et al., "Importance of Physical Attractiveness in Dating Behavior," *Journal of Personality and Social Psychology* 4(1966): 508–16.

2. S. Peele and A. Brodsky, *Love and Addiction* (New York: New American Library, 1976).

3. R. L. Solomon, "The Opponent-Process Theory of Acquired Motivation: The Costs of Pleasure and the Benefits of Pain," *American Psychologist* 35(1980): 691–712.

4. E. Walster et al., "Playing Hard-to-Get: Understanding an Elusive Phenomenon," *Journal of Personality and Social Psychology* 26(1973): 113–21.

5. J. W. Brehm, *A Theory of Psychological Reactance* (New York: Academic Press, 1966); S. S. Brehm and J. W. Brehm, *Psychological Reactance: A Theory of Freedom and Control* (New York: Academic Press, 1981).

6. E. W. Burgess and P. Wallin, *Engagement and Marriage* (Philadelphia: Lippincott, 1953); D. Byrne, *The Attraction Paradigm* (New York: Academic Press, 1971).

7. S. C. Saegert, W. Swap, and R. Zajonc, "Exposure, Context, and Interpersonal Attraction," *Journal of Personality and Social Psychology* 25(1973): 234–42.

8. A. C. Kerckhoff and K. E. Davis, "Value Consensus and Need Complementarity in Mate Selection," *American Sociological Review* 27(1962): 295–303; G. Levinger, "Development and Change," in H. H. Kelley et al., eds., *Close Relationships*, pp. 315–59 (New York: W. H. Freeman, 1983); B. I. Murstein, *Who Will Marry Whom? Theories and Research in Marital Choice* (New York: Springer, 1976); I. L. Reiss, *Premarital Sexual Standards in America* (New York: Free Press, 1960).

9. E. Berscheid and E. H. Walster, *Interpersonal Attraction*, 2nd ed. (Reading, Mass: Addison-Wesley, 1978).

10. I. Altman and D. A. Taylor, *Social Penetration: The Development of Interpersonal Relationships* (New York: Holt, Rinehart, & Winston, 1973).

11. R. J. Sternberg and S. Grajek, "The Nature of Love," *Journal of Personality and Social Psychology* 47(1984): 312–29.

12. E. Berscheid, "Emotion," in H. H. Kelley et al., eds., *Close Relationships*, pp. 110–68 (New York: W. H. Freeman, 1983).

Chapter 4. Liking versus Loving

1. *Webster's New World Dictionary of the American Language*, college edition (Cleveland: World Publishing, 1964).

2. E. Berscheid and E. H. Walster, *Interpersonal Attraction*, 2nd ed. (Reading, Mass.: Addison-Wesley, 1978); E. Hatfield and G. W. Walster, *A New Look at Love* (Reading, Mass.: Addison-Wesley, 1981).

3. A. J. Lott and B. E. Lott, "Group Cohesiveness, Communication Level, and Conformity," *Journal of Abnormal and Social Psychology* 62(1961): 408–12; A. J. Lott and B. E. Lott, "The Role of Reward in the Formation of Positive Interpersonal Attitudes," in T. L. Huston, ed., *Foundations of Interpersonal Attraction*, pp. 171–89 (New York: Academic Press, 1974).

4. A. J. Lott and B. E. Lott, "A Learning Theory Approach to Interpersonal Attitudes," in A. G. Greenwald and T. M. Ostrom, eds., *Psychological Foundations of Attitudes*, pp. 67–88 (New York: Academic Press, 1968).

5. W. Griffitt, and R. Veitch, "Hot and Crowded: Influence of Population Density and Temperature on Interpersonal Affective Behavior," *Journal of Personality and Social Psychology* 17(1971): 92–98.

6. G. L. Clore and D. Byrne, "A Reinforcement-Affect Model of Attraction," in T. L. Huston, ed., *Foundations of Interpersonal Attraction*, pp. 143–70 (New York: Academic Press, 1974).

7. D. Byrne, *The Attraction Paradigm* (New York: Academic Press, 1971).

8. S. S. Brehm, *Intimate Relationships* (New York: Random House, 1985).

9. U. G. Foa and E. B. Foa, *Societal Structures of the Mind* (Springfield, Ill.: Charles C Thomas, 1974); E. B. Foa and U. G. Foa, "Resource Theory: Interpersonal Behavior as Exchange," in K. J. Gergen, M. S. Greenberg, and R. H. Willis, eds., *Social Exchange: Advances in Theory and Research* (New York: Plenum Press, 1980).

10. G. C. Homans, *Social Behavior: Its Elementary Forms*, rev. ed. (New York: Harcourt Brace Jovanovich, 1974); B. F. Skinner, *Science and Human Behavior* (New York: Macmillan, 1953).

11. E. Walster, G. W. Walster, and E. Berscheid, *Equity: Theory and Research* (Boston: Allyn & Bacon, 1978).

12. Ibid.

Notes

13. L. Festinger and J. M. Carlsmith, "Cognitive Consequences of Forced Compliance," *Journal of Abnormal and Social Psychology* 58(1959): 203–10.

14. D. J. Bem, "Self-Perception Theory," *Advances in Experimental Social Psychology* 6(1972): 1–62.

15. E. Berscheid, "Interpersonal Attraction," in G. Lindzey and E. Aronson, eds., *Handbook of Social Psychology*, vol. 2, pp. 413–84 (New York: Random House, 1985).

16. F. Heider, *The Psychology of Interpersonal Relations* (New York: John Wiley, 1958).

17. T. M. Newcomb, "Individual Systems of Orientation," in S. Koch, ed., *Psychology: A Study of a Science*, vol. 3 (New York: McGraw-Hill, 1959); T. M. Newcomb, "Interpersonal Balance," in R. P. Abelson et al., eds., *Theories of Cognitive Consistency: A Sourcebook*, pp. 25–51 (Chicago: Rand McNally, 1968).

18. L. Festinger, *A Theory of Cognitive Dissonance* (Stanford, Calif.: Stanford University Press, 1957).

19. K. E. Davis and E. E. Jones, "Changes in Interpersonal Perception as a Means of Reducing Cognitive Dissonance," *Journal of Abnormal and Social Psychology* 61(1960): 402–10.

20. E. Aronson and J. Mills, "The Effect of Severity of Initiation on Liking for a Group," *Journal of Abnormal and Social Psychology* 63(1959): 375–80.

21. E. Aronson, "Some Antecedents of Interpersonal Attraction," in W. J. Arnold and D. Levine, eds., *Nebraska Symposium on Motivation*, vol. 17, pp. 143–78 (Lincoln: University of Nebraska Press, 1969).

22. E. Aronson, B. Willerman, and J. Floyd, "The Effect of a Pratfall on Increasing Interpersonal Attractiveness," *Psychonomic Science* 4(1966): 227–28.

23. D. Tennov, *Love and Limerence* (New York: Stein & Day, 1979).

24. S. Freud, "Certain Neurotic Mechanisms in Jealousy, Paranoia, and Homosexuality," in *Collected Papers*, vol. 2, pp. 235, 240, 323 (London: Hogarth Press, 1922); T. Reik, *A Psychologist Looks at Love* (New York: Farrar & Rinehart, 1944).

25. M. Klein and J. Riviere, *Love, Hate, and Reparation* (London: Hogarth Press, 1953).

26. A. H. Maslow, *Motivation and Personality* (New York: Harper & Row, 1954).

27. Ibid.

28. E. Fromm, *The Art of Loving* (New York: Harper, 1956).

29. Tennov, *Love and Limerence*.

30. Hatfield and Walster, *A New Look at Love*.

31. S. Peele and A. Brodsky, *Love and Addiction* (New York: New

Notes

American Library, 1976); D. de Rougemont, *Love in the Western World*, M. Belgion, trans. (New York: Harcourt, Brace & World, 1940).

32. K. R. Livingston, "Love as a Process of Reducing Uncertainty," in K. S. Pope, ed., *On Love and Loving*, pp. 133–51 (San Francisco: Jossey-Bass, 1980).

33. M. S. Peck, *The Road Less Traveled: A New Psychology of Love, Traditional Values and Spiritual Growth* (New York: Simon & Schuster, 1978).

34. E. Walster and E. Berscheid, "A Little Bit about Love: A Minor Essay on a Major Topic," in T. L. Huston, ed., *Foundations of Interpersonal Attraction*, pp. 355–81 (New York: Academic Press, 1974).

35. S. Schachter and J. E. Singer, "Cognitive, Social, and Physiological Determinants of Emotional State," *Psychological Review* 69(1962): 379–99.

36. W. James, "What Is Emotion?" *Mind* 9(1884): 188–204; C. G. Lange, *The Emotions* (Baltimore: Williams & Wilkins, 1885/1922).

37. E. Berscheid, "Emotion," in H. H. Kelley et al., eds., *Close Relationships*, pp. 110–68 (New York: W. H. Freeman, 1983); G. Mandler, *Mind and Emotion* (New York: John Wiley, 1975).

38. G. Wilson, *The Coolidge Effect: An Evolutionary Account of Human Sexuality* (New York: William Morrow, 1981).

39. D. M. Buss, "Love Acts: The Evolutionary Biology of Love," in R. J. Sternberg and M. Barnes, eds., *The Psychology of Love*, pp. 100–18 (New Haven: Yale University Press, 1988).

40. J. Bowlby, *Attachment and Loss*, vol. 1: *Attachment* (New York: Basic Books, 1969).

41. Wilson, *The Coolidge Effect*.

42. Buss, "Love Acts."

43. Wilson, *The Coolidge Effect*.

44. C. Hazan and P. Shaver, "Love Conceptualized as an Attachment Process," *Journal of Personality and Social Psychology* 52(1987): 511–24.

45. Bowlby, *Attachment and Loss*, vol. 1; M. D. S. Ainsworth, "The Development of Infant-Mother Attachment," in B. M. Caldwell and H. N. Ricciuti, eds., *Review of Child Development Research*, vol. 3, pp. 1–94 (Chicago: University of Chicago Press, 1973).

46. Livingston, "Love as a Process of Reducing Uncertainty."

47. Tennov, *Love and Limerence*.

48. Hatfield and Walster, *A New Look at Love*.

49. G. Schwartz and D. Weinberger, "Patterns of Emotional Responses to Affective Situations: Relations among Happiness, Sadness, Anger, Fear, Depression, and Anxiety," *Motivation and Emotion* 4(1980): 175–91.

50. Z. Rubin, "Measurement of Romantic Love," *Journal of Personality and Social Psychology* 16(1970): 265–73; Z. Rubin, *Liking and Loving:*

Notes

An Invitation to Social Psychology (New York: Holt, Rinehart, & Winston, 1973).

51. Rubin, "Measurement of Romantic Love."

52. Ibid.

53. Ibid.

54. R. J. Sternberg and S. Grajek, "The Nature of Love," *Journal of Personality and Social Psychology* 47(1984): 312–29.

55. R. J. Sternberg and M. Barnes, "Real and Ideal Others in Romantic Relationships: Is Four a Crowd?" *Journal of Personality and Social Psychology* 49(1985): 1589–96.

56. Sternberg and Grajek, "The Nature of Love."

57. G. H. Thomson, *The Factorial Analysis of Human Ability* (London: University of London Press, 1939).

58. S. Freud, *Three Contributions to the Theory of Sex* (New York: E. P. Dutton, 1905/1962); T. Reik, *A Psychologist Looks at Love* (New York: Farrar & Rinehart, 1944); Tennov, *Love and Limerence.*

59. J. A. Lee, "A Typology of Styles of Loving," *Personality and Social Psychology Bulletin* 3(1977): 173–82.

60. M. Lasswell and N. M. Lobsenz, *Styles of Loving* (New York: Ballantine, 1980).

61. C. Hendrick and S. Hendrick, "A Theory and Method of Love," *Journal of Personality and Social Psychology* 50(1986): 392–402.

62. Lee, "A Typology of Styles of Loving."

63. K. E. Davis, "Near and Dear: Friendship and Love Compared," *Psychology Today* 19(February 1985): 22–30.

64. K. E. Davis and M. K. Roberts, "Relationships in the Real World: The Descriptive Approach to Personal Relationships," in K. J. Gergen and K. E. Davis, eds., *The Social Construction of the Person* (New York: Springer-Verlag, 1985).

65. R. J. Sternberg, "A Triangular Theory of Love," *Psychological Review* 93(1986): 119–35.

66. Davis, "Near and Dear"; Sternberg, "A Triangular Theory of Love."

67. Lee, "A Typology of Styles of Loving."

68. Byrne, *The Attraction Paradigm.*

69. Livingston, "Love as a Process of Reducing Uncertainty."

70. Tennov, *Love and Limerence.*

71. J. Mills and M. S. Clark, "Exchange and Communal Relationships" in L. Wheeler, ed., *Review of Personality and Social Psychology*, vol. 3 (Beverly Hills, Calif.: Sage, 1982).

72. Heider, *The Psychology of Interpersonal Relations.*

73. Reik, *A Psychologist Looks at Love.*

74. A. H. Maslow, *Toward a Psychology of Being* (Princeton, N.J.: Van Nostrand, 1962); Freud, "Certain Neurotic Mechanisms."

75. Walster and Berscheid, "A Little Bit about Love."

76. Peele and Brodsky, *Love and Addiction.*

77. Peck, *The Road Less Traveled*; E. Fromm, *The Art of Loving* (New York: Harper, 1956).

78. Wilson, *The Coolidge Effect.*

79. C. Hazan and P. Shaver, "Love Conceptualized as an Attachment Process," *Journal of Personality and Social Psychology* 52(1987): 511–24; Bowlby, *Attachment and Loss*, vol. 1; Ainsworth, "Infant-Mother Attachment."

80. Rubin, "Measurement of Romantic Love"; Sternberg and Grajek, "The Nature of Love."

81. Davis, "Near and Dear."

82. R. J. Sternberg and M. Barnes, eds., *The Psychology of Love* (New Haven: Yale University Press, 1988).

Chapter 5. Attraction: What Makes It? What Breaks It?

1. Two excellent reviews of the literature on interpersonal attraction, upon which this chapter draws, have been written recently by Sharon Brehm and by Clyde Hendrick and Susan Hendrick: S. S. Brehm, *Intimate Relationships* (New York: Random House, 1985); C. Hendrick and S. Hendrick, *Liking, Loving, and Relating* (Monterey, Calif.: Brooks/Cole Publishing, 1983).

2. E. Walster et al., "Importance of Physical Attractiveness in Dating Behavior," *Journal of Personality and Social Psychology* 4(1966): 508–16.

3. E. Berscheid et al., "Physical Attractiveness and Dating Choice: A Test of the Matching Hypothesis," *Journal of Experimental Social Psychology* 7(1971): 173–89.

4. B. I. Murstein, "Physical Attraction and Marital Choice," *Journal of Personality and Social Psychology* 22(1972): 8–12; B. I. Murstein, *Who Will Marry Whom?* (New York: Springer, 1976).

5. E. Berscheid and E. Walster, "Physical Attractiveness," in L. Berkowitz, ed., *Advances in Experimental Social Psychology*, vol. 7 (New York: Academic Press, 1974).

6. K. Dion, E. Berscheid, and E. Walster, "What Is Beautiful Is Good," *Journal of Personality and Social Psychology* 24(1972): 285–90.

7. H. Sigall and D. Landy, "Radiating Beauty: The Effects of Having a Physically Attractive Partner on Person Perception," *Journal of Personality and Social Psychology* 28(1973): 218–24.

Notes

8. D. Landy and H. Sigall, "Beauty Is Talent: Task Evaluation as a Function of the Performer's Physical Attractiveness," *Journal of Personality and Social Psychology* 29(1974): 299–304.

9. D. Bar-Tal and L. Saxe, "Perceptions of Similarly and Dissimilarly Attractive Couples and Individuals," *Journal of Personality and Social Psychology* 33(1976): 772–81.

10. Berscheid et al., "Physical Attractiveness and Dating Choice."

11. M. Snyder, E. Berscheid, and P. Glick, "Focusing on the Exterior and the Interior: Two Investigations of the Initiation of Personal Relationships," *Journal of Personality and Social Psychology* 48(1985): 1427–39.

12. Ibid.

13. M. Snyder, E. D. Tanke, and E. Berscheid, "Social Perception and Interpersonal Behavior: On the Self-Fulfilling Nature of Social Stereotypes," *Journal of Personality and Social Psychology* 35(1977): 656–66.

14. D. G. Dutton and A. P. Aron, "Some Evidence for Heightened Sexual Attraction under Conditions of High Anxiety," *Journal of Personality and Social Psychology* 30(1974): 510–17.

15. Ibid.

16. L. Festinger, S. Schachter, and K. W. Back, *Social Pressures in Informal Groups: A Study of Human Factors in Housing* (New York: Harper, 1950).

17. T. M. Newcomb, *The Acquaintance Process* (New York: Holt, Rinehart, & Winston, 1961).

18. M. W. Segal, "Alphabet and Attraction: An Unobtrusive Measure of the Effect of Propinquity in a Field Setting," *Journal of Personality and Social Psychology* 30(1974): 654–57.

19. R. B. Zajonc, "Attitudinal Effects of Mere Exposure," *Journal of Personality and Social Psychology Monograph Supplement* 9(1968): 1–27.

20. S. Saegert, W. Swap, and R. B. Zajonc, "Exposure, Context, and Interpersonal Attraction," *Journal of Personality and Social Psychology* 25(1973): 234–42.

21. E. B. Ebbesen, G. L. Kjos, and V. J. Konecni, "Spatial Ecology: Its Effects on the Choice of Friends and Enemies," *Journal of Experimental Social Psychology* 12(1976): 505–18.

22. C. W. Backman and P. F. Secord, "The Effect of Perceived Liking on Interpersonal Attraction," *Human Relations* 12(1959): 379–84.

23. R. E. Stapleton, P. Nacci, and J. T. Tedeschi, "Interpersonal Attraction and the Reciprocation of Benefits," *Journal of Personality and Social Psychology* 28(1973): 199–205.

24. M. Worthy, A. L. Gary, and G. M. Kahn, "Self-Disclosure as an

Exchange Process," *Journal of Personality and Social Psychology* 13(1969): 59–63.

25. E. W. Burgess and P. Wallin, *Engagement and Marriage* (Philadelphia: Lippincott, 1953).

26. A. Skolnick, "Married Lives: Longitudinal Perspectives on Marriage," in D. Eichorn et al., eds., *Present and Past in Middle Life* (New York: Academic Press, 1981).

27. D. Byrne, *The Attraction Paradigm* (New York: Academic Press, 1971); A. Tesser and M. Brodie, "A Note on the Evaluation of a 'Computer Date,' " *Psychonomic Science* 23(1971): 300.

28. T. L. Huston and G. Levinger, "Interpersonal Attraction and Relationships," in M. R. Rosenzweig and L. W. Porter, eds., *Annual Review of Psychology*, vol. 29 (Palo Alto, Calif.: Annual Review, 1978).

29. R. Driscoll, K. W. Davis, and M. E. Lipetz, "Parental Interference and Romantic Love," *Journal of Personality and Social Psychology* 24(1972): 1–10.

30. E. Walster et al., "Playing Hard-to-Get: Understanding an Elusive Phenomenon," *Journal of Personality and Social Psychology* 26(1973): 113–21.

31. R. A. Wright and R. J. Contrada, "Dating Selectivity and Interpersonal Attractiveness: Support for a 'Common sense' Analysis" (unpublished manuscript, University of Texas, Austin, 1983).

Chapter 6. What Matters When?

1. Z. Rubin, "Measurement of Romantic Love," *Journal of Personality and Social Psychology* 16(1970): 265–73; Z. Rubin, *Liking and Loving: An Invitation to Social Psychology* (New York: Holt, Rinehart, & Winston, 1973).

2. Rubin, "Measurement of Romantic Love."

3. C. T. Hill, Z. Rubin, and L. A. Peplau, "Breakups before Marriage: The End of 103 Affairs," *Journal of Social Issues* 32(1976): 147–67.

4. R. S. Cimbalo, V. Faling, and P. Mousaw, "The Course of Love: A Cross-Sectional Design," *Psychological Reports* 38(1976): 1292–94.

5. Rubin, *Liking and Loving*; G. Levinger, M. Rands, and R. Talaber, *The Assessment of Involvement and Rewardingness in Close and Casual Pair Relationships* (National Science Foundation Technical Report DK; Amherst: University of Massachusetts Press, 1977).

6. R. J. Sternberg, "A Triangular Theory of Love," *Psychological Review* 93(1986): 119–35; R. J. Sternberg, "Construct Validation of a Triangular Theory of Love" (submitted for publication, 1987).

Notes

7. Rubin, *Liking and Loving*; Levinger, Rands, and Talaber, *Assessment of Involvement*.

8. R. J. Sternberg and S. Grajek, "The Nature of Love," *Journal of Personality and Social Psychology* 47(1984): 312–29.

9. E. Berscheid, "Emotion," in H. H. Kelley et al., eds., *Close Relationships*, pp. 110–68 (New York: W. H. Freeman, 1983); Sternberg, "A Triangular Theory of Love."

10. Sternberg, "Construct Validation."

11. G. Levinger, "Toward the Analysis of Close Relationships," *Journal of Experimental Social Psychology* 10(1980): 510–44.

Chapter 7. Beginnings, Middles, and Endings: The Course of a Relationship

1. R. F. Winch, *Mate Selection: A Theory of Complementary Needs* (New York: Harper, 1958); H. A. Murray, *Explorations in Personality* (New York: Oxford University Press, 1938).

2. A. C. Kerckhoff and K. E. Davis, "Value Consensus and Need Complementarity in Mate Selection," *American Sociological Review* 27(1962): 295–303.

3. G. Levinger, D. J. Senn, and B. W. Jorgensen, "Progress toward Permanence in Courtship: A Test of the Kerckhoff-Davis Hypotheses," *Sociometry* 33(1970): 427–43.

4. D. M. Buss, "Love Acts: The Evolutionary Biology of Love," in R. J. Sternberg and M. L. Barnes, eds., *The Psychology of Love*, pp. 100–118 (New Haven: Yale University Press, 1988).

5. B. I. Murstein, "Stimulus-Value-Role: A Theory of Marital Choice," *Journal of Marriage and the Family* 32(1970): 465–81.

6. R. A. Lewis, "A Developmental Framework for the Analysis of Premarital Dyadic Formation," *Family Process* 11(1972): 17–48.

7. G. Levinger and J. D. Snoek, *Attraction in Relationship: A New Look at Interpersonal Attraction* (Morristown, N.J.: General Learning Press, 1972).

8. G. Levinger, "The Embrace of Lives: Changing and Unchanging," in G. Levinger and H. L. Raush, eds., *Close Relationships: Perspectives on the Meaning of Intimacy* (Amherst: University of Massachusetts Press, 1977).

9. G. Levinger, "Development and Change," in H. H. Kelley et al., eds., *Close Relationships*, pp. 315–59 (New York: W. H. Freeman, 1983).

Notes

10. I. Altman and D. A. Taylor, *Social Penetration: The Development of Interpersonal Relationships* (New York: Holt, Rinehart & Winston, 1973).

11. R. S. Cimbalo, V. Faling, and P. Mousaw, "The Course of Love: A Cross-Sectional Design," *Psychological Reports* 38(1976): 1292–94.

12. P. C. Pineo, "Disenchantment in the Later Years of Marriage," *Marriage and Family Living* 23(1961): 3–11.

13. W. G. Graziano and L. M. Musser, "The Joining and the Parting of the Ways," in S. Duck, ed., *Personal Relationships*, vol. 4: *Dissolving Relationships* (New York: Academic Press, 1982).

14. B. Rollins and K. Cammon, "Marital Satisfaction over the Family Life Cycle: A Reevaluation," *Journal of Marriage and the Family* 36(1974): 271–82; B. C. Rollins and R. Galligan, "The Developing Child and Marital Satisfaction of Parents," in R. M. Lerner and G. B. Spanier, eds., *Child Influences on Marital and Family Interaction* (New York: Academic Press, 1978).

15. A. Skolnick, "Married Lives: Longitudinal Perspectives on Marriage," in D. Eichorn et al., eds., *Present and Past in Middle Life* (New York: Academic Press, 1981); N. D. Glenn, "Psychological Well-Being in the Post-Parental Stage: Some Evidence from National Surveys," *Journal of Marriage and the Family* 37(1975): 105–10.

16. S. S. Brehm, *Intimate Relationships* (New York: Random House, 1985).

17. B. R. Orvis, H. H. Kelley, and D. Butler, "Attributional Conflict in Young Couples," in J. H. Harvey, W. J. Ickes, and R. E. Kidd, eds., *New Direction in Attribution Research*, vol. 1 (Hillsdale, N.J.: Lawrence Erlbaum, 1976).

18. E. Berscheid et al., "Outcome Dependency: Attention, Attribution, and Attraction," *Journal of Personality and Social Psychology* 34(1976): 978–89; T. W. Smith and S. S. Brehm, "Person Perception and the Type A Coronary-Prone Behavior Pattern," *Journal of Personality and Social Psychology* 40(1981): 1137–49.

19. H. H. Kelley, "An Application of Attribution Theory to Research Methodology for Close Relationships," in G. Levinger and H. L. Raush, eds., *Close Relationships: Perspectives on the Meaning of Intimacy* (Amherst: University of Massachusetts Press, 1977).

20. W. J. Doherty, "Cognitive Processes in Intimate Conflict: I. Extending Attribution Theory," *American Journal of Family Therapy* 9(1981): 1–13; H. H. Kelley, *Personal Relationships: Their Structures and Processes* (Hillsdale, N.J.: Lawrence Erlbaum, 1979).

21. W. J. Doherty, "Attribution Style and Negative Problem Solving in Marriage," *Family Relation* 31(1982): 201–5.

22. F. Fincham and K. D. O'Leary, "Casual Inferences for Spouse

Notes

Behavior in Maritally Distressed and Nondistressed Couples," *Journal of Clinical and Social Psychology* 1(1983): 42–57.

23. N. S. Jacobson et al., "Attributional Processes in Distressed and Nondistressed Married Couples," *Cognitive Therapy and Research* 9(1985): 35–50.

24. N. S. Jacobson, W. C. Follette, and D. W. McDonald, "Reactivity to Positive and Negative Behavior in Distressed and Nondistressed Married Couples," *Journal of Consulting and Clinical Psychology* 50(1982): 706–14.

25. M. E. Madden and R. Janoff-Bulman, "Blame, Control, and Marital Satisfaction: Wives' Attributions for Conflict in Marriage," *Journal of Marriage and the Family* 43(1981): 663–74.

26. D. Phillips and R. Judd, *How to Fall Out of Love* (New York: Fawcett, 1978).

27. Berscheid, "Emotion."

28. D. Vaughan, *Uncoupling* (New York: Oxford University Press, 1986).

29. R. Weiss, *Marital Separation* (New York: Basic Books, 1975).

Chapter 8. The Triangle of Love

1. A. H. Maslow, *Toward a Psychology of Being* (Princeton: Van Nostrand, 1962).

2. A. Penney, *How to Make Love to a Man* (New York: Dell, 1981); A. Penney, *How to Make Love to Each Other* (New York: Berkley, 1982); A. Penney, *Great Sex* (New York: G. P. Putnam, 1985).

INDEX

Index

Index

Index

Index

Index

Index